Computer Communications and Networks

The **Computer Communications and Networks** series is a range of textbooks, monographs and handbooks. It sets out to provide students, researchers and non-specialists alike with a sure grounding in current knowledge, together with comprehensible access to the latest developments in computer communications and networking.

Emphasis is placed on clear and explanatory styles that support a tutorial approach, so that even the most complex of topics is presented in a lucid and intelligible manner.

Also in this series:

An Information Security Handbook
John M.D. Hunter
1-85233-180-1

Multimedia Internet Broadcasting: Quality, Technology and Interface
Andy Sloane and Dave Lawrence (Eds)
1-85233-283-2

The Quintessential PIC Microcontroller
Sid Katzen
1-85233-309-X

Information Assurance: Surviving in the Information Environment
Andrew Blyth and Gerald L. Kovacich
1-85233-326-X

UMTS: Origins, Architecture and the Standard
Pierre Lescuyer (Translation Editor: Frank Bott)
1-85233-676-5

OSS for Telecom Networks
Kundan Misra: An Introduction to Network Management
1-85233-808-3

Ian J. Taylor

From P2P
to Web Services
and Grids

Peers in a Client/Server World

Springer

Ian J. Taylor, PhD
School of Computer Science, University of Cardiff, Cardiff, Wales

Series editor
Professor A.J. Sammes, BSc, MPhil, PhD, FBCS, CEng
CISM Group, Cranfield University, RMCS, Shrivenham, Swindon SN6 8LA, UK

British Library Cataloguing in Publication Data
Taylor, Ian J.
    From P2P to Web Services and Grids. — (Computer communications and networks)
    1. Client/server computing   2. Internet programming   3. Middleware
    4. Peer-to-peer architecture (Computer networks)   5. Web services
    6. Computational grides (Computer systems)   I. Title

004.3′6
ISBN 1852338695

A catalog record for this book is available from the Library of Congress.

Computer Communications and Networks ISSN 1617-7975
ISBN 1-85233-869-5 Springer London Berlin Heidelberg
Springer is a part of Springer Science+Business Media
springeronline.com

Printed and bound in the United States of America
34/3830–543210 Printed on acid-free paper SPIN 10975107

Preface

Current users typically interact with the Internet through the use of a Web browser and a client/server based connection to a Web server. However, as we move forward to allow true machine-to-machine communication, we are in need of more scalable solutions which employ the use of decentralized techniques to add redundancy, fault tolerance and scalability to distributed systems. Distributed systems take many forms, appear in many areas and range from truly decentralized systems, like Gnutella and Jxta, centrally indexed brokered systems like Web services and Jini and centrally coordinated systems like SETI@Home.

From P2P to Web Services and Grids: Peers in a client/server world provides a comprehensive overview of the emerging trends in peer-to-peer (P2P), distributed objects, Web services and Grid computing technologies, which have redefined the way we think about distributed computing and the Internet. This book has two main themes: applications and middleware. Within the context of applications, examples of the many diverse architectures are provided including: decentralized systems like Gnutella and Freenet; brokered ones like Napster; and centralized applications like SETI and conventional Web servers. For middleware, the book covers Jxta, as a programming infrastructure for P2P computing, along with Web services, Grid computing paradigms, e.g., Globus and OGSA, and distributed-object architectures, e.g., Jini. Each technology is described in detail, including source code where appropriate, and their capabilities are analysed in the context of the degree of centralization or decentralization they employ.

To maintain coherency, each system is discussed in terms of the generalized taxonomy, which is outlined in the first chapter. This taxonomy serves as a placeholder for the systems presented in the book and gives an overview of the organizational differences between the various approaches. Most of the systems are discussed at a high level, particularly addressing the organization and topologies of the distributed resources. However, some (e.g., Jxta, Jini, Web services and, to some extent, Gnutella) are discussed in much more detail, giving practical programming tutorials for their use. Security is paramount throughout and introduced with a dedicated chapter outlining the many approaches to security within distributed systems.

Why did I decide to write this book?

I initially wrote the book for my lecture course in the School of Computer Science at Cardiff University on *Distributed Systems*. I wanted to give the students a broad overview of distributed-computing techniques that have evolved over the past decade. The text therefore outlines the key applications and middleware used to construct distributed applications today. I wrote each lecture as a book chapter and these notes have been extremely well received by the students and therefore I decided to extend this into a book for their use and for others ... so:

Who should read this book?

This book, I believe, has a wide-ranging scope. It was initially written for BSc students, with an extensive computing background, and MSc students, who have little or no prior computing experience, i.e., some students had never written a line of code in their lives !... Therefore, this book should appeal to people with various computer programming abilities but also to the casual reader who is simply interested in the recent advances in the distributed systems world.

Readers will learn about the various distributed systems that are available today. For a designer of new applications, this will provide a good reference. For students, this text would accompany any course on distributed computing to give a broader context of the subject area. For a casual reader, interested in P2P and Grid computing, the book will give a broad overview of the field and specifics about how such systems operate in practice without delving into the low-level details. For example, to both casual and programming-level readers, all chapters will be of interest, except some parts of the Gnutella chapter and some sections of the deployment chapters, which are more tuned to the lower-level mechanisms and therefore targeted more to programmers.

Organization

Chapter 1: Introduction: In this chapter, an introduction is given into distributed systems, paying particular attention to the role of middleware. A taxonomy is constructed for distributed systems ranging on a scale from centralized to decentralized depending on how resources or services are organized, discovered and how they communicate with each other. This will serve as an underlying theme for the understanding of the various applications and middleware discussed in this book.

Chapter 2: Peer-2-Peer Systems: This chapter gives a brief history of client/server and peer-to-peer computing. The current P2P definition is stated and specifics of the P2P environment that distinguish it from client/server are provided: e.g., transient nodes, multi-hop, NAT, firewalls etc. Several examples of P2P technologies are given, along with application scenarios for their use and categorizations of their behaviour within the taxonomy described in the first chapter.

Chapter 3: Web Services: This chapter introduces the concept of machine-to-machine communication and how this fits in with the existing Web technologies and future scopes. This leads onto a high-level overview of Web services, which illustrates the core concepts without getting bogged down with the deployment details.

Chapter 4: Grid Computing: This chapter introduces the idea of a computational Grid environment, which is typically composed of a number of heterogeneous resources that may be owned and managed by different administrators. The concept of a "virtual organization" is discussed along with its security model, which employs a single sign-on mechanism. The Globus toolkit, the reference implementation that can be used to program computational Grids, is then outlined giving some typical scenarios.

Chapter 5: Jini: This chapter gives an overview of Jini, which provides an example of a distributed-object based technology. A background is given into the development of Jini and into the network plug-and-play manner in which Jini accesses distributed objects. The discovery of look-up servers, searching and using Jini services is described in detail and advanced Jini issues, such as leasing and events are discussed.

Chapter 6: Gnutella: This chapter combines a conceptual overview of Gnutella and the details of the actual Gnutella protocol specification. Many empirical studies are then outlined that illustrate the behaviour of the Gnutella network in practice and show the many issues which need to be overcome in order for this decentralized structure to succeed. Finally, the advantages and disadvantages of this approach are discussed.

Chapter 7: Scalability: In this chapter, we look at scalability issues by analysing the manner in which peers are organized within popular P2P networks. First, social networks are introduced and compared against their P2P counterparts. We then explore the use of decentralized P2P networks within the context of file sharing. It is shown why in practice, neither extreme (i.e., completely centralized or decentralized architectures) gives effective results and therefore why most current P2P applications use a hybrid of the two approaches.

Chapter 8: Security: This chapter covers the basic elements of security in a distributed system. It covers the various ways that a third party can gain access to data and the design issues involved in building a distributed security system. It then gives a basic overview of cryptography and describes the various ways in which secure channels can be set up, using public-key pairs or by using symmetric keys, e.g., shared secret keys or session keys. Finally, secure mobile code is discussed within the concept of sandboxing.

Chapter 9: Freenet: This chapter gives a concise description of the Freenet distributed information storage system, which is real-world example of how the various technologies, so far discussed, can be integrated and used within a single system. For example: Freenet is designed to work within a P2P environment; it addresses scalability through the use of an adaptive routing algorithm that creates a centralized/decentralized network topology dynamically; and it address a number of privacy issues by using a combination of hash functions and public/private key encryption.

Chapter 10: Jxta: This chapter introduces Jxta that provides a set of open, generalized, P2P protocols to allow any connected device (cell phone to PDA, PC to server) on the network to communicate and collaborate. An overview of the motivation behind Jxta is given followed by a description of its key concepts. Finally, a detailed overview of the six Jxta protocols is given.

Chapter 11: Distributed Object Deployment Using Jini: This chapter describes how one would use Jini in practice. This is illustrated through several simple RMI and Jini applications that describe how the individual parts and protocols fit together and give a good context for the Jini chapter and how the deployment differs from other systems discussed in this book.

Chapter 12: P2P Deployment Using Jxta: This chapter uses several Jxta programming examples to illustrate some issues of programming and operating within a P2P environment. A number of key practical issues, such as out-of-date advertisements and peer configuration, which have to be dealt with in any P2P application are discussed and illustrated by outlining the potential solutions employed by Jxta.

Chapter 13: Web Services Deployment: This chapter describes the Web services deployment technologies, typically used for representing and invoking Web services. Specifically, three core technologies are discussed in detail: SOAP for wrapping XML messages within an envelope, WSDL for representing the Web services interface description, and UDDI for storing indexes of the locations of Web services.

Chapter 14: OGSA: This chapter discusses the Open Grid Service Architecture (OGSA), which extends Web services into the Grid computing arena by using WSDL to achieve self-descriptive, discoverable services that can be referenced during their lifetime, i.e., maintain state. OGSI is discussed, which provides an implementation of the OGSA ideas. This is followed by OGSI's supercessor, WSRF, which translates the OGSI definitions into representations that are compatible with other emerging Web service standards.

Disclaimer

Within this book, I draw in a number of examples from file-sharing programs, such as Napster, Gnutella (e.g., Limewire), Fastrack and KaZaA to name a few. The reason for this is to illustrate the different approaches in the organization of distributed systems in a computational scientific context. Under no circumstances, using this text, am I endorsing or supporting any or all of these file-sharing applications in their current legal battles concerning copyright issues.

My focus here is on the use of this infrastructure in many other scientific situations where there is no question of their legality. We can learn a lot from such applications when designing future Grids and P2P systems, both from a computational science aspect and from a social aspect, in the sense of how users behave as computing peers within such a system, i.e., do they share or not? These studies give us insight about how we may approach the scalability issues in future distributed systems.

English Spelling

I struggled with the appropriate spelling of some words, which in British English, should (arguably) be spelt with an 's' but in almost all related literature within this subject area, they are spelt with a 'z', e.g., organize, centralize, etc. After much dialogue with colleagues and Springer, we decided on a compromise; that is, I shall use an amalgamation of America English and British English known as mid-Atlantic English.... Therefore, for the set of such words, I will use the 'z' form. These include derivatives of: authorize, centralize, decentralize, generalize, maximize, minimize, organize, quantize, serialize, specialize, standardize, utilize, virtualize and visualize. Otherwise, I will use the British English spelling e.g. advertise, characterise, conceptualise, customise, realise, recognise, stabilise etc. Interestingly, however, even the Oxford Concise English Dictionary lists many of these words in their 'z' form....

Acknowledgements

I would like to thank a number of people who provided sanity checks and proof-reading for a number of chapters in this book. In particular, I'd like to thank Shalil Majithia, Andrew Harrison, Omer Rana and Jonathon Giddy. Also, many thanks to the numerous members of the GridLab, Triana and NRL groups for their encouragement and enlightening discussions during the writing of this book. So, to name a few, thanks to Alex Hardisty, Andre Merzky, Andrei Hutanu, Brian Adamson, Bernard Schutz, Joe Macker, Ed Seidel, Gabrielle Allen, Ian Kelley, Jason Novotny, Roger Philp, Wangy, Matthew Shields, Michael Russell, Oliver Wehrens, Felix Hupfeld, Rick Jones, Sheldon Gardner, Thilo Kielmann, Jarek Nabrzyski, Sathya, Tom Goodale, David Walker, Kelly Davis, Hartmut Kaiser, Dave Angulo, Alex Gray and Krzysztof Kurowski.

Most of this book was written in Sicily and therefore, I'd like to thank everyone I met there who made me feel so welcome and for those necessary breaks in B&Js in *Ragusa Ibla* and *il Bagatto* in Siracusa.... Finally, thanks to Matt for keeping his cool during some pretty daunting deadlines towards the end of the writing of this book.

Cardiff, UK.   *Ian Taylor*
April 2004

Contents

Part II Middleware, Applications and Supporting Technologies

Part IV From Web Services to Future Grids

1

Introduction

Recently, there has been an explosion of applications using peer-to-peer (P2P) and Grid-computing technology. On the one hand, P2P has become ingrained in current grass-roots Internet culture through applications like Gnutella [6] and SETI@Home [3]. It has appeared in several popular magazines including the *Red Herring* and *Wired*, and frequently quoted as being crowned by *Fortune* as one of the four technologies that will shape the Internet's future. The popularity of P2P has spread through to academic and industrial circles, being propelled by media and widespread debate both in the courtroom and out. However, such enormous hype and controversy has led to the mistrust of such technology as a serious distributed systems platform for future computing, but in fact in reality, there is significant substance as we shall see.

In parallel, there has been an overwhelming interest in Grid computing, which is attempting to build the infrastructure to enable on-demand computing in a similar fashion to the way we access other utilities now, e.g., electricity. Further, the introduction of the Open Grid Services Architecture (OGSA) [21] has aligned this vision with the technological machine-to-machine capabilities of Web services (see Chapter 3). This convergence has gained a significant input from both commercial and non-commercial organizations ([27] and [28]) and has a firm grounding in standardized Web technologies, which could perhaps even lead to the kind of ubiquitous uptake necessary for such a infrastructure to be globally deployed.

Although the underlying philosophies of Grid computing and P2P are different, they both are attempting to solve the same problem, that is, to create a *virtual overlay* [23] over the existing Internet to enable collaboration and sharing of resources [24]. However, in implementation, the approaches differ greatly. Whilst Grid computing connects virtual organizations [32] that can cooperate in a collaborative fashion, P2P connects individual users using highly transient devices and computers living at the *edges of the Internet* [46] (i.e., behind NAT, firewalls etc).

The name "Peers in a Client/Server World" describes the transitionary evolution from the widespread client/server based Internet, dominant over the past decade, back to the roots of the Internet where every peer had equal status. Inevitably, both history and practicality will influence the next generation Internet as we attempt to migrate from the technical maturity and robustness of the current Internet to its future vision. Therefore, as we move forward, we must build upon the current infrastructure to address key issues of widespread availability and deployment.

In this book, the key influential technologies are addressed that will help to shape the next-generation Internet. P2P and distributed-object based technologies, through to the promised pervasive deployment of Grid computing combined with Web services will be needed in order to address the fundamental issues of creating a scalable ubiquitous next-generation computing infrastructure. Specifically, a comprehensive overview of current distributed-systems technologies is given, covering P2P environments (Chapters 2,6,7, 9,10,12), security techniques (Chapter 8), distributed-object systems (Chapters 5 and 11), Grid computing (Chapter 4) and both *stateless* (Chapters 3 and 13) and *stateful* Web services (Chapter 14).

1.1 Introduction to Distributed Systems

A distributed system can be defined as follows:

"A distributed system is a collection of independent computers that appears to its users as a single coherent system" [1]

There are two aspects to this: hardware and software. The hardware machines must be autonomous and the software must be organized in such a way as to make the users think that they are dealing with a single system. Expanding on these fundamentals, distributed systems typically have the following characteristics; they should:

- be capable of dealing with heterogeneous devices, i.e., various vendors, software stacks and operating systems should be able to interoperate
- be easy to expand and scale
- be permanently available (even though parts of it may not be)
- hide communication from the users.

In order for a distributed system to support a collection of heterogeneous computers and networks while offering a single system view, the software stack is often divided into two layers. At the higher layers, there are applications (and users) and at the lower layer there is **middleware**, which interacts with the underlying networks and computer systems to give applications and users the transparency they need (see Fig. 1.1).

Middleware abstracts the underlying mechanisms and protocols from the application developer and provides a collection of high-level capabilities to

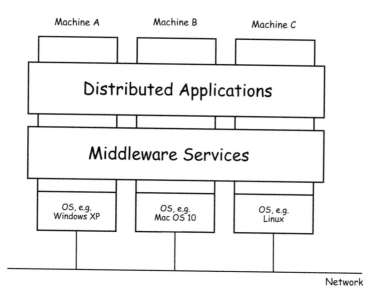

Fig. 1.1. The role of **middleware** in a distributed system; it hides the underlying infrastructure away from the application and user level.

make things far easier for programmers to develop and deploy their applications. For example, within the middleware layer, there maybe simple abstract communication calls that do not specify which underlying mechanisms they actually use, e.g., TCP/IP, UDP, Bluetooth etc. Such concrete deployment bindings are often decided at run time through configuration files or dynamically, thereby being dependent on the particular deployment environment.

Middleware therefore provides the *virtual overlay* across the distributed resources to enable transparent deployment across the underlying infrastructures. In this book, we will take a look at a number of different approaches in designing the middleware abstraction layer by identifying the kinds of capabilities that are exposed by the various types.

1.2 Some Terminology

Often, a number of terms are used to define a device or capability on a distributed network, e.g., node, resource, peer, agent, service, server etc. In this section, common definitions are given which are used consistently throughout this book. The definitions presented here do represent a compromise however, because often certain distributed entities are not identified in all systems in the same way. Therefore, wherever appropriate, the terminology provided here is given within the context of the system they described within. The terms are defined as follows:

- **Resource:** any hardware or software entity being represented or shared on a distributed network. For example, a resource could be any of the following: a computer; a file storage system; a file; a communication channel; a service, i.e., algorithm/function call; and so on
- **Node:** a generic term used to represent any device on a distributed network. A node that performs one (or more) capabilities is often exposed as a service
- **Client:** is a consumer of information, e.g., a Web browser
- **Server:** is a provider of information, e.g., a Web server or a peer offering a file-sharing service
- **Service:** is "a network-enabled entity that provides some capability" [21]; e.g., a Web server provides a remote HTTP file-retrieval service. A single device can expose several capabilities as individual services
- **Peer:** a peer is when a device acts as both a consumer and provider of information.

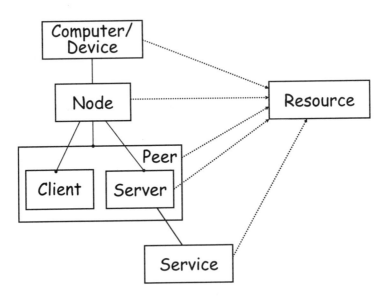

Fig. 1.2. An overview of the terms used to describe distributed resources.

Figure 1.2 organizes these terms by associating relationships between the various terminologies. Here, we can see that any *device* is a entity on the network. Devices can also be referred to in many different ways, e.g., a node, computer, PDA, peer etc. Each *device* can run any number of *clients, servers, services* or *peers*. A peer is a special kind of node, which acts as both a client and a server.

There is often confusion about the term *resource*. The easiest way to think of a resource is any capability that is shared on a distributed network. Sharing resources can be exposed in a number of ways and can also be used to represent a number of physical or virtual entities. For example, you can share: files (so a file is a resource), CPU cycles, storage capabilities (i.e., a file system), a service, e.g., a Web server or Web service, and so on. Therefore, everything in 1.2 is a resource except a client, who does not share.

A service is a software entity that can be used to represent resources, and therefore capabilities, on a network. There are numerous examples, e.g., Web servers, Web services, Jini services, Jxta peers providing a service, and so forth and so on. In simple terms, services can be thought of as the network counterparts of local function calls. Services receive a request (just like the arguments to a function call) and (optionally) return a response (as do local function calls). To illustrate this analogy, consider the functionality of a standard HTTP Web server: it receives a request for an HTTP file and returns the contents of that file, if found. If this was implemented as a local function call in Java, it would look something like this:

String getWebPage(String httpfile)

This simple function call takes a file-name argument (including its directory, e.g., /mydir/myfilename.html) and it returns the contents of that local file within a Java *String* object. This is basically what a Web server does. However, within the Web server scenario, the user would provide an HTTP address (e.g., *http://www.google.com/index.html*) and this would be converted into a remote request to the specified Web server (e.g., http://www.google.com) with the requested file (index.html). The entire process would involve the use of the DNS (Domain Name Service) but the client (e.g., the Web browser) performs the same operation as our simple local reader but renders the information in a specific way for the user, i.e., using HTML.

1.3 Centralized and Decentralized Systems

In this section, the middleware and systems outlined in this book are classified onto a taxonomy according to a scale ranging between centralized and decentralized. The distributed architectures are divided into categories that define an axis on the comparison space. On one side of this spectrum, we have centralized systems, e.g., typical client/server based systems. and on the other side, we have decentralized systems, often classified as P2P. In the centre is a mix of the two extremes in the form of hybrid systems, e.g., brokered, where a system may broker the functionality or communication request to another service. This taxonomy sets the scene for the specifics of each system which will be outlined in the chapters to follow and serves as a simple look-up table for determining a system's high-level behaviour.

The boundaries are not clean-cut however and there are a number of factors that can determine the centralized nature of a system. Even systems that are considered fully decentralized can, in practice, employ some degrees of centralization, albeit often in a self-organizing fashion [2]. Typically, decentralized systems adopt immense redundancy, both in the discovering of information and content, by dynamically repeating information across many other peers on the network.

Broadly speaking, there are three main areas that determine whether a system is centralized or decentralized:

1. Resource Discovery
2. Resource Availability
3. Resource Communication

One important consideration to bear in mind as we talk about the degree of centralization of systems is that of scalability. When we say a resource is centralized, we do not mean to imply that there is only one server serving the information, rather, we mean that there are a fixed number of servers (possibly one) providing the information which does not scale proportionately with the size of the network. Obviously, there are many levels of granularities here and hence the adoption of a sliding scale, illustrating the various levels on a resource-organization continuum.

1.3.1 Resource Discovery

Within any distributed system, there needs to be a mechanism for discovering the resources. This process is referred to as *discovery* and a service which supplies this information is called a *discovery service* (e.g., DNS, Jini Lookup, Jxta Rendezvous, JNDI, UDDI etc.). There are a number of mechanisms for discovering distributed resources, which are often highly dependent on the type of application or middleware. For example, resource discovery can be organized centrally, e.g., DNS, or decentrally, e.g., Gnutella.

Discovery is typically a two-stage process. First, the discovery service needs to be located; then the relevant information is retrieved. The mechanism of how the information is retrieved can be highly decentralized (as in the lower layers of DNS), even though access to the discovery service is centralized. Here, we are concerned about the discovery mechanism as a whole. Therefore, a system that has centralized access to a decentralized search is factored by its lowest common denominator, i.e., the centralized access. There are two examples given below that illustrate this.

As our first example, let's consider DNS which is used to discover an Internet resource. DNS works in much the same way as a telephone book. You give a DNS an Internet site name (e.g., www.cs.cf.ac.uk) and the DNS server returns to you the IP address (e.g., 131.251.49.190) for locating this site. In the same way as you keep a list of name/number pairs on your mobile phone, DNS keeps a list of name/IP number pairs.

DNS is not centralized in structure but the access to the discovery service certainly is because there are generally only a couple of specified hosts that act as DNS servers. Typically, users specify a small number of DNS servers (e.g., one or two), which are narrow relative to the number of services available to it. If these servers go down then access to DNS information is disabled. However, behind this small gateway of hosts, the storage of DNS information is massively hierarchical, employing an efficient decentralized look-up mechanism that is spread amongst many hosts.

Another illustration here is the Web site Google. Google is certainly a centralized Web server in the sense that there is only one Google machine (at a specific time) that binds to the address http://www.google.com. When we ask DNS to provide the Google address, it returns the IP Address 168.127.47.8, which allows you to contact the main Google server directly. However, Google is a Web search engine that is used by millions of people daily and consequently it stores a massive number of entries (around 1.6 billion). To access this information, it relies on a database that uses a parallel cluster of 10,000 Linux machines to provide the service (at the time of writing). Therefore, the access and storage of this information, from a user's perspective, is centralized but from a search or computational perspective, it is certainly distributed across many machines.

1.3.2 Resource Availability

Another important factor is the availability of resources. Again, Web servers fall into the centralized category here because there is only one IP address that hosts a particular site. If that machine goes down then the Web site is unavailable. Of course, machines could be made fault tolerant by replicating the web site and employing some internal switching mechanisms but the availability of the IP address remains the same.

Other systems, however, use a more decentralized approach by offering many duplicate services that can perform the same functionality. Resource availability is tied in closely to resource discovery. There are many examples here but to illustrate various availability levels, let's briefly consider the sharing of files on the internet through the use of three approaches, which are illustrated in Fig. 1.3:

1. MP3.com
2. Napster
3. Gnutella.

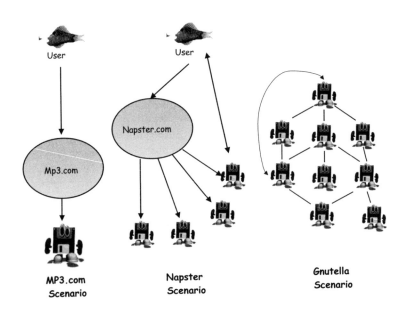

Fig. 1.3. A comparison of service availability from centralized, brokered and decentralized systems.

MP3.com contains a number of MP3 files that are stored locally at (or behind) the Web site. If the Web site or the hard disk(s) containing the database goes down, then users have no access to the content.

Napster, on the other hand, stores the MP3 files on the actual users' machines and *napster.com* is used as a massive index (or meeting place) for connecting users. Users connect to Napster to search for the files they desire and thereafter connect to users directly to download the file. Therefore, each MP3 file is distributed across a number of servers making it more reliable against failure.

However, as the search is centralized, it is dependent on the availability of the main Web site; i.e., if the Web site goes down then access to the MP3 files would also be lost. Interestingly, the difference between MP3.com and Napster is smaller than you may think: one centralizes the files, whilst the other centralizes the addresses of the files. Either is susceptible to failure if the Web site goes down. The difference in Napster's case is that, if the Web site goes down then current users can still finish downloading the current files they have discovered since the communication is decentralized from the main search engine. Therefore, if a user has already located the file and initiated the download process, then the availability of the Web site does not matter and they can quite happily carry on using the service (but not search for more files).

Thirdly, let's consider Gnutella. Gnutella does not have a centralized search facility nor a central storage facility for the files. Each user in the network runs a *servent* (a client and a server), which allows him/her to act as both a provider and consumer of information (as in Napster) but furthermore acts as a search facility also. Servents search for other files by contacting other servents they are connected to, and these servents connect to the servents they are connected to and so on. Therefore, if any of the servents are unavailable, users can almost certainly still reach the file they require (assuming it is available at all).

Here, therefore, it is important to insert redundancy in both the discovery and availability of the resources for a system to be truly robust against single-point failure. Often, when there are a number of duplicated resources available but the discovery of such resources is centralized, we call this a brokered system; i.e., the discovery service brokers the request to another service. Some examples of brokered systems include Napster, Jini, ICQ and Corba

1.3.3 Resource Communication

The last factor is that of resource communication. There are two methods of communication between resources of a distributed system:

1. **Brokered Communication**: where the communication is always passed through a central server and therefore a resource does not have to reference the other resource directly
2. **Point-to-Point (or Peer-to-Peer) Communication**: this involves a direct connection (although this connection may be multi-hop) between the sender and the receiver. In this case, the sender is aware of the receiver's location.

Both forms of communication have their implications on the centralized nature of the systems. In the first case for brokered communication, there is always a central server which passes the information between one resource and another (i.e., centralized). Further, it is almost certainly the case that such systems are centralized from the resource discovery and availability standpoints also, since this level of communication implies fundamental central organization. Some examples here are J2EE, JMS chat and many publish/subscribe systems.

Second, there are many systems that use point-to-point connections, e.g., Napster and Gnutella but also, so do Web servers! Therefore, this category is split horizontally across the scale and the significance here is in the centralization of the communication with respect to the types of connections.

For example, in the Web server example, communication always originates from the user. There exists a **many-to-one** relationship between users and the Web server and therefore this is considered centralized communication. This is illustrated in Fig. 1.4, where an obvious centralized communication pattern is seen for the Web server case.

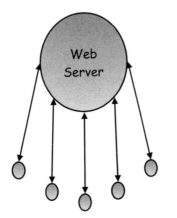 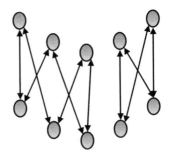

Many-to-one relationship between users and the Web server and therefore this can be considered centralized communication

Equal Peers: communication is *supposed* to be even; i.e., each provider is also a server of information and each node has an equal number of connections

Fig. 1.4. The centralization of communication: a truly decentralized system would have even connections across hosts, rather than a many-to-one type of connectivity.

However, in more decentralized systems, such as Napster and Gnutella, communication is more evenly distributed across the resources; i.e., each provider of information is also a server of information, and therefore the connectivity leans more towards a one-to-one connectivity rather than many-to-one. This equal distribution across the resource (known as equal peers) decentralizes communication across the entire system. However, in practice this is almost never the case because of the behavioural patterns depicted by users of such networks; e.g., some users do not share files and others share many (see Section 7.7).

1.4 Examples of Distributed Applications

In this section, the criteria defining the taxonomy are applied to several well-known examples of existing distributed applications and middleware. The examples given here serve as a point of reference for each chapter that describes the particular application or middleware in more detail.

1.4.1 A Web Server: Centralized

A good example of a centralized system is a Web server. Clients (i.e., users) use their Web browser to navigate Web pages on one or more Web sites. Each Web

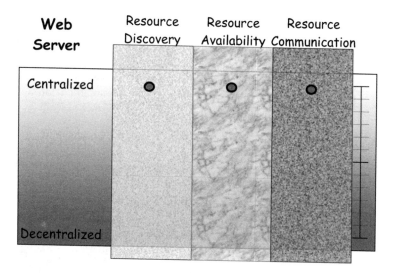

Fig. 1.5. Taxonomy for a Web server.

site is static to the particular domain with which it is associated. A Web server therefore is centralized in every sense. It has centralized discovery (through DNS), it is either available or not and all communication is centralized to the particular Web server being contacted. Communication is point to point but there is a many-to-one relationship between the users of this service and the server itself.

The circles in Fig. 1.5 show the position where a Web server lies on the centralized/decentralized scale for the three categories listed: resource discovery, resource availability and resource communication. The scale at the right-hand side of this graph indicates the broad granularity of our measurements (finer levels would not really change the outcome much anyway) but somewhere around the mid-point would denote the brokered case.

With brokering, typically one service brokers the request to another. DNS does not fall into this category since it has no intrinsic functionality or semantics itself. Web forwarding is a kind of brokering in this sense but this is a one-to-one forwarding. Typically, brokering involves making a decision about where to broker the request and therefore typically, there are many services offering the same functionality from which to choose. Communication can also be brokered by the server acting as a coordinator between the sender and receiver.

1.4.2 SETI@Home: Centralized

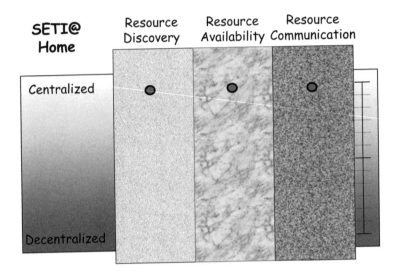

Fig. 1.6. Taxonomy for SETI@Home.

SETI@Home (Search for Extraterrestrial Intelligence) [3] is a project that analyses data from a radio telescope to search for signs of extraterrestrial life. Each user who takes part in this project downloads a data set and executes some signal-processing tasks. The actual program is implemented as a screen saver and therefore only operates when the computer is idle. The SETI@Home project has used over a billion years of CPU time at the time of writing.

Here, the entire system is run from the SETI@Home Web site. Users download the code and also the data when they are available to process. Therefore, the discovery is centralized (DNS) and the communication is centralized to the Web site. Resource availability is also centralized because without the availability of the Web site, the many SETI nodes cannot do anything since they need this server to download the next chunk of data. This taxonomy also applies to BOINC [38], which is the new open source release of the SETI@Home infrastructure. SETI is discussed in more detail in Chapter 2.

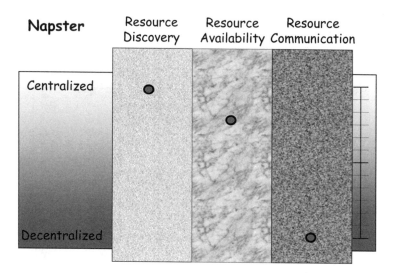

Fig. 1.7. Taxonomy for Napster.

1.4.3 Napster: Brokered

A good example of a brokered system is Napster [4]. Napster stores information about the location of peers and music files in a centralized way but then lets the peers communicate directly when they transfer files.

Here therefore, the discovery and availability are centralized through the Napster Web site but the communication between the peers is decentralized. However, the availability of the resources (i.e., files) is less centralized to a degree because users can still download the file even if the Napster server goes down. However, users cannot search for new resources when the Web site is unavailable and therefore limited in this respect. Napster is described in more detail in Chapter 2.

1.4.4 Gnutella: Decentralized

A popular example of a decentralized system is Gnutella [6] where discovery, availability and communication are completely decentralized over the network. Gnutella is discussed in detail in Chapter 6.

In theory Gnutella is completely decentralized but in practice is this really true? Decentralized networks are inherently self-organizing and so it is not only possible but indeed very likely that strong servers of information (the

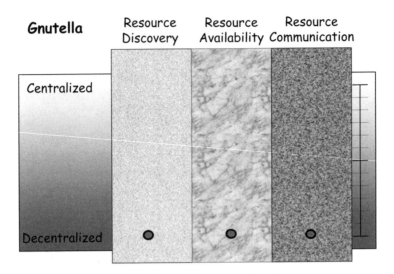

Fig. 1.8. Taxonomy for Gnutella.

so-called super-peers in Gnutella) could easily turn a decentralized network
into a semi-centralized one when peers contain an uneven amount of content.
Whether this is achieved by behavioural patterns or by artificially creating
a centralized-decentralized structure, the resulting network is no longer completely decentralized. This is discussed in detail in Chapter 7.

It is no coincidence, for example, that this evolution of hybrid decentralized and centralized systems echoes the evolution of other types of systems
such as Usenet [62]. The history of Usenet shows us that peer-to-peer (decentralization) and client/server (centralization) are not mutually exclusive.
Usenet was originally peer-to-peer. Sites connected via a modem and agreed
to exchange information (news and mail) with each other (UUCP). However,
over time, it became obvious that certain sites had better servers than others
and these sites went on to form the Usenet backbone. Today, the volume of
Usenet is enormous and servers on the backbone can elect how much information they want to serve and they get added to the Usenet network in a
decentralized fashion. Even the addition of new newsgroups is not centralized
as users have to vote for a newsgroup before it gets initiated.

1.5 Examples of Middleware

1.5.1 J2EE and JMS: Centralized

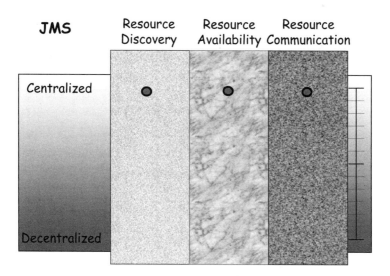

Fig. 1.9. Taxonomy for JMS

The Java development kit enterprise edition J2EE [13] is an example of a centrally controlled system. Here, one Web site is the manager of all interaction between clients. Clients in the Java Messaging System (JMS) do not know the whereabouts of other clients because this knowledge is stored within the central manger on the J2EE server. The entire system is based around a Web site and therefore the discovery is central.

JMS is used as a publish/subscribe mechanism within the J2EE environment (amongst other things) and is quite typical of other messaging systems, e.g., ICQ where messages are brokered through a central server in order to get to their destination. Therefore, the communication is brokered through the Web site. Further, there is only one copy of the Web site (typically these are quite complicated to set up) and therefore the availability is centralized also.

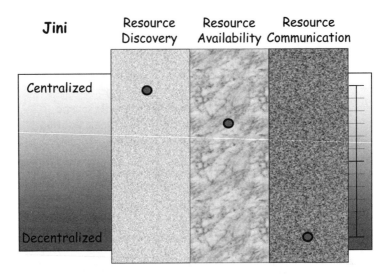

Fig. 1.10. Taxonomy for Jini.

1.5.2 Jini: Brokered

Jini [78] allows Java objects to become network-enabled services that can be distributed in a network 'plug and play' manner. In a running Jini system, there are three main players. There is a service, such as a printer, a supercomputer running a software service etc. There is a client which would like to make use of this service. Third, there is a lookup service (service locator) which acts as a broker/trader/locator between services and clients. Jini is discussed in detail in Chapters 5 and 11.

Jini is another example of a brokered system. Jini clients find out about services by using the lookup server. The lookup server brokers the request to a matching service and thereafter the communication takes place directly between the client and services. Therefore, the availability is centralized in the sense that it is dependent on the Jini lookup service but on the other hand, once a client discovers a service it wishes to use, the client and service can carry on communicating without the availability of the lookup service. Therefore, as in previous brokered systems, the availability is better than a strict centralized system.

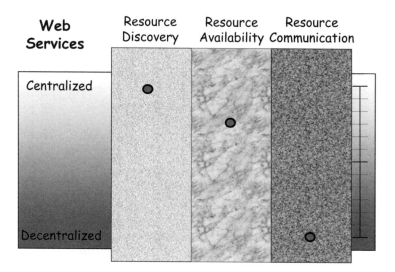

Fig. 1.11. Taxonomy for Web services.

1.5.3 Web Services: Brokered

At the core of the Web services model is the notion of a service, which can be described, discovered and invoked using standard XML technologies such as SOAP, WSDL and UDDI. Conventionally, Web services are described by a WSDL document, advertised and discovered using a UDDI server and invoked with a message conforming to the SOAP specification.

Web services therefore use the same brokered model as other systems, such as Napster, Jini or CORBA and therefore have a similar taxonomy to those systems. However, Web services differentiates itself by being based completely on open standards that has gained enormous support from thousands of companies and have been adopted by several communities, including the GGF. Web services are discussed in detail in Chapters 3, 13 and 14.

1.5.4 Jxta: Decentralized

Project Jxta [15] defines a set of protocols that can be used to construct peer-to-peer systems using any of the centralized, brokered and decentralized approaches but its main aim is to facilitate the creation of decentralized systems. Jxta's goal is to develop basic building blocks and services to enable P2P applications for interested groups of peers. Jxta will be discussed, both

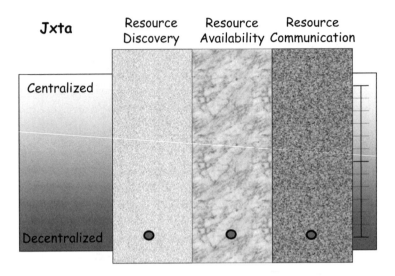

Fig. 1.12. Taxonomy for JXTA.

conceptually and from a programmers perspective in Chapters 10 and 12, respectively.

Jxta can support any level of centralization/decentralization but its main focus (and hence power) is to facilitate the development of decentralized applications. Therefore, in this context, Jxta peers can be located in a decentralized fashion; they have much redundancy in their availability and their communication is point to point and therefore no central control authority is needed for their operation.

1.6 Conclusion

In this chapter, the critical components of any distributed system were outlined concentrating particularly on the role of *middleware*. Distributed-systems terminology was introduced, along with notion of a service, which will be used frequently within this book. We then discussed a taxonomy for distributed systems based on a scale ranging from centralized to decentralized, which factored in: resource discovery, resource availability and resource communication. Several well-known distributed applications and middleware have been classified using this taxonomy, which will serve as a placeholder and give context to the distributed systems described in the rest of this book.

Part I

Distributed Environments

In this book, there are four main themes: distributed environments, middleware and applications, middleware deployment and future trends. We begin by setting the scene and introducing three diverse, yet somewhat complimentary technologies, that have evolved over the past several years. These are peer to peer, Web services and Grid computing. Each of these technological areas addresses specific issues within the distributed system spectrum and, as we look ahead, it is highly likely that each will play an important role in contributing to our future distributed-systems infrastructure.

2

Peer-2-Peer Systems

At the time of writing, there are one and a half billion devices worldwide (e.g., PCs, phone, PDAs, etc.), a figure which is rising rapidly. Surveys have stated that Internet users surpassed 530 million in 2001 and predictions indicate that this will double to 1.12 billion by year-end 2005 [175].

The computer hardware industry has also been characterised by exponential production volumes. Gordon Moore, the co-founder of Intel, in his famous observation in 1965 [140] (made just four years after the first planar integrated circuit was discovered), predicted that the number of transistors on integrated circuits would double every few years. Indeed this prediction, thereafter called *Moore's law*, remains true up until today and Intel predicts that this will remain true at least until the end of this decade [141].

Such acceleration in development has been made possible by the massive investment by companies who deal with comparatively short product life cycles. Each user now in this massive network has the CPU capability of more than 100 times that of an early 1990s supercomputer and surprisingly, GartnerGroup research reveals that over 95% of today's PC power is wasted. The potential of such a distributed computing resource has been in some ways demonstrated by the SETI@Home project [3], having used over a million years of CPU time at the time of writing.

In this chapter, peer-to-peer computing, a possible paradigm for making use of such devices, is discussed. An historical perspective is given, followed by a definition, taxonomy and justification for P2P computing. A background into the P2P environment is given followed by examples of several P2P applications that operate within such an environment.

2.1 What is Peer to Peer?

This section gives a brief background and history of the term "peer to peer" and describes its definition in the current context. Examples of P2P technologies are given followed by categorizations of their behaviour within the taxonomy described in the first chapter.

2.1.1 Historical Peer to Peer

Peer to peer was originally used to describe the communication of two peers and is analogous to a telephone conversation. A phone conversation involves two people (peers) of equal status, communication between a point-to-point connection. Simply, this is what P2P is, a point-to-point connection between two **equal** participants.

The Internet started as a peer-to-peer system. The goal of the original ARPANET was to share computing resources around the USA. Its challenge was to connect a set of distributed resources, using different network connectivity, within one common network architecture. The first hosts on the ARPANET were several US universities, e.g., the University College of Los Angeles, Santa Barbara, SRI and University of Utah. These were already independent computing sites with equal status and the ARPANET connected them as such, not in a master/slave or client/server relationship but rather as equal computing peers.

From the late 1960s until 1994, the Internet had one model of connectivity. Machines were assumed to be always switched on, always connected, and assigned permanent IP addresses. The original DNS system was designed for this environment, where a change in IP address was assumed to be abnormal and rare, and could take days to propagate through the system.

However, with the invention of Mosaic, another model began to emerge in the form of users connecting to the Internet from dial-up modems. This created a second class of connectivity because PCs would enter and leave the network frequently and unpredictably. Further, because ISPs began to run out of IP addresses, they began to assign IP addresses dynamically for each session, giving each PC a different, possibly masked, IP address. This transient nature and instability prevented PCs from being assigned permanent DNS entries, and therefore prevented most PC users from hosting any data or network-facing applications locally.

For a few years, treating PCs as clients worked well. Over time though, as hardware and software improved, the unused resources that existed behind this veil of second-class connectivity started to look like something worth getting at. Given the vast array of available processors mentioned earlier, the software community is starting to take P2P applications very seriously. Most importantly, P2P research is concerned in addressing some of the main difficulties of current distributed computing: scalability, reliability, interoperability.

2.1.2 Binding of Peers

Within today's Internet, we rely on fixed IP addresses. When a user types an address into his/her Web browser (such as http://www.google.com/), the

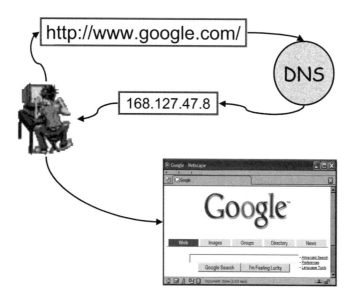

Fig. 2.1. The process whereby an Internet address is converted into the IP address for locating a Web page on the Internet.

Web server address is translated into the IP address (e.g., 168.127.47.8) by a domain name server (DNS). The Internet protocol (IP) then makes a routing decision based on the IP Address. If DNS is unavailable then typing http://168.127.47.8/ into a browser would be equivalent since the Web page is permanently bound to the IP address.

This is known as static or early binding. Figure 2.1 illustrates this process graphically. Early bindings form a simple architecture very similar to an address book on a mobile phone; e.g., the person's name is statically bound to his/her telephone number. This works in practice because typically people have long-term (early) bindings with their phone numbers and Web sites have long-term bindings with their IP addresses.

However, if a Web site changed its IP address several times a day then this type of binding starts to become impractical. Within P2P networks this is the norm. Often devices do not have a fixed address as they are hidden behind Network Address Translation (NAT) systems and therefore need a **late binding** of their addresses with their network identifier.

2.1.3 Modern Definition of Peer to Peer

With the emergence of new technologies in the late 1990s a new definition for peer to peer has begun to emerge, as follows:

> P2P is a class of applications that takes advantage of resources e.g. storage, cycles, content, human presence, available at the edges of the Internet (Shirky [46]).

Computers/devices "at the edges of the Internet" are those operating within transient and often hostile environments. Devices within this environment: can come and go frequently; can be hidden behind a firewall or operate outside of DNS, e.g., by NAT (see next section); and often have to deal with differing transport protocols, devices and operating systems (see Fig. 2.2 below). Often the number of computers in a P2P network is enormous consisting of millions of interconnecting peers.

This modern definition rather defines the P2P environment of devices and resources rather than previous definitions that focused on the *servent* methodology and decentralized nature of systems like Gnutella [6]. For example, in Gnutella, there are two key differences compared to client/server based systems:

- A peer can act as both a client and a server (they call these *servents* i.e. *serv*er and cli*ent* in Gnutella.)
- The network is completely decentralized and has no central point of control. Peers in a Gnutella network are typically connected to three or four other nodes and to search the network a query is broadcast throughout the network.

Certainly, within P2P systems, peers exist as defined in Gnutella. However, P2P networks do not have to be completely decentralized. This is evident in modern Gnutella implementations [51], which employ a centralized/decentralized approach in order to be able to scale the network and increase efficiency of search. Such networks are implemented using super-peers that cache file locations so that peers only have to search a small fraction of the network in order to satisfy their search requests.

Therefore, Shirky's definition here is more appropriate to describe a new class of applications that are designed to work within this highly transient environment (see also section 2.2), something previously unattainable.

Systems like Gnutella are now often referred to as **True P2P** (see Section 2.1.5) because of their pure decentralized approach, where everyone participates equally in the network. However, this ideal can never really be realised by a P2P system simply because certainly not all peers are equal within actual P2P networks, which has been proven by several empirical studies [69], [37] and [67]. See the next two chapters for a detailed overview of the evolving network topologies employed by recent decentralized file-sharing networks.

Other authors have noted the same. From [24], the authors state that "they prefer this definition to the alternative 'decentralized, self-organizing distributed systems, in which all or most communication is symmetric,' because it encompasses large-scale deployed (albeit centralized) P2P systems (such as Napster and SETI@Home) where much experience has been gained".

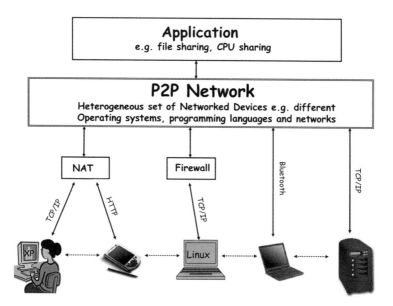

Fig. 2.2. A P2P environment: devices are connected behind NATs and firewalls; they run on different platforms, potentially using different programming languages, e.g. Jxta [15].

Examples of recent P2P technologies include:

- File sharing/storage programs, e.g., Gnutella [6], Napster [4], Limewire [51], KaZaA [52], Freenet [58] and Popular Power [53], some of which have taken the spotlight by providing a way of sharing any type of digital file, of which, users typically provide audio and video files
- CPU resource-sharing systems, e.g., SETI@Home [3], United Devices[54], Entropia [55] and XtremWeb [191]
- Instant messaging (e.g., ICQ [56] and Jabber [5])
- Conferencing applications e.g.,netmeeting [57] for white-boarding, voice over IP.

What makes these similar is that they are all leveraging previously unused resources by tolerating and even working with the variable connectivity that many devices connected to these networks exhibit.

2.1.4 Social Impacts of P2P

The legal connotations and social impacts of P2P are ongoing. No doubt, it has opened the eyes and imaginations of people from numerous disciplines to the massive sharing of resources across the Internet. Even within the context of the sharing of copyrighted material, there are compulsive arguments for and against the use of such technologies. There are a number of articles and books written on the subject that support the concept of P2P and those that give legal context for it. For example, on the *Open Democracy* Web site, there are a number of articles that give a social context for P2P, both from a cultural perspective and a legal one. In this section, a very brief summary of some of the points raised is given.

Vaidhyanathan [178], in his five-part article on the new information ecosystem, paints a picturesque account of a deep cultural change that is taking place through the introduction of P2P technologies. He argues that "what we call P2P communicative networks actually reflect and amplify - revise and extend - an old ideology or cultural habit. Electronic peer-to-peer systems like Gnutella merely simulates other, more familiar forms of unmediated, uncensorable, irresponsible, troublesome speech; for example, anti-royal gossip before the French revolution, trading cassette tapes among youth subcultures as punk or rap, or the illicit Islamist cassette tapes through the streets and bazaars of Cairo."

He argues against the current clampdown strategy that is being employed by companies and governments. Such a strategy involves radically redesigning the communication technologies so that information can be monitored more closely. These restrictions would destroy the current openness of the current Internet and could bring about a new type of Internet which, he says, would "not be open and customisable. Content - and thus culture - would not be adaptable and malleable. And what small measures of privacy these networks now afford would evaporate".

Rainsford [179] uses the term "information feudalism", which was taken from an analogy given by Peter Drahos [181]. Drahos suggests that

> The current push for control over intellectual property rights has bred a situation analogous to the feudal agricultural system in the medieval period. In effect, songwriters and scientists work for corporate feudal lords, licensing their own inventions in exchange for a living and the right to 'till the lands' of the information society.

Rainsford quotes a number of authors who believe that the struggle that we are experiencing has deep underlying roots in cultural transformations, which will inevitably bring about a change in the decaying business models of today. Rainsford also notes that "the links asserted between p2p systems and terrorism, or the funding of terrorism" are "a concept which is laughably ironic as p2p by its very nature is a non-profit system".

Rimmer [180] gives a legal case for the argument and argues that "if claims by peer-to-peer distributors that they are supporting free speech and contributing to knowledge want to find a sympathetic ear in the courtroom, then they have to mean it". He discusses the current use of P2P and argues that they have not lived up to their revolutionary promise, being used mostly for circulating copyrighted media around the world. He lists several cases which have been brought against companies, which have resulted in infringements, and some that have not.

Rimmer states that P2P networks are "vulnerable to legal actions for copyright infringements because they have facilitated the dissemination of copyright media for profit and gain." He concludes that "the courts would be happy to foster such technology if it promoted the freedom of speech, the mixing of cultures, and the progress of science".

For further reading, see the articles listed or the Open Democracy Web site [177], which hosts a series of articles in response to these comments. Similar articles appear on other Web sites, such as OpenP2P [65].

2.1.5 True Peer to Peer?

Within P2P, there are three categories of systems (as outlined in Chapter 1):

- **Centralized systems:** where every peer connects to a server which co-ordinates and manages communication. Some examples here include the CPU sharing applications, e.g., SETI@Home
- **Brokered systems:** where peers connect to a server in order to discover other peers, but then manage the communication themselves (e.g., Napster). This is also called Brokered P2P.
- **Decentralized systems:** where peers run independently without the need for centralized services. Here, the discovery is decentralized and the communication takes place between the peers. Peers do not need a known centralized service for them to operate, e.g., Gnutella, Freenet

Most Internet services are distributed using the traditional client/server (centralized) architecture. In this architecture, clients connect to a server using a specific communications protocol (e.g., TCP) to obtain access to a specific resource. Most of the processing involved in delivering a service usually occurs on the server, leaving the client relatively unburdened. Most popular Internet applications, including the World Wide Web, FTP, telnet, and email, use this service-delivery model. Unfortunately, this architecture has a major drawback; that is, as the number of clients increases (and therefore load and bandwidth) the server becomes a bottleneck and can eventually result in the server not being able to handle any additional clients.

The advantage of the client/server model is that it requires less computational power on the client side. However, this has been somewhat circumvented due to ever-increasing CPU power and therefore most desktop PCs are ludicrously overpowered to operate as simple clients, e.g., for browsing and email.

P2P, on the other hand, has the capability of serving resources with high availability at a much lower cost, while maximizing the use of resources from every peer connected to the P2P network. Whereas client/server solutions rely on costly bandwidth, equipment, and location to maintain a robust solution, P2P can offer a similar level of robustness by spreading network and resource demands across the network. Note though that some middleware architectures used to program such systems are often capable of operating in one or more of these modes.

Further, the more decentralized the system, the better the fault tolerance, since the services are spread across more resources. Therefore, at the far side of the scale, you have true P2P systems, which employ a completely decentralized structure, both in look-up and in communication. Hong [62] gives a useful description for communication within P2P systems. He defines P2P systems as being a class of distributed systems that are biased to more of a decentralized approach, where there is no global notion of centralization. He argues that such systems are primarily concerned with smaller distributed levels of centralization with respect to communication.

When designing a P2P system therefore, there is a trade-off between inserting the correct amount of decentralization for the network to be fault tolerant against failure but centralized enough to scale to large number of participants. These issues are discussed in detail in Chapter 7.

2.1.6 Why Peer-to-Peer?

So why is P2P important. What's new?

Although the term P2P, in many peoples' minds, is linked with distributing copyrighted material illegally, it has in fact much more to offer. P2P file-sharing applications have addressed a number of important issues when dealing with large-scale connectivity of transient devices. There are a number of practical real-world applications for such a technology, both on the Internet [54] [3] and on wireless networks, e.g., for mobile sensors applications [176], and in many different kinds of scientific and social experiments.

P2P could provide more useful and robust solutions over current technologies in many different situations. For example, current search engine solutions centralize the knowledge and their resources. This is an inherent limitation. Google, for example, relies on a central database that is updated daily by scouring the Internet for new information. Simply due to the massive size of this database (more than 1.6 billion entries) not every entry gets updated every day, and as a result, information can often be out of date. Further, it is impractical (from a cost perspective) that such solutions will be scalable for the future Internet.

For example, even though Google, at the time of writing, runs a cluster of 10,000 machines to provide its service, it only searches a subset of available Web pages (about 1.3×10^8) to create its database. Furthermore, the world produces two exabytes (2×10^{18} bytes) each year but only publishes about 300 terabytes (3×10^{12} bytes) i.e. for every megabyte of information produced, one byte gets published. Therefore, finding useful information in real-time is becoming increasingly difficult.

A similar service could be implemented using P2P technology. One possibility is that every person runs a personal Web server on a desktop computer that has the capability to process requests for information about the documents it manages. A user's server could receive a query, check the local documents and respond with a list of matching documents. Each server would be responsible for indexing its own documents and would therefore be capable of providing more specialized, accurate and up-to-date information.

This decentralization of indexing is much more manageable than the task facing Google. Corporations could also provide specialized information available that current search engines cannot reach. Further, if the user's server disconnected from the network then the search service would also become unavailable and therefore users searching would not receive results for unavailable resources as they do at present. This solution outlines an extreme P2P solution, but in practice some combinational technique could prove very effective.

2.2 The P2P Environment

This section covers the technology that makes the P2P environment so difficult to work within. In Fig. 2.2, this environment was illustrated; that is, peers are: extremely transient (they are continually disappearing and reappearing), connections are often multi-hop (i.e., packets travel via several intermediaries before they reach their destination), and peers reside in hostile environments (i.e., they live behind NAT routing systems and firewalls).

In this section, a background is given into some of the technologies behind P2P networks, which helps set a more realistic P2P scene. The first section makes a brief excursion into switching technology for networks. The second section describes a particular subset of these that contains NAT systems. Lastly, firewalls are discussed.

2.2.1 Hubs, Switches, Bridges, Access Points and Routers

This section gives a brief overview of the various devices used to partition a network, which gives the context for the following two sections on NAT and firewalls often employed within a P2P network. Briefly, the critical distinction between these devices is the level or layer at which they operate within the International Standard Organization's Open System Interconnect (ISO/OSI) model, which defines seven network layers [98].

- **Hubs:** A hub is a repeater that works at the physical (lowest) layer of OSI. A hub takes data that comes into a port and sends it to the other ports in the hub. It doesn't perform any filtering or redirection of data. You can think of a hub as a kind of Internet chat room. Everyone who joins a particular chat is seen by everyone else. If there are too many people trying to chat, things get bogged down.

- **Switches and Bridges:** These are pretty similar. Both operate at the Data Link layer (just above Physical) and both can filter data so that only the appropriate segment or host receives a transmission. Both filter packets based on the physical address (i.e. Media Access Control (MAC) address) of the sender/receiver although newer switches sometimes include the capabilities of a router and can forward data based on IP address (operating at the network layer), referred to as IP switches. In general, bridges are used to extend the distance capabilities of the network while minimizing overall traffic, and switches are used primarily for their filtering capabilities to create multiple, smaller virtual local area networks (LANs) out of one large LAN for easier management/administration (V-LANs).

- **Routers:** These work at the Network layer of OSI (above Data Link) and operate on the IP address. Like switches and bridges, they filter by only forwarding packets destined for remote networks thus minimizing traffic, but are significantly more complex than any other networking device; thus they require much more maintenance and administration. The home networker typically uses a DSL or cable modem router that joins the home's LAN to the wide area network (WAN) of the Internet. By maintaining configuration information in a "routing table" routers also have the ability to filter traffic, either incoming or outgoing, based on the IP addresses of senders and receivers. Most routers allow the home networker to update the routing table from a Web browser interface. DSL and cable modem routers typically combine the functions of a router with those of a switch in a single unit.

2.2.2 NAT Systems

For a computer to communicate with other computers and Web servers on the Internet, it must have an IP address. An IP address is a unique 32-bit number that identifies the location of your computer on a network. There are, in theory, 2^{32} (4,294,967,296) unique addresses but the actual number available is much smaller (somewhere between 3.2 and 3.3 billion). This is due to the way that the addresses are separated into classes and also because some are set aside for multicasting, testing or other special uses.

With the explosion of the Internet and the increase in home networks and business networks, the number of available IP addresses is simply not enough. An obvious solution is to redesign the address format to allow for more possible addresses. This is being developed and is called IPv6, but it may take several years to deploy because it requires modification of the entire infrastructure of the Internet.

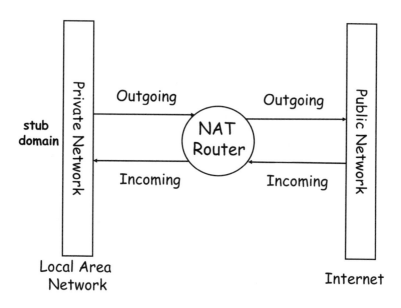

Fig. 2.3. A NAT System divides a local network from the public network and offers local-to-public mapping of addresses. This allows the number of machines on the Internet to increase past the physical limit. A NAT system converts local addresses within the *stub domain* into one Internet address.

A network address translation system (see Fig. 2.3) allows a single device, such as a router, to act as an agent between the Internet (public network) and a local (private) network. This means that only a single, unique IP address is required to represent an entire group of computers. The internal network is usually a LAN; commonly referred to as the *stub domain*. A stub domain is a LAN that uses IP addresses internally. Any internal computers that use unregistered IP addresses must use NAT to communicate with the rest of the world.

There are two types of NAT translation, static or dynamic, which are illustrated in Fig. 2.4. Static NAT involves mapping an unregistered IP address to a registered IP address on a one-to-one basis. Particularly useful when a device needs to be accessible from outside the network (i.e., in static NAT), the computer with the IP address of 192.168.0.0 will always translate to 131.251.45.110 (see upper part of Fig. 2.4).

Dynamic NAT, on the other hand, maps an unregistered IP address to a registered IP address from a group of local dynamically allocatable IP addresses, i.e., the stub domain computers will be allocated an address from a specified range of addresses, e.g., 192.168.0.0 to 192.168.0.50, in Figure 2.4 and

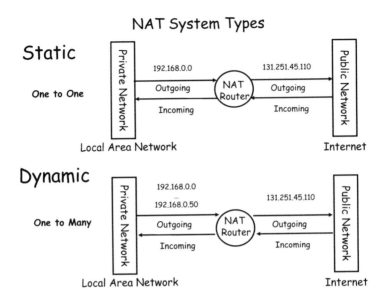

Fig. 2.4. A NAT system can be allocate dynamic address or translate from fixed stub domain address to outside ones.

will translate these to 131.251.45.110 for the outside world. In this circumstance, it is easy to see why NAT systems are problematic since you could have potentially hundreds of stub domain computers masquerading as one external IP address.

2.2.3 Firewalls

A firewall is a system designed to prevent unauthorized access to or from a private network. All messages entering or leaving the computer system pass through the firewall, which examines each message and blocks those that do not meet the specified security criteria. Specifically, firewalls are implemented by blocking certain ports, thereby disabling certain types of services that operate on those ports.

Some firewalls permit only email traffic, thereby protecting the network against any attacks other than attacks against the email service. Other firewalls provide less strict protections, and block services that are known to be problematic. Generally, firewalls are configured to protect against unauthenticated interactive logins from the outside world. This, more than anything, helps prevent unauthorized users from logging into machines on your network.

More elaborate firewalls block traffic from the outside to the inside, but permit users on the inside to communicate freely with the outside. Figure 2.5

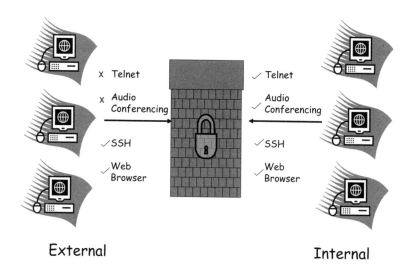

External   Internal

Fig. 2.5. A firewall blocks traffic to and from specified ports, here only SSH and Web browsing are allowed by external computers.

illustrates a scenario where both telnet and audio conferencing are blocked from the outside world but Web browsing and SSH connections are acceptable. However, internal users can freely open up external connections using any of these services but, in this example, they would not be able to hear the other participants in the audio conference because incoming audio is blocked.

A firewall therefore can essentially protect you against most types of network attack. Firewalls are also important since they can provide a single choke point where security and audit can be imposed, i.e., they can provide an important logging and auditing function and provide summaries to the administrator about what kinds and amount of traffic passed through it and how many attempts there were to break into it. Within P2P applications, it is often necessary to traverse such firewalls, for example, by rerouting the data over the HTTP port.

2.2.4 P2P Overlay Networks

P2P implementations frequently involve the creation of overlay networks ([23]) with a structure that is completely independent of that of the underlying network of connected devices. The purpose of overlay networks is that they abstract the complicated connectivity of a P2P network to a higher-level programmatical view of the peers that make up the network. This is illustrated in Fig. 2.6 which shows the programmer's view of the network (see top cloud of peers) that simplifies and abstracts the network structure and underlying transport mechanisms (see bottom part) into a collection of cooperating peers.

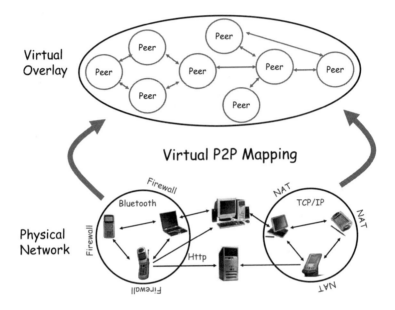

Fig. 2.6. An illustration of the notion of an overlay network. Modern P2P infrastructures typically overlay a virtual view of the nodes on the network to abstract the underlying mechanisms that actually connect these devices; this example was taken from Jxta [15].

There are several different types of overlay networks. For example, within Jxta, a virtual network overlay sits on top of the physical devices and is organized into transient or persistent relationships, which they call peer groups. Peers in Jxta are not required to have direct point-to-point network connections and such connections are represented through the use of virtual pipes. Virtual pipes simply define the endpoints of the connection and leave it to the underlying mechanisms to implement the appropriate behaviour for that environment, e.g., for TCP, a fixed point-to-point connection is created for the pipe but for UDP pipes this is not required and therefore the pipe remains connectionless. Other network overlays include the use of distributed hashtables e.g. Chord [45] or Pastry [44].

2.3 P2P Example Applications

2.3.1 MP3 File Sharing with Napster

Napster [4], the famous MP3 file sharing program, was launched in 1999. It had a revolutionary impact on the Internet due to its infamous reputation for sharing illegal MP3 files and its unique design; i.e., after the initial centralized Napster search, clients connected to each other and exchanged data directly from one system's disk to another. Figure 2.7 illustrates this process.

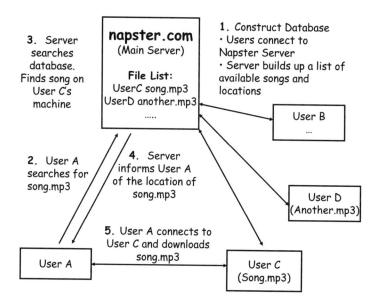

Fig. 2.7. The Napster scenario for providing a distributed file system for music files.

Users first connect to the main Napster server and register themselves to join the network. The main server obtains a list of MP3s that the user has and adds this to the list of songs in the central database. When a user (User A) performs a search, Napster searches the local database on the main server and then returns the address of the peer that has a copy of the file. User A then connects directly to the peer that has the file (User B) and downloads the file directly from this user's disk without any further intervention from the host, unless communication is interrupted (because the peer has logged off, for example).

Napster is P2P because the Napster peers bypass DNS and because once the Napster server resolves the IP address of the PCs hosting a particular song, it shifts control of the file transfers to the nodes. However, Napster is an example of brokered P2P for the same reasons.

2.3.2 Distributed Computing Using SETI@Home

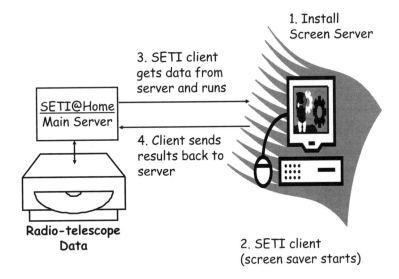

Fig. 2.8. SETI algorithm for performing distributed data analysis on radio-telescope data.

In 1996, SETI@Home [3] was launched, which is a scientific experiment that uses Internet-connected computers in the **S**earch for **E**xtra**T**errestrial **I**ntelligence. SETI distributes a screen saver based application to users that uses various signal analysis algorithms to process radio-telescope data. At the time of writing, it had signed up more than three million users (around a half million active contributors) and had used over a million years of CPU time. The client software (i.e., the screen saver) contacts a server to download the data to process and then processes this until the problem is solved, then returns the results back to the server (see Fig. 2.8). If the run does not succeed then this data segment is assumed to be lost and therefore ignored.

There are other similar projects:

- Distributed.net [64] uses computing power to crack previously unbreakable encrypted messages.

- Companies such as United Devices [54] and Entropia [55] which solve a varied number of problems for both non-profit and commercial gains. For example, United Devices in February 2003 used their meta processor to help the United States Department of Defence (DoD) to find a cure for smallpox [40].

2.3.3 Instant Messaging with ICQ

One of the most popular instant messaging programs, ICQ [56], was released in November 1996. ICQ notifies users when their friends come online and allows them to send messages to each other. Furthermore, apart from its instant messaging capabilities it allows users to exchange files.

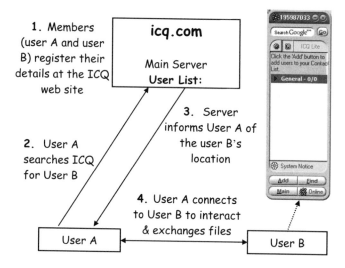

Fig. 2.9. ICQ scenario uses a brokered approach using a central database to store user's information. To the right, the current ICQ user interface is given.

ICQ is a hybrid of the decentralized and client/server architectures (see Fig. 2.9). It uses a central server to monitor the users that are currently on line and to notify interested parties when new users connect to the network. All other communication between users is conducted between the users directly. Therefore, this employs a brokered P2P architecture, similar to Napster, having a central database of users (where Napster has files) for lookup purposes only, with communication taking place independently of this central authority.

2.3.4 File Sharing with Gnutella

Gnutella is a 'true P2P' system. It does not rely on central control for lookup, organization and communication. The internal mechanisms of Gnutella will be discussed in detail in Chapter 6 but briefly; the scenario is given here in Fig. 2.10.

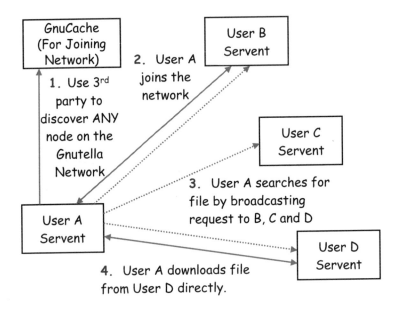

Fig. 2.10. Gnutella decentralized approach. There are two aspects to discovery: joining the network and then discovering other peers.

There are several ways of joining a Gnutella network. The one given in Figure 2.10 uses a *GnuCache* as a lookup server for a list of Gnutella nodes, but one could easily use another method; e.g., use newsgroups to get lists of nodes, Web sites, etc. The node joins the network by connecting initially to one Gnutella node, which can be any node on the network making it generally easy to join in a decentralized fashion.

Once it has joined the node discovers other nodes through the first node by issuing *ping* and receiving *pong* descriptors from peers accepting connections. Gnutella nodes typically connect to three nodes and then search by broadcasting their search request to all connected neighbours, as illustrated here. Each neighbour repeats this search request to his/her neighbours and so on, which is known as *flooding the network*. Here, User D has the required file so User A connects directly to User D and downloads the file using this point-to-point connection.

2.3.5 Conclusion

There are many aspects to categorising a system as P2P. Although, a true P2P system employs a completely decentralized structure (e.g., Gnutella), there also exist other systems that have other structures, e.g., Napster has a hybrid P2P structure and SETI has a centralized structure. Therefore, although decentralization is not a required consideration of P2P systems, it is a desired one. The real key features of P2P that make it a new computing paradigm is that P2P applications:

1. operate at the *edges of the Internet*; behind Firewalls and NAT Translation systems
2. operate in hostile environments, e.g., transient connections where failure is the norm
3. take advantage of unused resources, e.g., storage, cycles, content, human presence, etc.

3

Web Services

Tim Berners-Lee, the inventor of the World Wide Web, noted:

> As we look forward, we are tempted to distinguish between the multimedia world of information targeted for human perception, and the well-defined world of data which machines handle.... The Web technology must allow information intended for a human to be effectively presented, and also allow machine processable data to be conveyed. Only then can we start to use computers as tools again [155].

3.1 Introduction

Up until recently, data has been exported on the World Wide Web for human consumption in the form of Web pages. Most people therefore use the Web to read news/articles, to buy goods and services, to manage on-line accounts and so on. For this purpose, we use a Web browser and access information mostly through this medium.

From a publishing perspective, this involves converting the raw information, from a database, for example, into HTML or similar language so that it can be rendered in the correct form. Further, many Web sites collate information from other sites via Web pages, which is a bizarre occurrence involving decoding and parsing human-readable information not intended for machines at all (see Fig. 3.1).

This scenario works well for many applications but it is highly redundant because the conversion from the raw data into human-readable format for publication and availability does not support software interactions very well. What we really need to do is to provide a mechanism whereby the raw data can be accessed in a similar fashion by machines as humans read Web pages now. Therefore, a more efficient mechanism is required in order to enable true

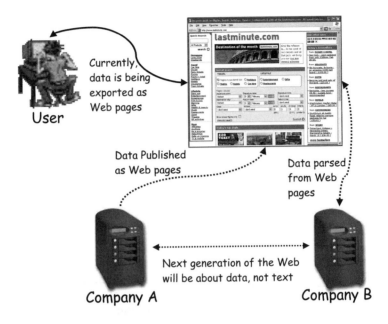

Fig. 3.1. We use the Web for Web browsing at the moment but the next generation will be more focused on machine-to-machine interaction.

machine-to-machine communication to provide a machine-processable Web. This is illustrated in Fig. 3.1.

Many believe, including Berners-Lee, that the next generation of the Web will be about data, not text. Providing ubiquitous mechanisms for representing and providing data in a machine-readable fashion is at the core of *Web services*. Companies are increasingly in need of standard mechanisms to be able to publish, advertise and discover links to actual data sources, rather than Web pages.

3.1.1 Looking Forward: What Do We Need?

In order to see what we need to build a new infrastructure that allows such machine-to-machine Web communication, let's take a brief look at why, and how, the World Wide Web started.

Berners-Lee created the first Web browser in 1990 at CERN in Switzerland, where a few thousand scientists worked using a variety of different computers. He soon found it frustrating to exchange data with different collaborators because he had to log onto the various computers to be able to share information.

After writing various similar programs to transfer and convert information from one system to another, he started to think about better ways of achieving

Browsers

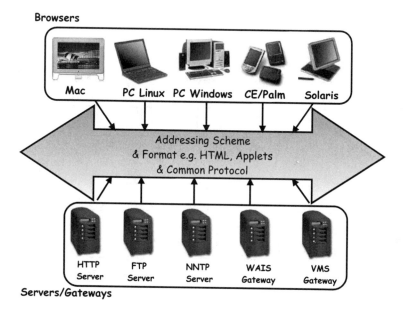

Servers/Gateways

Fig. 3.2. The model for the World Wide Web. Multiple types of browsers can talk to multiple types of machines if they share common address schemes, formats and protocols.

this. He then came up with the idea of creating some imaginary information system which everyone could read. He took the existing *hypertext* idea[1] [173] and wrote the first Web browser that connected via DNS and TCP to create the start of the World Wide Web; but that, he says, was the easy bit ... the difficult bit was to get people to join in.

Figure 3.2 illustrates this idea. The Web allows many disparate information systems to serve data by creating an abstract imaginary space where these differences do not exist. A Universal Resource Identifier(URI) identified the document and a suite of protocols (e.g., HTTP) and data formats (e.g., HTML) formed a *bus* which allowed computers to exchange information by mapping from their **local formats** into **standards** that provided global interoperability. The Web therefore was deployed as a set of protocols, not a single program, as shown.

This layer provided the interface for interoperability between the diverse clients and servers that existed on the Internet. The initial so-called *World-WideWeb* browser was developed on a NeXT workstation and the first Web server was *nxoc01.cern.ch*, later changing its name to *info.cern.ch*. The follow-

---

[1] Vannevar Bush was the conceptual creator, laying out the notion of the modern hyperlink in 1945, and in 1965, Ted Nelson coined the word "hypertext."

Machine/Browser/Server

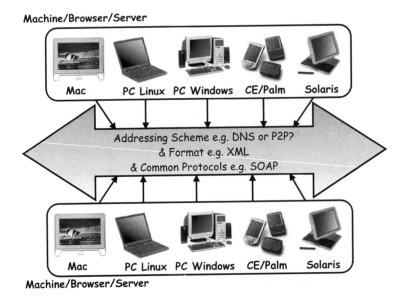

Machine/Browser/Server

Fig. 3.3. Creating a machine-to-machine communicable Web involves building a common layer of protocols.

ing year the Stanford Linear Accelerator Center (SLAC) in California became the first Web server in the USA as the widespread distribution of the software began.

In 1992, there were 50 Web servers worldwide; in 1993 NCSA released the first alpha version of Marc Andreessen's "Mosaic for X." Then in October 1994, Berners-Lee founded the World Wide Web Consortium (W3C) for standardizing common protocols to promote the Web's evolution and ensure its interoperability. By this time, the WWW explosion had already set in. For example, Internet users increased from 40 million in 1995 to 150 million in 1998 and 320 million by year 2000. Further, It has been projected that there will be 1.12 billion Internet users by year-end 2005 [175].

For the machine-to-machine interoperable Web, we need the same kind of group of protocols that will allow machines to interoperate at the data level. To achieve this, we must build this layer out of standardized technologies in order to gain widespread adoption.

The first step was for commercial and non-commercial sectors to agree on a common data format in order to be able to expose their functionality to others in a truly interoperable fashion. This led to the standardization of XML through W3C [97], the latest version being 1.0, Third Edition [95].

Since then, a number of other technologies have been standardized through W3C and other organizations, such as OASIS [167]. Figure 3.4 shows a list of a subset of the standards that are used at each level, ranging from the network protocols, data transport and service descriptions, through to higher-level workflow orchestration languages, such as BPEL4WS [172]. For a more complete list, see [192].

The three core technologies will be described in detail in Chapter 13, but briefly they are: SOAP, which provides an *envelope* for the XML message; WSDL, which provides the description of the interface for the Web service; and UDDI, which provides a lookup service for dynamically locating Web services.

3.1.2 Representing Data and Semantics

The focus on representing and exchanging data on the Web is based around the eXtensible Markup Language (XML). XML is an initiative from the W3C defining an "extremely simple" dialect of the Standard Generalized Markup Language (SGML) [164] that can be served, received and processed on the World Wide Web in the way that is now possible with HTML.

XML is a structured document that is made up of storage units, containing either parsed or unparsed data. Basically, XML is to data what HTML is to text as XML allows you to define *self-describing data*. A description of XML is outside the scope of this book and therefore, for more information please see other resources, such as [95], [96], [99] and numerous books on the subject, e.g., [162] and [163].

The focus on representing and exchanging data using XML has led to two main thrusts in this direction. These are:

- **The Semantic Web:** is an extension of the current World Wide Web in which information is given well-defined meaning, better enabling computers and people to work in cooperation [160]. It is focused on the representation of data and seeks to create a machine-processable Web. The effort is led by W3C [161] with participation from a large number of researchers and industrial partners. The Semantic Web is based on the Resource Description Framework (RDF), which integrates a variety of applications using XML for syntax and URIs for naming.
- **Web Services:** are a software system designed to support interoperable machine-to-machine interaction over a network [166]. In simple terms, Web services provide the definitions (and infrastructure) to allow applications to exchange XML messages with each other.

These two technologies do not compete, but rather they complement each other. In a keynote speech [159], Berner-Lee said "Web services meet immediate technology needs, while the Semantic Web has the potential for future exponential growth." Such convergence has led to a number of groups that are focusing on this integration, e.g., [156] and [157]. In a recent paper the authors noted [158] "Semantic Web Enabled Web Services (SWWS) will transform the

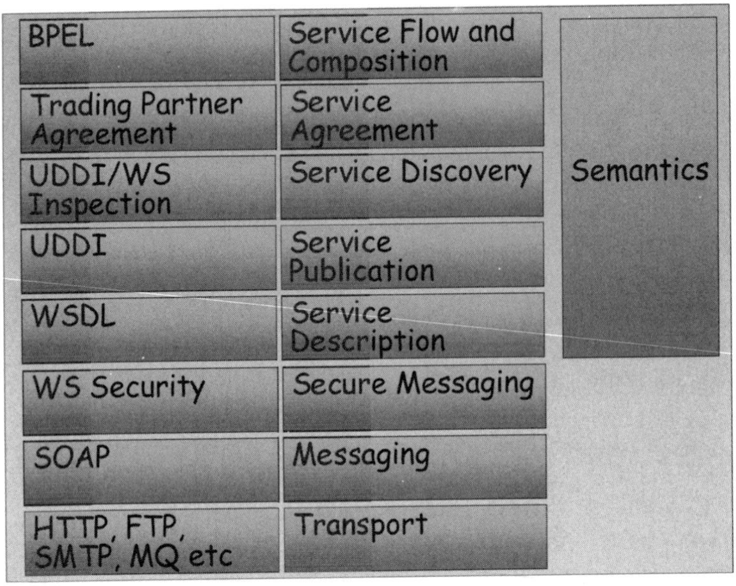

BPEL	Service Flow and Composition	
Trading Partner Agreement	Service Agreement	
UDDI/WS Inspection	Service Discovery	Semantics
UDDI	Service Publication	
WSDL	Service Description	
WS Security	Secure Messaging	
SOAP	Messaging	
HTTP, FTP, SMTP, MQ etc	Transport	

Fig. 3.4. A taxonomy of the various technologies used to represent and deploy Web services and those that can be influenced by semantics.

Web from a static collection of information into a distributed device of computation on the basis of Semantic Web technology making content within the World Wide Web machine-processable and machine-interpretable."

Further, the authors define a taxonomy (see Fig. 3.4) that illustrates the various Web services technologies with those that can be influenced by semantics. Anything from the service description upwards can be enhanced to include a rich layer of semantics that can be understood by applications.

In this chapter, we will take a look at the core infrastructure that can enable machine-to-machine interactions now using Web services. For more information on the Semantic Web, see the references listed above.

3.2 Web Services

Web services are a distributed systems technology that uses standard Internet protocols to move XML documents between service processes [86]. Simply therefore, Web services are software programs that enable applications to talk to each other remotely via XML messages.

Briefly, a program sends a *request* to a remote Web service containing an XML message and (optionally) *receives* a response (see Fig. 3.5). The specifics about how such services are represented, advertised, discovered and communicated with are all defined by Web service standards, such as WSDL, UDDI and SOAP, described in Chapter 13.

In a sense, Web services can be thought of as Internet-oriented text-based integration adapters [87] and since any data format can be mapped in and out of text, their applicability is widespread. Since Web services are based on XML documents and document exchange, the technological underpinning of Web services is often called *document-oriented* computing [86].

Although Web services are centred around documents, it does not necessarily follow that such documents should be readable by people, which is reflected in the core goal of Web services, that is, to enable machine-to-machine communication at the same scale and using the same style of protocols as the human interface-centred World Wide Web.

The recent hype of Web services has been amplified by the current implementations of Web services, which are based on core Internet technology (i.e., Web servers), and since such text-based systems have been behind the success of the World Wide Web, it therefore follows that Web services are the next generation Internet. In fact, however, Web services do not need a Web server to run at all (see Section 3.4.2).

3.2.1 A Minimal Web Service

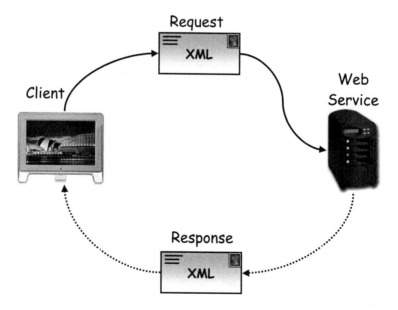

Fig. 3.5. An illustration of the role of a Web service.

A minimal Web service has three components [86]:

1. **The Service:** a service is a software component which is capable of processing an XML document. The particular transport and application protocols, e.g., what programming language the service is written in, whether it operates as a stand-alone process or is part of a Web or application server, etc., is of no importance.
2. **The Document:** the XML document that is sent to a service which contains the application-specific information.
3. **The Address:** this describes the protocol binding (e.g., TCP or HTTP) along with the network address that can be used to access the service. The address is also called a port reference.

Even though in principle, these should be enough to build a Web service, in practice, at least one more component is added, that is, the *Envelope* or *message encapsulation protocol*, which adds things like routing and security information to the message without the need to modify the actual XML document.

Typically, services use SOAP to define its envelope. Further, comprehensive descriptions of Web services have also been adopted (i.e., WSDL) and if you introduce these then it is useful to have a yellow pages for looking up such descriptions (e.g., UDDI). These three technologies provide the programming backbone for current Web services and are outlined later in this chapter and described in detail in Chapter 13.

3.2.2 Web Services Architecture

Web services can be used to exchange simple or extremely complex XML documents that can contain either document-oriented or procedural-oriented information. They are based on standardized XML protocols which are supported globally by most major technology firms.

Web services are *interoperable* and *loosely coupled*, which go hand in hand to create a powerful but flexible infrastructure for document exchange that can work on all platforms. The key to this interoperability is XML which provides the message-passing and service definitions in a operating system and programming language neutral fashion. Messages, wherever they originated from, are *converted* into XML **before** being transported to the remote service.

This is illustrated in Fig. 3.6, which shows this conversion process from language-dependent clients (in C++ here) and services (in Java here), which can interoperate through a common representation of the data, i.e., XML. This leads to a many-to-one situation that is perfectly scalable; i.e., vendors only have to write a data-to-XML and XML-to-data convertors once for each supported language. Many already exist (e.g., for Java [171] and [170]). XML provides the common ground for all diverse service implementations. Similar architectures have been employed elsewhere; for example, Jxta uses an XML

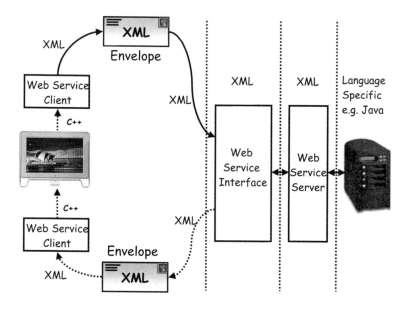

Fig. 3.6. A Web service is loosely coupled, meaning that the Web service interface is separated from its implementation.

data representation [15] but the protocols implemented around this are not based on open standards.

Web services extend this approach to decouple the logic of the client and the server by providing XML descriptions for the service interface (WSDL). This means that a Web service can be accessed through a common-ground interface which is independent of the back-end implementation.

Figure 3.6 illustrates this by showing a C client talking to a Web service written in Java. Further, each Web service can have multiple language bindings, which makes it easy to change the back-end implementation without the client needing to update its code. For example, a company could keep the same Web service interface but re-implement its C++ implementation of this service in Java and the client would not even realise that it had been changed.

A service model that can provide diverse implementation behind a single interface definition is defined to be a *virtual service*. The fact that Web services are virtual was one of the compelling factors that led to the convergence of Grid computing and Web services that will be discussed in Chapter 14.

An useful analogy of the decoupling of a Web service interface and its implementation is a Java interface and implementation. Java interfaces are similar to abstract classes except all of their methods are automatically public and abstract. They provide an extensible mechanism for defining external interfaces to objects that are used to represent some (or all) of its functionality.

Java interfaces are similar to Web service interfaces in that they allow multiple back-end implementations of the same interface. Within Web services, this may involve implementations from different programming languages whereas within Java, this typically involves creating objects that conform to the same interface but provide different behaviour[2]. Such an approach is fundamental to the Factory Method Design Pattern [174], which has proved to be popular and good programming practice.

Due to the structure of Web services, they are suited to expose *coarse-grained* functionality. The overhead of converting from programming language to text and vice-versa means that the functionality exposed by a Web service must justify this process and therefore typically several components are combined. For example, a service, such as a method call in a Java class is far too fine an operation for a Web service.

Having looked at the key features and architecture of Web services, let's look at a more advanced definition, which represents these features in more detail:

> Web services are loosely coupled, reusable software components that semantically encapsulate discrete functionality and are distributed and programmatically accessible over standard Internet protocols [165].

3.2.3 Web Services Development

As Web services decouple the Web service interface from the back-end implementation, there are a number of ways that a developer can integrate applications. There have been four common development practices identified [93] that are useful to illustrate such possible scenarios:

1. **Greenfield:** the developer starts from scratch, creating not only the Web service but also the application functionality being exposed as a Web service.
2. **Bottom up:** the functionality being exposed as a Web service (i.e., the back-end application) already exists and the programmer needs to design a suitable interface.
3. **Top down:** you start with an existing Web service interface and then create the application functionality capable of implementing that interface.
4. **Meet in the middle:** this is a combination of the bottom-up and top-down scenarios. Here, the Web services interface (abstract WSDL) and existing application code exist already and you need to integrate them. This may involve creating a bridge between the Web service interface and the underlying operations implemented in the application.

---

[2] Objects could use Java interfaces to bind to different languages also, using JNI.

A number of companies are now using the bottom-up approach to expose current functionality as Web services, thus enabling better machine-to-machine communication of such services.

3.3 Service-Oriented Architecture

The Service-Oriented Architecture (SOA) is an example of the *composite computing model*, which is defined as:

> The composite computing model is an architecture that uses distributed, discovery-based execution to expose and manage a collection of service-oriented software assets [94].

At the fundamental level, an SOA is a collection of services on a network that communicate with each other. The services are loosely coupled, have well-defined interfaces and are reusable. An SOA therefore has a higher-level view of coarse-grained application development that uses standard interfaces to hide the underlying technical complexity.

In an SOA, the capabilities (i.e., software assets) should be dynamically discoverable, there should be a clear separation of the software's capabilities and its implementation and it should be possible to quickly assemble impromptu computing communities with minimal coordinated planning efforts, installation technicalities or human intervention. For more details on SOAs see [106].

It is important to note that an SOA does not require Web services and further, Web services can be deployed without an SOA. However, many believe that building an SOA using Web services is the ideal approach.

3.3.1 A Web Service SOA

A service can be described, discovered and invoked using standardized XML technologies in the current Web services technology stack. There are three main components:

1. **SOAP:** the envelope for a Web service that contains the XML message
2. **WSDL:** an XML format for describing the interface to a Web service
3. **UDDI:** the repository (the yellow pages) for a number of deployed Web services.

SOAP messages (when used for Web service requests and responses) conform to the WSDL definition of available Web services. Typically, WSDL defines the interface and location of the Web service, the SOAP message used to access the Web services and the protocols over which such SOAP messages can be exchanged and the WSDL descriptors can be accessed via a UDDI repository (or another directory service).

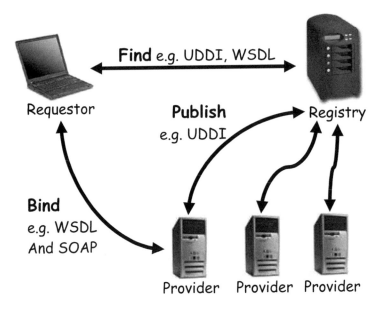

Fig. 3.7. An overview of the service-oriented architecture.

Services are implemented and published by *service providers*, discovered and invoked by *service requesters* and information about a service may be kept within a *service registry*. Therefore, we have three essential operations that you would want to perform:

- **Publish:** Performed by the service provider to advertise the existence and capabilities of a service
- **Find or Locate:** Performed by the service requester to locate a service that meets a particular need or technology fingerprint
- **Bind or Invoke:** Performed by the service requester to invoke the service being provided by the service provider.

Figure 3.7 illustrates how these operations map to the underlying Web service protocols. Service providers create a WDSL interface for their Web service that specifies its functionality. The WSDL document also contains the location (address) of the service and the transport mechanism that is used to contact the service. Therefore, to publish a service, the service provider registers the WSDL document with the UDDI registry (typically by providing a link to the location of the document).

When a service requester wishes to use a service, it contacts the UDDI server, searches through its database and finds a service that closely matches the search criteria to obtain the location of the WSDL file. Then, the service requester uses the WSDL file to create a request/response invocation on the Web service. The message for the invocation is typically wrapped in an envelope, using SOAP, and sent to the Web service. SOAP includes various transport bindings and data encoding mechanisms, which are described in Chapter 13.

3.4 Common Web Service Misconceptions

In this section, some common Web service misconceptions are discussed. The brief notes here are a summary of the key points raised by Vogels [86], so for more information please read the original article.

3.4.1 Web Services and Distributed Objects

Web services are simply a mechanism for exchanging structured XML documents. This is a very different concept from requesting the instantiation of an object, and therefore Web services should not be confused with distributed object systems. For example, in Jini (see Chapter 5, for example), which is an example of a distributed object system, objects can be remotely invoked by using a local proxy which maintains a reference to the particular instance of the remote object. Using this proxy, the client can alter the *state* of the remote object since it is persisted within the distributed environment.

A system that can maintain the state of remote objects is referred to as a *stateful* distributed system. Web services however have no notion of state, and they fall into the category of distributed system techniques that enable *stateless* computing; i.e., invoking the same Web service twice in succession will be treated as two independent invocations to separate instances of the same service. Once the invocation is finished, the session cleans up and all local data is lost. Of course, an application could be constructed in such a way that state could be retained but this would involve a layer over the core Web services technology; e.g., identification numbers could be used to update remote databases (a notion addressed by OGSA [21] and WSRF [25]).

3.4.2 Web Services and Web Servers

There is a common misconception that Web services require HTTP and a Web server in order to run. This is not true but the confusion is amplified because most Web services are deployed within a Web server environment.

As we'll see in Chapter 13, the use of SOAP, WSDL or UDDI does not require the use of a Web server but the most popular hosting environments do actually use one. To invoke a Web service, SOAP is typically used, which can run over a number of different transport protocols apart from HTTP. For example, SOAP can work using JMS or SMTP and can be therefore hosted in a number of different ways. For SOAP to work within a Web server, it basically uses the HTTP protocol to deliver the data to a back-end SOAP server, typically implemented using a Java servlet. It is the SOAP server itself that communicates and translates the information to and from the Web service. The Web server itself is simply a delivery mechanism.

The advantages of using a Web server to host Web services however are numerous. First, they alleviate a number of administrative problems with respect to firewalls because well-known trusted ports are used. Second, the Web server technology is tried and trusted and has been shown to be robust, therefore providing a solid backbone for the Web service environment.

Alternatively, there are a number of toolkits that can be used to develop and integrate Web services that do not rely on a Web server to function. For example, PocketSoap [88], WASP [89], the Emerging Technologies Toolkit [90] and the WSE [91]. As the adoption increases, I'm sure we'll see other hosting environments appear within the community, e.g., within P2P.

3.5 Conclusion

In this chapter, a historical perspective and conceptual overview of Web services was given. The next stage of the Web evolution is more focused on the representation and machine-to-machine communication of data, rather than the textual representation within a Web browser that has been the quintessence of the modern Internet. To this end, a number of protocols and data formats have been introduced to provide a common layer of technologies that are capable of enabling such machine-to-machine interaction.

Web services are focused on building such capabilities on top of today's Internet and therefore the role of standardization is playing an important role in defining this environment. The standardized technologies that are at the core of Web services are XML, SOAP, WSDL and UDDI, which form the core of the Web services technology stack that will be discussed in Chapter 13.

4

Grid Computing

Over the past decade there has been a huge shift in the way we perceive and utilize computing resources. Previously, computing needs were typically achieved by using localised resources and infrastructures and high-end scientific calculations would be performed on dedicated parallel machines. However, nowadays, we are seeing an increasing number of wide-area distributed-computing applications, which has led to the development of many different types of middleware, libraries and tools that allow geographically distributed resources to be unified into a single application. This approach to distributed computing has come under a wide number of different names, such as meta-computing, scalable computing, global computing, Internet computing and more recently, Grid computing.

4.1 The Grid Dream

The name Grid takes its name from an analogy with the electrical *power grid*. The Grid *dream* is to allow users to tap into resources off the Internet as easily as electrical power can be drawn from a wall socket. To make this happen, not only does the underlying infrastructure (called the *power grid* for electricity and simply *the Grid* for computing) have to be pervasive, but we would need a number of levels of security and accountancy to provide transparent access, just as one has with power. For example, imagine when you plug in your kettle, your only concern is, have you filled it with water. You should not have to worry about where the electricity comes from, whether it is bought from other countries or generated from coal, windfarms, etc. You should simply take for granted that when your appliance is plugged in it will get the power it needs.

The Grid is trying to implement this same scenario for a different type of utility, i.e., when you sit at your computer, your only concern should be that you have a smart idea (e.g., some scientific analysis, etc.) and you want this idea to be realised without knowing (or caring) what other computer resources you are using and where they are located. Just as a power grid is a utility (i.e., you ask for electricity, you get it and pay accordingly), the Grid is also seen as a utility (i.e., you ask for computer power, storage or service capacities and you get it), and consequently you pay for it. Such issues are tackled by the Grid middleware.

Currently, however, Grid accountancy is not really practical or functional but a number of users and scientists have devoted their machines to form a prototype Grid for research development of these essential services needed for widespread adoption. In reality, however, there is not one single "Grid", rather there are many different types: some are evolving, some private, some public, some regional, some global, some specific (e.g., dedicated to one scientific application) and some generic. Such Grids have realistic goals but do not attempt to solve the whole Grid problem. It will be some time before the power grid analogy becomes reality (if ever).

Interestingly though, there are companies [137] that are starting to offer broadband high-speed Internet access through standard electrical sockets in homes and businesses. Such connections take advantage of the extensive electricity network already in place. A specially designed modem (that consumes power of the order of one quarter of a 40 W lightbulb) transmits the broadband information across existing electricity cables to the electricity substation. From here, the data is collected and transported over a local network and onto the Internet. Trials of such systems have indicated that symmetrical speeds of up to 1 Mbit/s can be achieved. Imagine, anywhere you have a power socket, you can tap into the Internet; combine this with the Grid computing dream and then perhaps it really could become a reality!

4.2 Social Perspective

For a Grid to be successful, we not only have to tackle the huge technological problems but also address the social aspects [33] of how to engage researchers, educators, businesses and consumers in using the Grid as part of their every-day work. In describing the Grid, the authors noted [32] that the first recognisable grid was Edisons power distribution grid in New York. Its goal was to supply power to Wall Street in 1882 at the same price as the current existing technology and therefore costs needed to be kept down at every step.

At the core of his economic analysis was Ohms Law, which was used to control the cost of generating, distributing and using electricity [35]. Edison chose Wall Street because he could only compete with gas if there were a high enough population density to yield economic return, given the cost relationships defined by Ohms Law (he also had to choose an area where he could find capital for the switching costs). Here, it is plain to see that the social good of any new infrastructure has wide social implications, i.e., if those investing in this new technology do not see an economic return then its progress will slow down and consequently, so will its widespread availability.

This is also true for today's Grid because its adoption within the wider community is also highly dependent on social acceptance and industrial success if the cost-volume relations are to break even. Grid computing has attempted to address these issues in a number of ways, for example, by gaining large industrial backing and by *conforming* to international standards. For example, there is much support for the lower-level infrastructure, and several companies and institutions have already committed massive amounts of resources to the Grid. For example, the U.S. National Science Foundation has committed $53 million on the TeraGrid [138], that will include 13.6 teraflops of computing power, over 450 terabytes of data storage, and high-resolution visualization systems, interconnected by a 40 Gbps network. The actual nodes are Linux clusters of Intel-based IBM computers with Sun and Oracle also being involved. Similar initiatives are also happening elsewhere. Also, the convergence of Web services and Grid computing in the form of the Open Grid Service Architecture (OGSA) [27] and more recently the Web Services Resource Framework (WSRF) [25], [26] are clear moves in support of globally accepted standards (also see Section 4.5.2).

4.3 History of the Grid

In this section, a context is given for the introduction of how Grids came into being by taking a look at early metacomputing techniques that led to the evolution of Grid technology. The sections here form a brief summary of some of the key systems in the development of Grid technologies. The authors [119] identify three different generations in the evolution of the Grid:

1. **First Generation:** Early metacomputing environments, such as FAFNER [120] and the I-WAY [121].
2. **Second Generation:** This saw the introductions of: core Grid technologies like the Globus toolkit [28] and Legion [123]; distributed object systems, e.g., Jini [78] and CORBA [126]; Grid resource brokers and Schedulers, e.g., Condor, [125], LSF [111], SGE [135]; a number of integrated systems including Cactus [134], DataGrid [118], UNICORE [132] and P2P computing frameworks, e.g., Jxta [15]; and application user interfaces for remote steering and visualization, e.g., Portals and Grid Computing Environments (GCE) [143].
3. **The Third Generation:** This saw the introduction of a service-oriented approach (e.g., OGSA [21]) and the increasing use of *metadata* (giving more detailed information describing services) through semantic Web research [129] and the introduction of collaborative technologies, such as the Access Grid [130].

The next three sections give a brief summary of the key technologies and explain the progression towards the current state of the art in Grid research.

4.3.1 The First Generation

In the early 1990s there was a shift in emphasis placed on wide-area distributed computing. A new wave of high-performance applications were being developed, which requires specific requirements that were not achievable on a single computer. Two representative, yet diverse, experiments are described here that provided an infrastructure for access to computational resources by high-performance applications: these are FAFNER [120] and the I-WAY [121].

As described in detail in Section 8.3.4, the RSA algorithm for asymmetric cryptography is based on the premise that large numbers are very difficult to factorize. In 1991, RSA Data Security Inc. initiated the Factoring Challenge in order to provide a test bed for factoring implementations. FAFNER (Factoring via Network-Enabled Recursion) was set up to factor via the Web and any computer with more than 4 MB of memory could participate in this experiment. Specifically, FAFNER was set up to factor RSA 130 using the Number Field Sieve (NFS) factoring method. They created a Web interface form in HTML for NFS and contributors could take this form and use it to invoke CGI scripts to perform the factoring. FAFNER is basically a collection of Perl scripts, HTML pages and associated documentation, which comprises the *server-side* of the factoring effort. The FAFNER software itself doesn't factor the RSA130, rather, it provides interactive registration, task assignment and solution database services to clients that perform the actual work. FAFNER was a forerunner to systems such as SETI [3], Distributed.net [64], Entropia [55] and United Devices [54], to name a few.

The I-WAY experiment was started as a project to link various supercomputing centres and to provide the infrastructure for a metacomputing [112] environment for high computational scientific applications [121]. This connectivity involved using high-speed networks, which gave application developers access to a wide variety of resources, e.g., supercomputers, databases and scientific instruments, all potentially located at geographically distributed sites. The I-WAY environment allowed the assembly of unique capabilities that could not otherwise be created in a cost-effective manner and was the forerunner for the Globus toolkit. The I-WAY connected supercomputers and other resources at 17 sites across North America based on ATM connectivity. The I-WAY consisted of a number of I-POP (point of presence) servers [122] that were connected by the Internet or ATM networks (see Fig. 4.1). The I-Soft software infrastructure could be used to access the configured I-POP machines and provided an environment that consisted of a number of services, including scheduling, security (authentication and auditing), parallel programming support (process creation and communication) and a distributed file system (using AFS, the Andrew File System).

Sixty different groups used this network to create a diverse set of applications, for example: to construct large-scale scientific simulations [115], [116], collaborative engineering [113], [114], and supercomputer-enhanced scientific instruments [113], [117]. The I-Soft toolkit formed the basis of the Globus

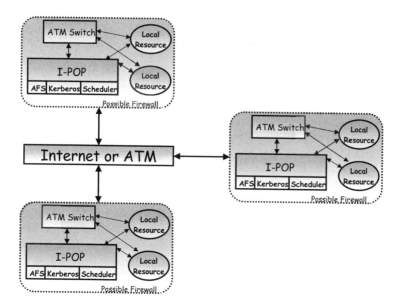

Fig. 4.1. The I-WAY network, consisting of cooperating I-POP servers that could communicate across the Internet or ATM networks.

toolkit, which is in widespread adoption throughout the Grid computing world today.

4.3.2 The Second Generation

The I-WAY paved the path for the second generation of metacomputing technologies that aimed to provide a common infrastructure for Grid applications through the development of the Globus toolkit (see Section 4.7) and Legion [123]. Legion is an integrated operating system for Grids or meta-systems. Its focus is to give the user the impression that he is using a global virtual computer, which transparently handles all the complexity involved with having such a distributed system (scheduling on processors, data transfer, communication and synchronization). Legion has an object-oriented design; every component (hosts, files, programs) is represented as an object. It is written in MPL (Mentat Programming Language) [124], which is a parallel version of C++, and supports applications written in MPL, FORTRAN and Java as well as the use of MPI and PVM.

During the second generation, we saw the widespread adoption of *distributed object systems*, such as Jini (see Chapter 5) and CORBA [126]. The Common Object Request Broker Architecture (CORBA) is developed by the Object Management Group [128] and defines an object-oriented model for accessing distributed objects. CORBA supports describing interfaces to active, distributed objects via an Interface Description Language (IDL), which can be linked to code written in any of the supported languages (C, C++, Java, COBOL, Smalltalk, Ada, Lisp, Python and IDLscript). Compiled object implementations use the Object Request Broker (ORB) to perform remote method invocations.

For many scientists, their research is highly dependent on computing throughput, which follows the SIMD (Single Instruction, Multiple Data) parallel computing model. Here, a scientist would require that the **same program** be iterated many times over **different data**. Such a class of problem is also called High-Throughput Computing (HTC). In this generation of the Grid, we saw a number of *Grid resource brokers* and *schedulers* that supported this class of application. These were either introduced or extended for operation on the Grid, e.g., Condor, [125], LSF [111] and SGE [135]. For example, Condor is a system that takes advantage of idle machines (e.g., at night or weekends) and allows the submission of many jobs at the same time. Source code does not have to be modified in any way to use Condor and it supports transparent *checkpointing* and *migration* of jobs across the network. *Checkpointing* involves saving a job's state to disk so that it can be resumed at a later stage, either locally or remotely by *migrating* (or moving) it to another machine.

Also, in this generation, we saw a number of integrated systems including Cactus [134], DataGrid [118], UNICORE [132] and P2P computing frameworks (e.g., Jxta [15]; see Chapter 10) and application user interfaces for remote steering and visualization, i.e., portals. Briefly, Cactus is a problem-solving environment designed for scientists and engineers. It has a modular structure which can be distributed across a parallel machine and the Grid. Cactus originated in academic research and is one of the driving applications in the Gridlab project [34] (Triana [29] being the other). Cactus runs on many architectures and supports checkpointing, which was demonstrated in the Cactus Worm experiment [133] that deployed Cactus on the Grid using the Globus toolkit. DataGrid's objective is to enable next-generation scientific exploration that requires intensive computation and the analysis of large-scale shared databases. Such databases range from hundreds of terabytes to petabytes and are used by widely distributed scientific communities. UNICORE attempts to make seamless Grid computing a reality for non-Grid experts. It has developed a user-friendly interface that allows easy and uniform access to distributed computing resources and provides support for running scientific and engineering applications.

4.3.3 The Third Generation

The second generation paved the way for the basic interoperability to enable large-scale distributed computation and sharing of resources. The key focus of the third generation extended this model to allow the flexible assembly of Grid resources by exposing the functionality through standard interfaces with agreed interpretation. This solution employed the use of the *service-oriented model* with increasing attention to metadata of such services. The defining paper of the Grid anatomy [22] focused on terms, such as *distributed collaboration* and *virtual organizations* and identified a model based on the Open Grid Service Architecture model. OGSA represents a convergence with the Web services and allows Grid protocols to be exposed through Web services' XML standardized technologies, such as WSDL, UDDI and SOAP, described in detail in Chapter 14. The following sections in this chapter introduce the foundations for some of these key concepts and give a broad overview of the functionality of the most widely used Grid toolkit, Globus.

4.4 The Grid Computing Architecture

In [22], the authors define Grid computing as "flexible, secure, coordinated resource sharing among dynamic collections of individuals, institutions, and resources". The emphasis here being on the flexible and dynamic environment that can be used to discover and interoperate with distributed resources. This coordinated resource sharing is undertaken via multi-institutional *virtual organizations*. Virtual Organizations provide a highly controlled environment to allow each resource provider to specify exactly what she wants to share, who is allowed to share it and the conditions whereby this sharing occurs. The set of individuals and/or institutions that provides such sharing rules is collectively known as a virtual organization (VO).

In Grid computing, users can share or have direct access to computers, software, data and other resources. This transparent access to distributed resources is achieved through the use of *middleware*, e.g, Globus (see Section 4.7).

VOs are not original in concept. In many ways, they are similar to Jxta peer groups (see Section 10.3.1), which also facilitate the dynamic creation of a collection of cooperating peers that have a common set of goals. In Jxta, groups share common group protocols that can provide authentication, authorization and other policies for their interaction. Sharing resources can also be set at finer levels of granularity within the peer group itself so that specific criteria can be set for each resource or person accessing that resource. The VO and peer group concepts are very similar but the terminology and terms used are different.

Figure 4.2 illustrates the Grid architecture. Here, users/clients use the standard Internet via a Grid middleware toolkit, e.g., Globus. This toolkit enables them to discover the existence of distributed resources, make reservations for their use and then gain direct access to them. The direct access is achieved via standard Internet technologies, such as FTP or the Grid-enhanced version GridFTP [108]. Therefore, the routing of the data is achieved by standard TCP/IP routing and therefore could pass through several intermediaries but is not controlled by higher-level mechanisms, e.g., like those employed by P2P

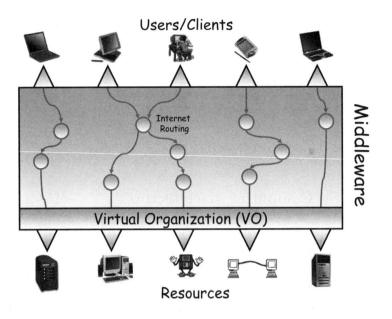

Fig. 4.2. The architecture of a computational Grid. The middleware (e.g., Globus) enables clients to access distributed resources from another administrative domain (i.e., virtual organization), whilst providing transparency across the various protocols of the underlying Internet, as shown.

infrastructures such as Jxta (see Chapter 10). Also shown here is the concept of the virtual organization which provides a blanket for every resource to define its sharing and security policies.

4.4.1 Virtual Organizations and the Sharing of Resources

VOs are dynamically accessible from a Grid application and applications are capable of spanning a number of different organizations, each running its own VO. The authors [22] identify a number of examples of different VOs and scenarios. Some of these are illustrated here:

- **Resource Providers:** application service providers, storage service providers and CPU cycle providers all can represent a VO.
- **Product Design:** for example, here, several organizations could form an industrial consortium in order to integrate sophisticated tools to simulate a next-generation supersonic aircraft. The simulation will need to integrate and aggregate multiple software and hardware resources, including sensitive proprietary software components developed by the various participants. Each component may operate on its machine but has access to the

necessary design databases and related information. Security is paramount because, although such organizations have agreed to collaborate, they do not want to lose intellectual copyright on their constituent software components, which may have been developed over many years. Such a scenario could enable the collaboration to prototype and cost-estimate the production of such an aircraft even though no one partner has complete knowledge of the entire process.

- **Crisis Management:** for example, a team may be set up to respond to a chemical spill by using local weather and soil models to estimate the spread of the spill. This could determine the impact based on factors such as the location of the population and environmental considerations, e.g., rivers, water supplies, etc. and create a short-term emergency plan that could evacuate and notify the relevant authorities and hospitals. Other examples here include using modules that could be developed to forecast extreme hazardous events such as avalanching, flooding, landslides, storms or forest fires. For example, for the case of a severe storm, the output from the operational meteorological forecast models could drive the suite of fine scale models for the primary target area of the storm. The fine-scale models could locally forecast maximum wind speeds, the snow loading of avalanche slopes, river run-off, or landslide danger.
- **Data Intense Applications:** for example, the members of a large, international, high-energy physics collaboration, such as DataGrid [118], described earlier, could also form a VO.

Although each of these examples differs in many ways, e.g., the number and type of participants, the activities, the duration and scale of the interaction, and the particular resources being shared, they each share a common set of goals, i.e., to collaborate. In every case, each organization will consist of a number of distrustful participants who may or may not have prior relationships with those who wish to share their resources. Further, in some cases the data could be sensitive, e.g., direct access to a sensor or an incoming physics data stream. Therefore, each participant must be sure that she only shares such resources with permissible participants.

The scope for the VO can span multiple organizations but its granularity depends on the specific collaboration at hand. Therefore, it could be convenient within a multi-institutional collaboration to have a specific policy and therefore fit the entire collaboration under one VO. However, in other scenarios several VOs representing the participating institutions could be integrated. The actual designing of how many VOs you want to use is completely flexible and an organization can participate in one or more VOs by sharing some or all of its resources. Figure 4.3 illustrates an example of one organization blanketed by its own VO (VO1) simultaneously accessing resources from two other virtual organizations, VO2 and VO3.

The pooling of resources at multiple sites is a key element in aggregating functionality that exposes new services to the community that could not have

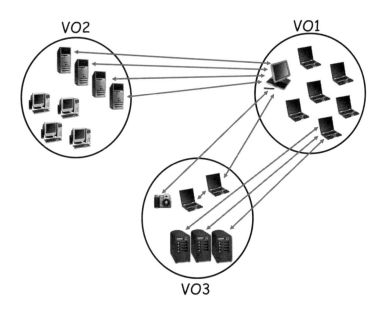

Fig. 4.3. Three virtual organizations. Users can access multiple VOs and access a number of different services across the multiple sites.

been previously achieved. The actual sharing of resources is dependent on the choices made by the resource owner, i.e., when, where and what can be done. For example, a participant in a VO may only accept *secure* computational resources by some defined policy.

The implementation of a VO must be flexible and allow mechanisms for users to express policies, to establish identities (of users and resources) for authentication and to authorize the use of the particular operation. Further, such relationships can vary over time depending on various factors, e.g., the availability of resources, the access to morphed data sets etc. Further, such sharing relationships are very much P2P in nature; e.g., providers can also be consumers and sharing can exist at many levels; e.g., there could be common sharing relationships to coordinate the use across many resources, spanning many different organizations. Here, the ability to delegate authority in controlled ways becomes very important along with the coordination mechanisms, e.g., co-scheduling. Such issues are addressed in the Globus toolkit; see Section 4.7.

4.5 To Be or Not to Be a Grid: These Are the Criteria...

The Grid is defined [139] as something that "coordinates distributed resources using standard, open, general-purpose protocols and interfaces to deliver required qualities of service" (also becoming known as "qualities of experience"). To qualify this vision, there have been specific criteria that have been identified, which an application must support to be classified as a Grid. In Foster's paper, [107], he outlines a three-point checklist; that is, a Grid:

1. coordinates resources that are not subject to **centralized control**
2. uses **standard, open, general-purpose protocols** and interfaces
3. delivers non-trivial **qualities of service**.

These criteria have been reiterated elsewhere [33] and form the basis for current guidelines from programming Grids[1]. The Globus toolkit, for example, supports the creation of Grids by meeting all criteria. These, perhaps somewhat contrived, criteria mean that other systems do not qualify as Grids for various reasons. For example, Jxta could not be considered a Grid because it does not use standard protocols and Condor [125] couldn't be considered a Grid because it has centralized control. In the following three sections these criteria are described in more detail.

4.5.1 Centralized Control

The first point in the checklist is talking about how the resources that make up the distributed system are controlled, whether they are:

- centrally controlled by one administrator (a non-Grid)
- consist of a number of interacting administrative domains that pull resources together using common policies.

There are a number of issues here that support these criteria. For example, resources within a collaborative development may be owned by different organizations, who would not be happy to surrender control of their resources under some central management infrastructure. Second, since the Grid aims to join a larger number of resources then any centralized control will certainly affect its scalability.

Therefore, computational Grids should connect resources at different administrative domains. Typically, this is achieved by defining and using a virtual organization (see Section 4.4.1 that provides a controlled environment for its set of individuals and/or institutions. However, other protocols and mechanisms exist elsewhere to achieve similar desirable results; e.g., most P2P applications achieve this, although at varying degrees of granularity.

---

[1] There are a number of researchers who think these criteria are too restrictive; see [20] for a collection of articles on the subject.

Jxta, for example, supports VO concepts but also much finer levels of granularity and has the capability of connecting a vast number of machines administered by different organizations or users. Other systems, e.g., FreeNet (see Chapter 9) provide a virtual overlay that allows secure encrypted storage and retrieval across millions of computers, potentially spanning millions of different administrative domains.

There are also several examples of systems that are not Grids under this category; e.g., Sun's Grid Engine [110] or Platform's Load-Sharing Facility [111] have a centralized control of the hosts they manage.

4.5.2 Standard, Open, General-Purpose Protocols

The Grid architecture is a protocol architecture [22]. It is important that such protocols and interfaces are multi-purpose, standard and open. If not then we are dealing with an application-specific system that will not generalize to the wider community. Within the Grid, such standards-based open protocols define the basic mechanisms of how users and resources (from within a VO) negotiate, establish, manage and exploit sharing relationships. The Grid *vision* therefore, is about creating or using existing standards for open and generalized protocols, interfaces and policies that enable this level of resource sharing within such a distributed system.

In essence, Grid computing is aiming to help standardize the way we do distributed computing rather than having a multitude of non-interoperable distributed systems. A standards-based open architecture promotes extensibility, interoperability and portability because it has general agreement within the community. To help with this standardization process, the Grid community has the successful and popular Global Grid Forum (GGF) [109], which hosts three conferences a year with both research groups (for researching areas) and working groups (for standardization) existing in a number of different areas.

For example, the newly adopted OGSA and OGSI (see Chapter 14) by Globus [28] have working groups concentrating on their standardization throughout the whole Grid community. Further, the de facto implementation of the core Grid standards, *Globus* [28], has over six years of experience dealing with the Grid community and the new version of its toolkit has embraced Web services (see Chapter 3) to create a standardized interface to their Grid services (see Chapter 14).

Many systems fail on this criterion but excel in the other two categories. For example, distributed computing systems that harness idle CPU cycles, e.g., Entropia [55] and United Devices [54] and file-sharing systems, such as Gnutella [6] all deliver high levels of QoS, albeit for specialized services, but for the most part are not based on open standards, and therefore are too specific for generalized use; e.g., it would be difficult to see how the Gnutella protocol could be useful for anything but searching for files or data content.

4.5.3 Quality Of Service

A key parameter in Grid systems is the *Quality of Service* (QoS). When a Grid job has QoS requirements, it is often necessary to negotiate a *service-level agreement* beforehand to enforce this certain level of service. There are three types of quality support that can be provided:

1. None: No QoS is supported at all.
2. Soft: You can specify QoS requirements and these will try to be met but they cannot be guaranteed. This is the most common form of QoS implemented in Grid applications.
3. Hard: This is where all nodes on the Grid support and guarantee the level of QoS requested.

A Grid should be able to deliver non-trivial QoS, whether, for example, this is measured by performance, service or data availability or data transfer. QoS is application specific and it completely depends on the needs of the application. For example, in a physics experiment, the QoS may be specified in terms of computational throughput but on other experiments, the QoS may be specified in terms of reliability of file transfers or data content.

4.6 Types of Grid

Broadly speaking, there are three types of Grid:

1. Computational Grids
2. Data Grids
3. Service Grids.

A *computational Grid* is a distributed set of resources that are dedicated to aggregate computational capacity. Computational Grids are highly suitable for *task farming* or *high-throughout computing* applications where there is typically one data set and a huge parameter space through which the scientist wishes to search. The scientist will be typically searching for some phenomenon (e.g., whilst searching for gravitational wave signals) or some stabilisation or convergence of network state (e.g., teaching a neural network). Such algorithms involve little or no communication between the nodes and therefore fit excellently onto a coarse-grained processor, such as the Grid. There are many infrastructures for this, including those outlined in Section 4.3.2.

A *data Grid* is a collection of distributed resources that are specifically set up for processing and transferring large amounts of data. Here, the European DataGrid project [118] is a good example, focusing on the development of middleware services to enable distributed analysis of physics data from CERN. At its core, DataGrid uses Globus but adds a rich set of functionality on top of this to support data Grids. For example, it employs a hierarchical structure that will distribute several petabytes of data to various sites across the world. They use global namespaces to differentiate between different and replicated data sets and this huge data Grid will load balance the analysis jobs from over 700 physicists for the largest throughput for this community.

A *service Grid* is a collection of distributed resources that provides a service that cannot possibly be achieved through one single computer. In this example therefore, the Grid will typically consist of several different resources, each providing a specific function that needs to be aggregated in order to collectively perform the desired services. For example, you could have a service that obtained its functionality by integrating and connecting databases from two separate VOs (representing two data streams from physics sensors/detectors) in order to output their correlation. Such a service could not be provided by one organization or the other since the output relies on the combination of both.

4.7 The Globus Toolkit 2.x

Over the past several years many protocols, services and tools have sprung from research and development efforts within the Grid community. Such tools have attempted to address the challenges of building scalable VOs through the use of services such as cross-institutional security management, resource management and co-allocation, information services and data management services for data replication and transfer. These tools have been implemented by the Globus toolkit [28], which enables applications to handle distributed heterogeneous computing resources as a single virtual machine. The Globus project is a U.S. multi-institutional research effort that seeks to enable the construction of computational grids and contains a core set of services that aim to provide solutions for the Grid infrastructure. These services use standards (some achieved through the GGF) wherever possible and have well-defined interfaces that can be integrated into applications in an incremental fashion.

The Globus toolkit consists of four layers, as outlined in Fig. 4.4. The first layer, the Grid fabric, consists of the actual resources that you want to make available to the Grid application. The components of this Grid fabric are integrated by Grid APIs that have been implemented by the Globus toolkit. Such APIs are now being exposed as Grid services in the Globus Toolkit 3.x (see Chapter 14). The third layer typically consists of a set of capabilities that are specific to an application or a set of applications. For example, DataGrid has created such a layer for flexible transportation of data and all DataGrid applications access the various Grid functionalities through this layer. More generalized application-level interfaces have also been recently implemented, for example, within the EU-funded Gridlab project [34]. Within these layers, other services that provide remote steering services (i.e., to dynamically change parameters of a remote application, for example) and to give access to the current state of the application are typically provided through the use

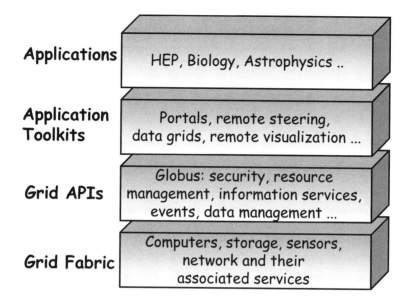

Fig. 4.4. The Globus Toolkit 2.x, showing the various layers in the Grid technology stack. The key building block for an application is the Globus toolkit.

of a Grid portal [143]) or another graphical interface, e.g., a visual problem solving environment [29].

Finally, the fourth layer is the actual application. There are a wide number of applications, i.e., hundreds that have used Globus to build multi-institutional Grids. Some examples of key worldwide projects and forums are given in Appendix A.

4.7.1 Globus Tools

This section outlines these main services provided by the 2.x version of the Globus toolkit. See Chapter 14 for details of the 3.x toolkit. the purpose of this section is to give the reader an overview of the types of services on which the Globus team have been focused. Rather than providing a uniform programming model, such as the object-oriented model, the Globus toolkit provides a bag of services that programmers developing both specific tools or applications can use to meet their needs. Such a methodology is only possible when such capabilities are distinct and have well-defined interfaces that can be incorporated into applications or tools in an incremental fashion. The Globus toolkit essentially consists of four elements:

1. **Security:** to provide authentication, delegation and authorization.

2. **Information Services:** to provide information about Grid services.
3. **Data Management:** involves accessing and managing data.
4. **Resource Management:** to allocate resources provided by a Grid.

These will be described in more detail in the following four sections.

4.7.2 Security

The Grid Security Infrastructure (GSI) provides security mechanisms, i.e., authentication and communication over an open network. GSI supports a number of features that a Grid user requires; e.g., authenticate using a single sign-on mechanism, delegation, integration with local security systems and trust-based relationships. GSI is based on public-key encryption (using X.509 certificates) and SSL but extensions have been added for single sign-on and delegation. The GSI implementation in Globus adheres to the IETF GSS-API standard [148].

X.509 certificates involve the use of the Certificate Authority (CA), which issues the certificates to the subjects (i.e., Grid users). The use of X.509 certificates therefore implies that each subject exchanging information trusts the given CA; i.e., a CA acts as a *trusted third party*

X.509 certificates contain information about the CA as well as the subject. They contain the subject's name, along with his public key, the name of the CA and other fields such as an ID of the encryption algorithms applied and identifiers. The certificates are also signed by the CA so that users can verify that the CA specified in the certificate actually issued the certificate; i.e., they can get the public key of the CA and test if it matches the private key used to sign the certificate. Private keys are also password protected by the user. Certificates can be obtained in a number of ways depending on the particular CA-approved mechanism. For examples, see [149] and [144].

GSI allows **mutual authentication**, i.e., allows two parties across the Grid to prove to each other that they are who they say they are (for a detailed overview of the underlying security techniques, see Chapter 8). Figure 4.5 illustrates how one person, B verifies that A is who she says she is. The steps are as follows:

1. A sends B her public key.
2. B then verifies that the key being sent to him has been issued by the listed CA in the certificate. This is achieved by checking the signature on the certificate against the CA's public key. (Note therefore that B has to trust the CA.)
3. B then sends a random message to A and asks A to encrypt this message.
4. A then encrypts this message using her private key and returns this message to B.
5. B then uses A's public key to decrypt the message. If the message is the same that was sent then B is sure that A is identified (since A is the only person that can have her private key).

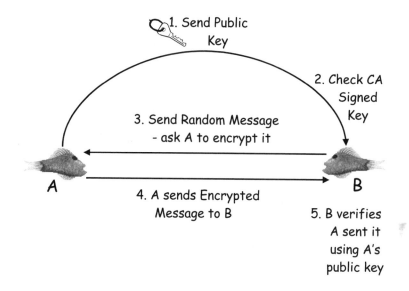

Fig. 4.5. Shows how a person verifies that the person with whom they are communicating is who she says she is; used for mutual authentication in Globus.

6. the exact same operation is then performed by A to verify that B is who he says he is.

Delegation is achieved in Globus by the use of **proxy** certificates. Proxy certificates are temporary certificates that are generated on the fly from a person's identity but bypass the need for password-protected private keys. Specifically a proxy consists of a new certificate containing a new public and private key. The new certificate is signed by the owner rather than the CA, which creates a *chain of trust*; i.e., the proxy is verified and trusted because it is signed by the certificate owner and the certificate is trusted because it is signed by the CA. For a detailed overview of the security mechanisms, see the Globus GSI Web page [144].

4.7.3 Information Services

The Monitoring and Discovery Service (MDS) is the collective interface to the various information services that are provided by Globus. Each of the information services can be accessed separately but MDS integrates these to provide a standard mechanism for publishing and discovering resource status and configuration information. This is a good example of the Globus hourglass approach to software writing (see Fig. 4.6). In their model, the Globus

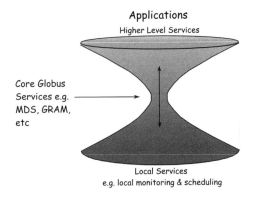

Fig. 4.6. The hourglass approach to Globus tool development.

toolkit components (e.g., MDS, GRAM, etc.) provide an API for many underlying components and Grid protocols. Therefore, MDS here is the neck of the hourglass that has applications and higher-level services or tools above it and the lower-level mechanisms (e.g., local monitoring services) below it.

MDS consists of three main components, illustrated in Fig. 4.7:

1. **GRIS (Grid Resource Information Servers)** that collect data on each resource and can be located on a well-known port (i.e., 2135).
2. **IP (Information Providers)** which provide the interface between local data collection service and the GRIS servers.
3. **GIIS (Grid Index Information Services)** that collect information from one or more GRIS servers and act as a lookup service for resource information.

Briefly, data flows from the local data collection services to the IPs, along to the GRIS servers and then are finally collected by the aggregate directory service, GIIS. IPs can collect data from a variety of sources, e.g., current load status, operating system type and version, file system information (e.g., free disk space, etc.), RAM and virtual memory levels. There can be several local data providers connected to one GRIS server, each interfaced through an IP as illustrated. Further, there can be several GRIS servers registered with one GIIS server and so on.

Therefore, when a request arrives at the GIIS, the GRIS checks its local cache and if the information is not there, or out of date, then it invokes the IP to gather the data and pass it along up the chain. For more information, see the Globus Information Services Web page [146].

4.7.4 Data Management

Data management in Globus consists of three distinct components:

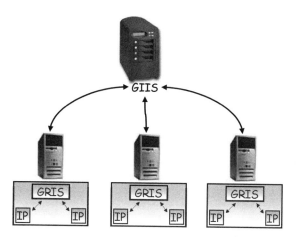

Fig. 4.7. An overview of the protocols you use within MDS.

- **GridFTP:** an extended version of the IETF's FTP (File Transport Protocol). It is secure; i.e., it authenticates via GSI security and adds new features, such as parallel data transfer, partial file transfer and server-to-server (i.e., third-party) data transfer. GridFTP is downloadable from the Web site [147] as an SDK (software development kit). There is also a community effort GGF GridFTP working group that focuses on improving the current GridFTP protocol [150].
- **Data Replication:** consists of a *Replica Catalog* component and a *Replica Management* tool. The Replica Catalog is a lookup directory that contains mappings between logical names for files and one or more copies of the files located on physical storage systems across the Grid. The Replica Management tool integrates this catalog and GridFTP to keep track of and replicate data files. Such tools are important for certain science experiments where either the data cannot be stored completely at one location or when a number of groups collaborate on data analysis and they need to obtain efficient access to the data files. Such data therefore would be replicated and moved closer to where the various groups perform the analysis.
- **GASS:** the Global Access to Secondary Storage system allows remote access to data via standard protocols. GASS includes both client libraries (for accessing remote files) and a server (which acts as a limited file server). Data therefore can be accessed by specifying a URL, in the form of an HTTP URL or an x-gass URL when an HTTP server is not accessible.

For more information, see the Globus Data Management Web page [147].

4.7.5 Resource Management

The Globus Resource Allocation Manager (GRAM) is used to allocate and monitor remote resources. The main component of GRAM is a server process, called the *Gatekeeper*, which typically runs on the machine on which the user wants to run a job. The Gatekeeper has the responsibility to authenticate the user and then satisfy the request[2]. Job requirements are specified using the Resource Specification Language (RSL). GRAM uses GASS to download the executable, to move stdin/stdout/stderr and access files to and from remote locations.

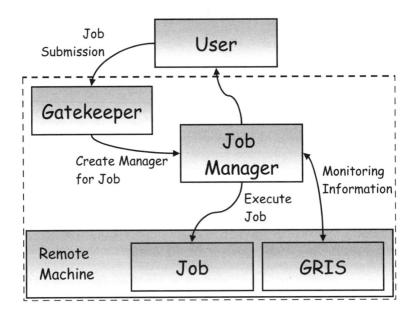

Fig. 4.8. An overview of how GRAM submits and monitors jobs.

Briefly, when a job is submitted in RSL to GRAM, the request is sent to the *Gatekeeper* for the remote computer (see Fig. 4.8). The gatekeeper then creates a *job manager* for the job, which starts and monitors the job during its lifetime. The job manager is the interface to the user and communicates state changes during the running of the job. Then, when the remote job terminates (either normally or by failing), the job manager terminates also. For more information, see the Globus Resource Management Web page [145].

---

[2] In fact, the Gatekeeper is really part of the security infrastructure, which checks the credentials and changes the user ID to the mapped user before running the specific service. However, the only services ever implemented to work with this, at the time of writing, were GRAM and GARA.

Globus has evolved from the I-Soft system, through version 1 (GT1) to version 2 (GT2) and recently, its emphasis has moved from supporting just high-performance applications towards supporting more pervasive services that can support virtual organizations. This evolution is continuing through OGSA (GT3), which is based on exposing its functionality as Web services; see Chapter 14.

4.8 Comments and Conclusion

Grid computing provides an infrastructure for wide-area distributed computing. The Grid process is a community-driven process (the GGF has a great deal of support) and its focus is to encapsulate and expose this functionality through standard open protocols and services. For example, in the P2P chapters (see Chapters 2, 6, 7 and 9), the focus was on a much more *top-down* view; that is, let's look at what infrastructure and connectivity exists in today's Internet and adapt a specific ad hoc protocol that will work with a specific application. This is addressed somewhat by Jxta (Chapter 10) but again Jxta does not work with standardized protocols; they are simply *Jxta protocols*, which were specified by Sun and a small number of other companies. This is not to say that the Jxta protocols are bad, in fact, they are extremely insightful, but without widespread agreement, which can lead to standardization, it is more difficult to gain widespread adoption (but not impossible).

The Grid approach is much more a bottom-up approach. The Grid community is focused on not only creating the necessary standards which have widespread agreement and standardized protocols but also on building the low-level infrastructure to provide a secure computing environment for accessing distributed resources. For example, within a Grid computing environment it is possible to schedule the execution of a piece of your code on a distributed resource, which is something that requires a concrete security policy as well as the technical specification of how you describe what it is you wish to execute and how this is accomplished (via environment variables, etc.). The core toolkit, Globus, tackles a number of these key issues including security, job submission, resource allocation, reliable (and fast) file transfer, data replication and information systems.

This chapter has outlined the concepts behind Grid Computing. Analogous to the power grid, Grid computing is aiming to provide computing resources as a utility, just as gas and electricity are provided to us now. To this goal, the underlying infrastructure needed to support this kind of interaction has evolved from middleware, such as I-Soft that supports wide-area high-performance computing to Globus 1 and 2, which introduces more interoperable solutions. In Chapters 13 and 14, we'll see how these technologies move to a more service-oriented approach (see Section 3.3) that exposes the Grid protocols using Web service standards (e.g. WSDL, SOAP etc), in the form of OGSA.

This continuing evolution is bringing us closer to systems for production Grids capable of running a wide range of applications. Key to this integration is the concept of virtual organizations that make it easier to establish cross-organizational sharing relationships. Today, Grids have three main properties; that they coordinate resources that are not subject to *centralized control*; use *standard, open, general-purpose protocols* and interfaces; and deliver non-trivial *qualities of service*.

Part II

Middleware, Applications and Supporting
Technologies

In this theme, we take a look at middleware and applications, along with the supporting techniques that make these possible. We first take a look at a distributed-object based system, called Jini, which provides an overview of some of the underlying techniques that have been used to support distributed systems development (Chapter 5).

We then revisit peer to peer by taking a look at Gnutella, a system that popularised and helped redefine P2P, through its novel decentralised search protocol (Chapter 6). We show how such a model can be efficiently scaled, though the introduction of caching peers, and discuss the advantages and disadvantages of such an approach (Chapter 7).

To set the scene for the last two chapters within this theme, security within distributed systems is introduced (Chapter 8). We then show how many of these security and P2P techniques discussed so far have been used within a real-world system called Freenet (Chapter 9). By generalizing on these ideas, Jxta is introduced, which attempts to provide a middleware infrastructure for programmers by creating a P2P overlay (Chapter 10).

5

Jini

This chapter gives an overview of Jini, thereby providing an example of a well-known distributed-object based system. Jini is similar in concept to industry-pervasive systems such as CORBA [126] and DCOM [127]. It is distinguished by being based on Java, and deriving many features purely from this Java basis (e.g., the use of RMI and Java serialization). There are other Java frameworks from Sun which would appear to overlap Jini, such as Enterprise Java Beans (EJBs) [16]. However, whereas EJBs make it easier to build business logic servers, Jini could be used to distribute these services in a network *plug-and-play* manner.

In this chapter, a background is given into the development of Jini and into the network plug-and-play manner in which Jini accesses distributed objects. Specifically, Java RMI is discussed, which forms the transportation backbone, along with Java serialization. The discovery of Jini services is described and the notion of a Jini *proxy* is introduced.

Jini implements three protocols that allow a service provider to register its service, a client to search for the service and both a client and service provider to discover the Jini look up server. The Jini look up server is central to the control of the Jini environment as it coordinates the discovery and registration of Jini objects. Jini runs a brokered architecture however, in that the discovery is centralized through the look up service but the communication thereafter between the client and the service is direct.

Finally, Jini advanced issues, such as leasing and distributed asynchronous events are discussed. In the following chapter, an overview of how to set the Jini runtime up and how Jini services are deployed using a simple application illustrates how these individual parts fit together.

5.1 Jini

5.1.1 Setting the Scene

Historically, operating systems have been designed with certain assumptions; that a computer will have a processor, some memory and a disk. When a computer is booted, it looks for a hard disk and if it can't find one then it cannot function.

In more recent times however, computers are used within different scenarios and have fundamentally different roles. For example, a mobile phone does not contain a hard disk but it does have a processor, some memory and a network connection and when it boots up, rather than searching for a disk, it looks for the telephone network. If a network cannot be located then it can't function as a mobile phone. This growing trend from disk-centric to network-centric within a wide range of embedded devices radically affects the way we organize software.

The main emphasis of Jini [78], [79] is to place the emphasis back onto the network and attempt to provide an infrastructure that would enable the many varied processors in devices that have no disk drive to operate and locate services. Jini therefore provides mechanisms to enable adding, removing and locating devices and services on the network.

In addition, Jini provides a programming model that makes it easier for programmers to get their devices talking to each other. Jini builds on top of Java, object serialization and RMI (see next section) to enable objects to move around the network from virtual machine to virtual machine and extend the benefits of object-oriented programming to the network. Instead of requiring device vendors to agree on the network protocols through which their devices can interact, Jini enables the devices to talk to each other through interfaces to objects. First, let's look some of the technologies that Jini integrates in order to implement this distributed mechanism.

5.2 Jini's Transport Backbone: RMI and Serialization

Although Jini can be implemented using more verbose networking communication techniques, e.g., XML-based message passing [81], most Jini applications sit on top of two of the core Java technologies implemented in the Java SDK, that is, RMI and the Java serialization of Objects.

If you are using the core Java SDK you have the following options for communicating across a network:

1. **Sockets:** these are one-to-one, duplex connections. With sockets you need to pack data for a socket and unpack it on other side; i.e., you also need to agree on predefined format and internal data protocol.

2. **RPC (Remote Procedure Call):** this abstracts the communication interface to the level of a procedure call. The programmer appears to be calling a local procedure but the procedure is hosted remotely. The arguments and return values are serialized using an external data representation, e.g., XDR.

3. **RMI (Remote Method Invocation):** this is similar to RPC but in Java it uses the Java serialization mechanism to pack objects for transportation.

5.2.1 RMI

RMI is a tightly coupled communication technology that requires an application to know a remote application's methods. Other more loosely coupled communication mechanisms (e.g., Jxta pipes, JMS etc.) are discussed elsewhere (see Chapter 10 and the JMS Web site [14]). RMI provides the mechanism by which the server and the client communicate and pass information back and forth and therefore allow Java objects to be distributed across a network.

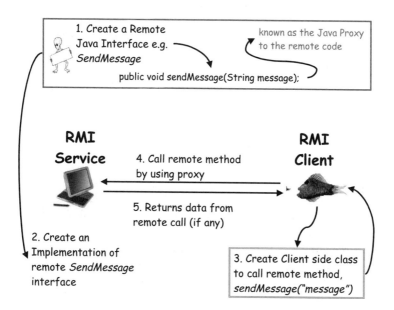

Fig. 5.1. An overview of remote method invocation (RMI).

RMI applications consist of two separate programs: a **server** and a **client**. The server application creates a number of remote objects (implementing different services), creates local references for them, and then waits for clients to invoke methods on these remote objects. The remote objects are created by a two-stage process:

1. by implementing a *proxy* (using a Java Interface)to the remote code (see Fig. 5.1, stage 1);
2. then, implementing this proxy in a class that is stored on the RMI server (see Fig. 5.1, stage 2).

A client application then gets a remote reference (i.e., the *proxy* interface defined for the remote object) using one of the following methods:

- an application can register its remote objects with RMI's simple naming facility, the *rmiregistry* application;
- or the application can pass and return remote object references as part of its normal operation.

These rather simple mechanisms of discovering remote reference to objects is where Jini, described in the next section, improves on the basic RMI functionality. It achieves this through the use of a Jini Lookup Service (LUS), which is a third party application that is used to register the location of remote objects. Incidentally, the LUS is a bit like a Napster server or a super-peer in Gnutella except that these store references to the locations of remote files and an LUS stores the location of remote Java objects (which in fact, also could be Java references to a file...).

Once a client gets the reference to the remote object, it uses its local copy of the Java proxy to invoke the remote method (see Fig. 5.1, stages 3 and 4) and RMI takes care of the rest. Within RMI, details of the communication between remote objects are completely handled by RMI; i.e., to the programmer, remote communication looks like a standard Java method call. So how does RMI transport the data across the network automatically?

5.2.2 Serialization

Fundamental to RMI's transport mechanism is the *Java Serialization* mechanism, which is used to transport any object that is passed as a parameter to or returned from a remote function. RMI uses the object serialization mechanism to transport objects by value across the network and between different Java Virtual Machines (JVMs). Serializable classes are capable of being able to be converted into a self-describing byte stream that can be used to reconstruct an exact copy of the serialized object when the object is read back from the stream. Therefore, serialization can be used to store an object's state in such a way that later it can be completely reconstructed.

Serialized Java objects can be stored to a disk file (for persistence), can be transferred across the network using a socket and can be used within a third party mechanism behind the scenes in order to transparently (to the programmer) pass objects between networked devices as in Jini (see Fig. 5.2).

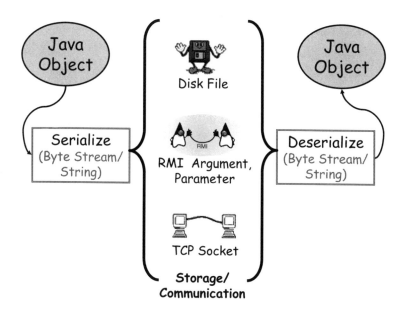

Fig. 5.2. Java serialization can be used to transport a Java object across a network or to store it to local disk for persistence.

In Java, the default serialization mechanism stores all (non-transient) data members of a class to a set of bytes, typically stored into a stream. This stream can then be passed across a network or stored to a local disk file. Note that serialization does not store the actual class *bytecode*; rather, it stores the name of the class needed in order to reconstruct the object. In this way, Java serialization with respect to actual classes is more of a dependency rather than part of the core serialization mechanism. In Java, there are two methods of serializing a class, by implementing either one of the following *Java Interfaces*:

1. **java.io.Serializable:** simple default mechanism, where only minimal modification to the code is necessary
2. **java.io.Externalizable:** implements a custom serialization policy. Using the Externalizable interface, you can specify precisely what, and how, you want to store and retrieve the information contained within the class.

Here, the default mechanism will be briefly illustrated using some simple Java code. For details of the *Externalizable* interface and its use, please take a look at the Java Tutorial [82]. Figure 5.3 illustrates, using a simple example, how you mark a class serializable. In Java, this is achieved by making the class implement the *java.io.Serializable* interface, which basically tags the class as being able to be serializable to the JVMs. The JVM does the rest and

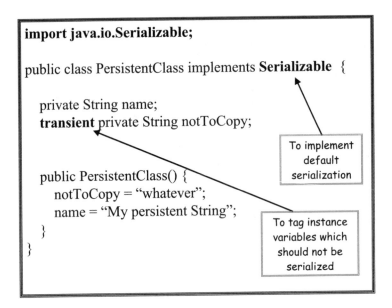

```
import java.io.Serializable;

public class PersistentClass implements Serializable {

    private String name;
    transient private String notToCopy;


    public PersistentClass() {
        notToCopy = "whatever";
        name = "My persistent String";
    }
}
```

To implement default serialization

To tag instance variables which should not be serialized

Fig. 5.3. A simple code fragment that shows how you make a Java class serializable and how you would exclude certain instance variables by using the transient key word.

serializes every instance variable (whether it be a simple variable, i.e., an int, double, an array, i.e., double[] or even an object). Java recursively serializes every variable by decomposing it into its constituent parts and applying the same procedure on them. To tell the JVM you do not want it to serialize an instance variable, you use the *transient* keyword (see Fig. 5.3).

The code in Fig. 5.4 shows how one would serialize any Java object to a file. In this example, we create a Java file output stream (so we can write to a file) and then stream an object output stream into this file, into which we can write our serialized Java objects. Using the same mechanism, this object output stream could be plugged into a different storage or networking device other than a file, e.g., a socket, etc. To serialize today's date therefore, we create a new Date object (i.e., *new Date()*) and write this object to our object output stream, which in turn gets written to the file.

To load this serialized object back in from the file, we perform the inverse operation; that is, we create a Java file input stream and attach an object input stream to this in order to convert the contents of the file and to *deserialize* them into a collection of Java objects (see Fig. 5.4). The *readObject()* function returns a Java Object but since we know we have stored a Java Date object previously, we can *typecast* this into what it should be.

Serialize today's date to a file:

```
FileOutputStream f = new FileOutputStream("tmp");
ObjectOutputStream s = new ObjectOutputStream(f);
s.writeObject(new Date());
s.flush();
```

Deserialize today's date from a file:

```
FileInputStream in = new FileInputStream("tmp");
ObjectInputStream s = new ObjectInputStream(in);
Date date = (Date)s.readObject();
```

Fig. 5.4. A Java code fragment that serializes a serializable Java object (java.util.Date) to a File output stream for persistence.

This simple mechanism (from the programmer's side anyway...), provides a powerful way of being able to transfer objects or persist their state. Java serialization is used extensively and RMI, for the programmer, abstracts such communication to a higher level, that is, at the *method* level. Therefore, within RMI, you have to tag your objects as serializable but then thereafter you simply invoke Java methods and the associated argument objects that are passed across the network are handled for you by the RMI subsystem.

In the next section, a brief overview of Jini is given, which is followed by a detailed description of each part.

5.3 Jini Architecture

Jini has a brokered architecture, discussed in Chapter 1, which will become apparent in the following overview.

Jini is a set of APIs and network protocols that can help you build and deploy distributed systems that are organized as federations of services. A service is a network-enabled entity that performs some function. Some examples of services include hardware devices (such as printers, scanners, hard drives, etc.), software, communications channels and even human users themselves. For example, a Jini-enabled disk drive could offer a "storage" service and a

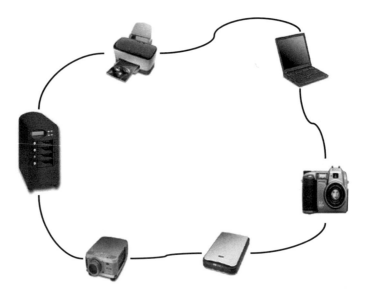

Fig. 5.5. A Jini federation

Jini-enabled printer could offer a "printing" service. The federation of services is a set of available services on the network that a client can utilize to help accomplish some goal.

Therefore, to perform a task, a client enlists the help of services. For example, a client program might upload an image from a scanning service, download this to a disk drive via a disk-drive service, and send it to the printing service of a colour printer. In this example, the client program builds a distributed system consisting of itself, the scanning service, the disk-drive storage service and the colour-printing service. The client and services of this distributed system work together to perform this task.

The concept of a Jini federation (see Fig. 5.5) reflects that the Jini network does not involve a central controlling authority and therefore the set of all services available on the network forms a federation. Jini's runtime infrastructure provides a mechanism for clients and services to find each other by using a lookup service that stores a directory of currently available services. Such a directory service allows a client to broker the task to a service available on the network.

Once services locate each other, they thereafter communicate directly and are independent of the Jini runtime infrastructure. This architecture is therefore brokered and similar in mechanism to systems such as Napster (see Section 2.3.1), although differing in functionality. As in Napster, if the Jini lookup

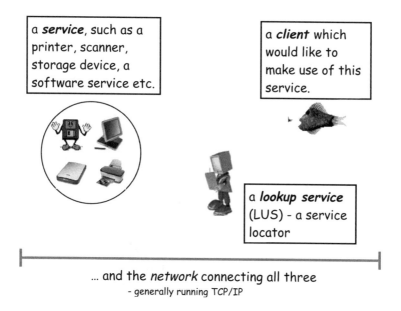

a **service**, such as a printer, scanner, storage device, a software service etc.

a **client** which would like to make use of this service.

a **lookup service** (LUS) - a service locator

... and the **network** connecting all three
- generally running TCP/IP

Fig. 5.6. The three players in a Jini system.

service crashes, any clients or servers brought together via the lookup service before it crashed can continue their work.

5.3.1 Jini in Operation

Jini defines a runtime infrastructure that provides mechanisms that enable you to add, remove, locate and access services. Briefly, in a running Jini system, there are three main players (see Fig. 5.6):

1. There is a service, such as a printer, scanner, storage device, a software service, etc.
2. There is a client which would like to make use of this service.
3. And there is a lookup service (LUS). This essentially is a service locator that acts as a broker/trader/locator between services and clients.

Of course, there is also an additional component, and that is a network connecting all three of these, and this network will generally be running TCP/IP. (Note that the Jini specification is fairly independent of network protocol, but the only current implementation is on TCP/IP).

When new services become available on the network, they register themselves with a lookup service. When clients wish to locate a service to assist with some task, they consult a lookup service.

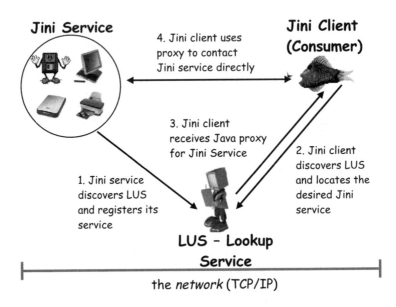

Fig. 5.7. Broad overview of Jini in operation.

The scenario of using Jini services is given in Fig. 5.7 and has the following steps:

1. The Jini service uses discovery (see Section 5.4.1) to locate the LUS and then registers its service with the LUS for use on the Jini network.
2. The Jini client uses discovery (see Section 5.4.1) to locate the LUS and then uses the LUS to find the particular Jini service(s) it wishes to use. The lookup service then returns information to the client (a proxy, see below), which allows the client to contact the service directly.
3. Thereafter, the client and service exchange information directly and the lookup server is no longer required.

Code is moved around among these three pieces, and this is done by marshalling the objects. This involves serializing the objects in such a way that they can be moved around the network and later reconstituted (deserialized) by using included information about the class files as well as instance data as discussed in Section 5.2.2.

Much of the power of Jini comes from the core nature of Java, that is, the ability to download bytecodes from the network and execute them locally, just as you do each time you use an applet. In Jini, services are always accessed via an object that is provided by the service itself, called a proxy (as in RMI; see Section 5.2.1). The client downloads this proxy from the lookup server and makes calls on this object just as it would on any other RMI object, in order to use the service.

In some ways, Jini proxies are analogous to Java applets. Applets provide a mechanism to acquire and use a remote application locally, while Jini proxies provide the same feature for the Jini services. You need to know the Web page to access the applet, whereas you need to know the Jini lookup server and service description to use the particular Jini service. However, typically applets are meant for human consumption, i.e., providing GUIs for Web browsers whereas Jini services are designed to be used programmatically. Further, Jini services are typically used remotely whereas applets are always run locally. Jini services are essentially network aware, on-demand device drivers. The way proxies interact with the service is up to the creator of the service proxy. Here are some possibilities:

1. **The proxy performs the service itself:** This is very similar to an applet: the Java proxy code is downloaded to the client and the client executes the function directly on the downloadable object. When it is executed, the object is completely self-contained and does not require any remote functionality.
2. **The proxy is an RMI stub for a remote service:** Here, the proxy is a minimal piece of code which is an interface to the remote object. The client makes a call on the proxy object; then RMI transfers this call and arguments to the remote object on the service provider, where the actual execution is made.
3. **The proxy acts as a smart adapter:** Here, the proxy contains enough code to be able to make decisions about how to execute the functionality. It could use whatever communication protocol it likes, e.g., sockets, CORBA, Jxta, etc. to broker the request to a remote service. Under this scenario, Jini services can gain access to hardware devices that have their own communication protocol or contact Jini services that are written in other programming languages.

5.4 Registering and Using Jini Services

The Jini runtime infrastructure defines one network-level protocol, called discovery, and two object-level protocols, called join and lookup. Briefly, discovery enables clients and services to locate lookup services, join enables a service to register itself in a lookup service and lookup enables a client to query a lookup service for available services.

5.4.1 Discovery: Finding Lookup Services

Discovery is the Jini mechanism that allows both clients and services to locate Jini lookup services. For a service provider, this allows their services to be registered with this LUS and made available to Jini clients/users. For a client, this enables the lookup of available Jini services on the network for use within a particular application. There are two ways of discovering Jini lookup services, by:

1. **The Unicast Discovery Protocol:** is used when the client or service already knows the location of the LUS, e.g., *jini://spectra.astro.cf.ac.uk.* This specifies the lookup service running on the host *spectra.astro.cf.ac.uk* on the default port (note that Jini uses its own protocol for this). Unicast lookup is used when static connections are needed between services and lookup services.

2. **The Multicast Request and Announcement Protocols:** uses multicast to a local (or well known) network. As soon as a Jini service connects to the network, it broadcasts a presence announcement by sending a multicast packet onto a well-known address. Included in this packet is an IP address and port number where the Jini service can be contacted by a lookup service. Lookup services monitor this port using a multicast request for appropriate packets and when received, a lookup service makes a TCP connection to the IP address and port number extracted from the packet.

When the lookup service is contacted, it uses RMI to send an object (called the service registrar, *net.jini.core.lookup.ServiceRegistrar*) to the Jini service provider. The service registrar object facilitates further communication with the lookup service. It can return information about the available Jini groups, service identifiers (for Unicast lookup), notification (for asynchronous discovery of new services) and last, services can use the join protocol and clients can use the lookup protocol, as described in the next two sections.

5.4.2 Join: Registering a Service (Jini Service)

Once a Jini service provider has obtained a service registrar object, it can join the federation of services that are registered with the particular lookup service. To join, the service provider invokes the *register()* method on the service registrar object (see Fig. 5.8).

There are two parameters to register: a parameter object called a *ServiceItem* and a *lease duration*. The service item is defined as follows:

```
ServiceItem(ServiceID id, Object service, Entry[] attrSets)
```

- **id:** universally unique identifier (UUID) for registered services (128-bit value). Service IDs are intended to be generated only by lookup services, not by clients.
- **service:** the object implementing the actual Jini Service, i.e., the Java proxy object.

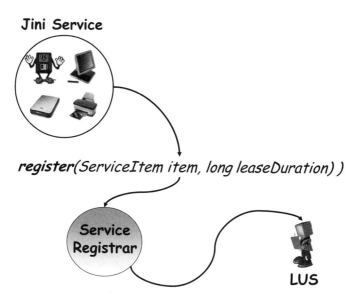

Fig. 5.8. Jini Services use the *register()* function of the *ServiceRegistar* object to join the Jini network.

- **attrSets:** attribute sets include extra information about the service. Examples of these are: icons; classes that provide GUIs for the service; and objects that give more information about the service.

The *leaseDuration* variable is used by Jini lookup services to keep track of active Jini services. The lease duration can be specified by the service itself or by the lookup server. Services can therefore choose either of the following defaults or set this duration themselves:

- **Lease.ANY:** the service lets the lookup service decide on the time
- **Lease.FOREVER:** the request is for a lease that never expires.

Leasing is a way for components to register that they are alive, but allow themselves to be "timed out" if they have failed or if they are unreachable. The lookup service acts as the *granter* of the lease.

The *register()* method sends a copy of the *ServiceItem* object (using RMI) to the lookup service, where the service item is stored. This completes the *join* process and its service is now registered in the lookup service.

5.4.3 Lookup: Finding and Using Services (Jini Client)

Once a service has registered with a LUS service via the join process, it is available for use by clients who query that lookup service. To find a service, clients query lookup services via a process called *lookup*.

First, a client discovers a lookup service and obtains a service registrar object, as described. It then invokes the *lookup()* method on this object to perform a lookup:

```
Object lookup(ServiceTemplate tmpl)
```

The client passes a *Service Template* argument to *lookup()*, which is a object containing the search criteria for the query. The service template can include a reference to an array of *Class* objects. These objects indicate to the lookup service the Java type (or types) of the service object desired by the client. The service template can also include a *service ID*, which uniquely identifies a service, and attributes, which must exactly match the attributes uploaded by the service provider in the service item. Attributes can contain a plaintext string for describing a service, e.g., "Epson 880 Service".

The *Service Template* can also contain wildcards for any of these fields. A wildcard in the *service ID* field, for example, will match any *service ID*. The *lookup()* method sends the service template to the lookup service, which performs the query and returns the matching service objects. The client gets a reference to the matching service objects as the return value of the *lookup()* method.

```
public interface JiniPrinter {
    /**
     * Print the document contained in the given String or
     * throw a PrinterException explaining why the call failed
     */
    public void print(String text) throws PrinterException;
}


public class LaserPrinter implements JiniPrinter {
    public void print(String text) throws PrinterException {
    // implement Laser-specific code here or throw exception
    }
}
```

Fig. 5.9. A simple example of how one might build a searchable Jini hierarchy for a definition of any printer.

In most cases, a client looks up a service by using a Java type, typically specified using a Java interface. For example, if a client wanted to use a printer, it would compose a service template that included a *Class* object for a well-known interface to printer services. All printer services would implement this well-known interface. For example, something like the code in Fig. 5.9 might be constructed to provide a generalized interface that could be implemented for any printer, whether it be a laser printer (as shown) or any other printer type.

The lookup service would return a service object (or objects) that implemented this JiniPrinter interface. Attributes can be included in the service template to narrow the number of matches for such a type-based search. The client would use the printer service by invoking the service object's methods declared in the printer service interface (in this case the print() method).

5.5 Jini: Tying Things Together

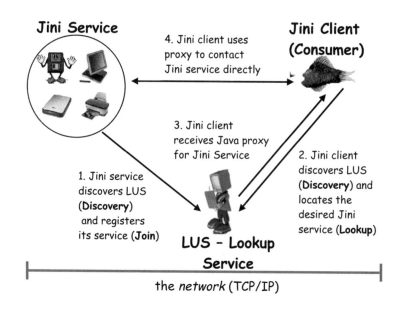

Fig. 5.10. An enhanced Jini example illustrating which Jini protocols are used at each stage of the scenario given in Fig. 5.7.

In summary therefore, in this section we insert the protocols and the relevant Java objects that are used at each stage of the Jini scenario given in

Fig. 5.7. In Fg. 5.10, the actual Jini protocols that are used by the three main Jini components are illustrated. For example here, when either the client or the service contacts the Jini LUS, it uses the discovery protocol; when the service wishes to add its service to the list of available Jini services, it uses the *join* protocol on the LUS; and finally, when the client wishes to search for available services that match its search criteria, it uses the *lookup* protocol.

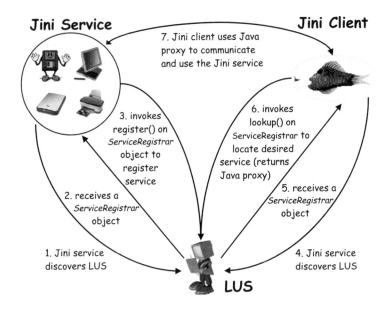

Fig. 5.11. An even more enhanced Jini example illustrating the Java objects along with the Jini protocols used at each stage of the scenario given in Fig. 5.10.

To enhance this scenario, we now add the actual Java objects that are involved at each stage of this process (see Fig. 5.11). This figure is a good overview of the entire Jini process. In Chapter 11, we will see how this is implemented and deployed within a Jini environment. Figure 5.11 gives a detailed scenario for our print example introduced in the previous section and has the following stages:

1. The Jini service uses *discovery* to locate the LUS, either by using multicast or unicast discovery.
2. The LUS returns a ServiceRegistrar object.
3. The Jini service can now use the ServiceRegistrar's register() function to register its print service with the LUS.
4. The Jini client uses discovery to locate the LUS, again either by using multicast or unicast discovery.

5. The LUS returns a ServiceRegistrar object.
6. The client uses the ServiceRegistrar's lookup() function to search for the LaserPrint service required.
7. The client receives the Java proxy (the LaserPrint interface).
8. The client executes the LaserPrint's print, which results in a remote method invocation of an implementation of the LaserPrint interface, which is connected to the remote printer and therefore the text is printed.

5.6 Organization of Jini Services

Jini communities are called groups, and during the discovery process, a service or client can specify the groups it wishes to find. The discovery protocols will then return any LUS services that are members of those groups. Therefore, grouping in Jini is based around the Jini LUS services.

An LUS can be a member of many groups and in most cases communities and groups can be thought of as the same things. Groups are simply the name used to represent communities. The most important distinction is that, due to network separation, different communities may have the same group name. Therefore, groups are not globally unique, nor are they necessarily globally accessible.

5.6.1 Events

Jini objects may also be interested in state changes in other Jini objects, and would like to be notified of such changes. The networked nature of Jini has led to a particular event model which differs slightly from the other models already in Java. Jini essentially extends the Java event model to work in a distributed environment. There are several factors which led to this new event model design, such as: messages maybe lost due to network delivery and therefore synchronous methods will fail; network delivery may delay events so events may appear in a different order than intended; and a remote listener may have disappeared by the time the event arrives so there needs to be a time-out mechanism.

Jini typically uses events of one type, the *RemoteEvent* or a small number of subclasses and conveys just enough information to allow state information to be found if needed. A remote event is *serializable* and can be moved around the network to its listeners.

In a synchronous system an interaction has the precise state and order of events. In a network system this is not so easy. Jini makes no assumptions about guarantees of delivery, and does not assume that events are delivered in order. The Jini event mechanism does not specify how events get from producer to listener (but are typically implemented by RMI calls).

The event source supplies a sequence number that could be used to construct state and ordering information if needed. This generalizes things such as timestamps on mouse events. For example, a message with id of ADD_NODE and sequence number of 3 could correspond to the state change *"added MIME type text/xml for files with suffix .tbx"*. Another event with id of RE-MOVE_NODE and sequence number of 4 would be taken as a later event even if it arrived earlier. The event source should be able to supply state information upon request, given the sequence number.

5.7 Conclusion

This chapter discussed the use of Jini for distributing Java objects across a network. First, an overview of RMI was given, which is the underlying communication technology that Jini builds upon to provide a network plug-and-play capability for distributed objects.

There are three main players in Jini: a service, such as a printer, scanner, storage device, a software service, etc.; a client which would like to make use of this service; and a lookup service that is a service registration and lookup facility.

Jini clients and services discover an LUS by using the discovery protocol. Services join a Jini federation (collection of Jini services) by using the join protocol and clients locate services by using the lookup protocol. These concepts are illustrated through the use of a simple scenario which outlines the various Jini protocols and how one uses the Java objects that are used to implement these protocols.

6

Gnutella

Gnutella defined and popularised modern P2P technology through its truly decentralized design and implementation. It arrived right around the time when centrally organized solutions were being targeted and provided a mechanism that offered a much more tolerant structure, where no single entity could be isolated to bring down the entire network. The Gnutella network consists of thousands of information providers, which are not indexed in a central place. Therefore, to shut down such the network is not trivial since a vast number of peers (i.e., many hundreds) would have to be eliminated.

This chapter provides an overview of the original 0.4 version of the Gnutella network. It combines a conceptual overview and a user-friendly rewrite of the Gnutella protocol specification [47]. An historical perspective is provided, along with usage scenarios, which include joining and searching the Gnutella network. This is followed by a detailed account of its protocol specification that provides the fundamental information required for a competent programmer to build a Gnutella network from scratch.

6.1 History of Gnutella

Gnutella was born sometime in early March 2000. Justin Frankel and Tom Pepper, working under the dot-com pen name of Gnullsoft [9], are Gnutella's inventors. Their last life-changing product, Winamp [7], was the beginning of a company called NullSoft [8], which was purchased by America Online (AOL) in 1999. Winamp was developed for playing music files. According to Tom Pepper, Gnutella was developed primarily to share cooking recipes.

Gnutella was developed in just fourteen days by two guys without college degrees. It was released as an experiment but was then abruptly stopped by AOL shortly afterwards (see [10] and [11]). It was supposed to be released as Version 1.0 under the GNU General Public License but never actually grew beyond version 0.56. The Gnutella name is a merging of GNU and Nutella (see Fig. 6.1). GNU is short for GNU's Not Unix, open source developing and

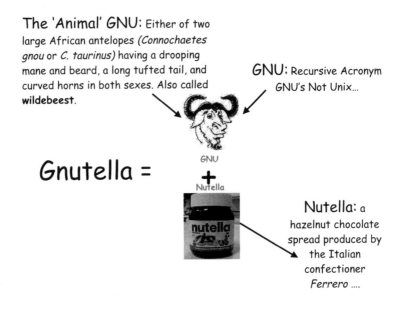

The 'Animal' GNU: Either of two large African antelopes *(Connochaetes gnou* or *C. taurinus)* having a drooping mane and beard, a long tufted tail, and curved horns in both sexes. Also called **wildebeest**.

GNU: Recursive Acronym GNU's Not Unix...

Gnutella =

GNU

+

Nutella

Nutella: a hazelnut chocolate spread produced by the Italian confectioner Ferrero ....

Fig. 6.1. The Gnutella name explained with animals and all....

Nutella is a hazelnut chocolate spread produced by the Italian confectioner Ferrero, which the authors liked...

Just as Gnutella was about to disappear, open source developers intervened and Bryan Mayland reverse-engineered Gnutella's communication protocol and released the findings on the *http://gnutella.nerdherd.net*. This site hosted the protocol documentation but also hosted a link to Gnutella's Internet Relay Chat (IRC) channel *#gnutella*, which had a massive response and significantly affected the future development.

6.2 What Is Gnutella?

Gnutella is a protocol for a distributed search. In this model, every peer in the network is both a client and a server. This is illustrated in Fig. 6.2. These so-called Gnutella *servents* (**server** + **client**) provide client-side interfaces through which users can issue queries and view search results, while at the same time they also accept queries from other servents, check for matches against their local data set, and respond with applicable results. Due to its distributed nature, a network of servents that implements the Gnutella protocol is highly fault tolerant, as the operation of the network as a whole is not affected if a subset of servents goes off line.

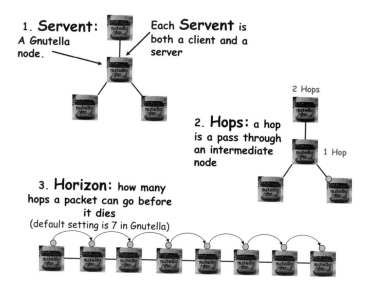

1. **Servent:** A Gnutella node.

Each **Servent** is both a client and a server

2. **Hops:** a hop is a pass through an intermediate node

2 Hops

1 Hop

3. **Horizon:** how many hops a packet can go before it dies
(default setting is 7 in Gnutella)

Fig. 6.2. Gnutella terms defined.

Each Gnutella node is connected to a small number of other Gnutella nodes (typically around four) and such connections are formed on a random ad hoc basis depending on where new peers happen to join the network. This structure is shown in Fig. 6.3, which illustrates the flat nature of the Gnutella network. Gnutella nodes have no central lookup service or caching servers and therefore only see other peers to whom they are connected.

Therefore, when a peer wishes to search the network for a file it has to ask its neighbours. Requests are answered if the peer has a copy of the requested file otherwise they are forwarded to all its connected peers, and so on. In this way, the network is flooded with a request in an inherently massively parallel fashion, which in theory should result in ultra fast searching. Well it does, but in practice of course, the amount of traffic that such a request generates can often saturate the capacity of the network and leave little bandwidth left for actually retrieving files, which defeats the point of the exercise! Such limitations are discussed in great detail in the next chapter, but it is important to understand the core Gnutella technology before understanding how these issues are addressed.

As a consequence of this method of searching a network, the Gnutella protocol defines a term to measure the number of nodes the packet travels through before it reaches its destination. This term is referred to as the *number of hops*, i.e., how many peers a request hops through (see Fig. 6.2).

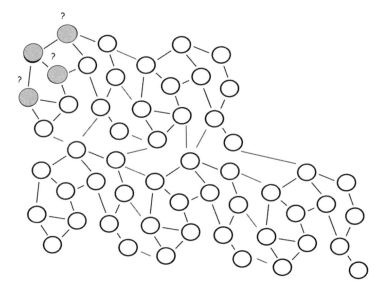

Fig. 6.3. An illustration of a basic Gnutella network containing tens of nodes.

In practice, a real-world Gnutella network would not be as organized as Fig. 6.3 due to the semi-random fashion that peers join the network and discover other peers. It would almost certainly be the case that peers will be connected in such a way that they will form loops. For example, peer A may connect to peer B, which may connect to peer C , which may, in turn, connect back to peer A. In this circumstance, it is important to make sure that the request doesn't loop indefinitely. For this reason, a unique identifier is attached to the message so that peers can drop requests that they have already seen. This is described in more detail in Section 6.3.3 but this principle is used in all P2P searchable networks.

Networks of this nature can become incredibly large and therefore you need a mechanism to limit the searchable area. For this reason, the Gnutella specification includes a TTL (Time To Live, see Fig. 6.2) for the request. TTL is also known as the Gnutella horizon, i.e., how far a packet can go before it dies.

The "standard" TTL is 7 hops, so, how far is that? A 7-hop radius combined with network conditions (i.e., 4 connections) means that around 10,000 nodes are reachable within a fully connected network. Another way to look at a TTL is with an analogy of a "large crowd" i.e. when you're in a large crowd (e.g., a rock/pop concert, a demonstration) you can only see so far.

The crowd appears to go on forever and also, you don't know exactly where you are in relation to the rest of the crowd; that's a peer in Gnutella.

6.3 A Gnutella Scenario: Connecting and Operating Within a Gnutella Network

This section provides an overview of how a servent joins the Gnutella network and, once joined, how it then discovers other servents available on the network. The next section illustrates this by using a typical Gnutella scenario.

6.3.1 Discovering Peers

There are various ways to discover a peer, both initially, when joining a Gnutella network, and when already connected to a Gnutella node:

1. **Out of Band Methods:** e.g., IRC and Web: In the early days, users used IRCs (Internet Relay Chat) to locate a host to which to connect. Otherwise, users checked a handful of Web pages to see which hosts were available. Users tried a number of hosts using the Gnutella software until one worked.
2. **Host Caches:** GnuCache was used to cache Gnutella hosts, which was included in Gnut software for UNIX. This gave users a permanent server for users to connect to in order to find out other users on the Gnutella network.
3. **Internal Peer Discovery:** involves issuing Ping messages, waiting for Pong responses with invitations to connect.

Note: peers must be willing to receiving incoming connections from "unknown" peers. Peers maybe picky about accepting connections for many reasons; for example, nodes may have too many connections already or prospective nodes may not have good properties, e.g., sharing few files, slow connections, and so on. Also, peers leaving a network can cause additional shuffling. Therefore, establishing a good set of connections can be haphazard.

6.3.2 Gnutella in Operation

Figure 6.4 illustrates the steps involved in connecting and searching within a Gnutella network.

User A performs the following steps in order to join and become an active participant in the Gnutella network:

1. User A uses one of the techniques discussed in Section 6.3.1 to join the Gnutella network. In this case, the user connects to a GnuCache server.
2. GnuCache returns a list of nodes on the Gnutella network. User A chooses one of these (User B) and attempts to contact it.

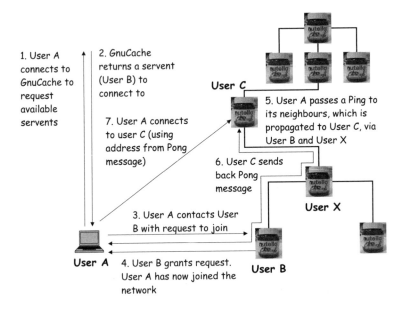

Fig. 6.4. Joining and discovering peers within a Gnutella network.

3. User A sends a "Gnutella Connect" (see section 6.4) to User B to request to join the network
4. User B accepts and returns a "Gnutella OK" to User A, who finalises the connection. User A is now connected to the Gnutella network.
5. User A now announces its presence by issuing a *Ping* to its neighbour (User B); User B forwards this to User X, who, in turn, forwards it to User C.
6. User C returns a *Pong* message, which gets passed along the same path as the ping descriptor travelled. *Pong* messages contain the address of the sender.
7. User A connects to User C by using the address specified in C's pong message to create another connection. User A continues in this fashion until it has reached its maximum connection count (typically set to around 4).

6.3.3 Searching Within Gnutella

In order to locate a file, a servent sends a query request to all its direct neighbours, which in turn forward the query to their neighbours, and the process repeats. When a servent receives a *query request*, it searches its local files and returns a *query response* containing all the matches it finds. *Query responses* follow the reverse path of *query requests* to reach the initiating servents for the request. Servents along the path do not cache the *query responses*.

To avoid *query requests* and *responses* flooding the network, each query contains a TTL field (typically set to 7, see Fig. 6.2). When a servent receives a query with a positive TTL, it decrements it before forwarding the query to its neighbours. Queries received with a TTL of 0 are not forwarded. In other words, queries are propagated using a controlled flooding.

It is easy to see that the same query can visit a servent more than once during the controlled flooding, i.e., through different neighbours of that servent. To make sure that each node does not serve the same query more than once, each message (i.e., descriptor) is identified by a 128-bit Unique IDentifier (UID). Servents memorise these UIDs and when a servent receives a query with a UID it has encountered previously, it simply drops the query.

6.4 Gnutella 0.4 Protocol Description

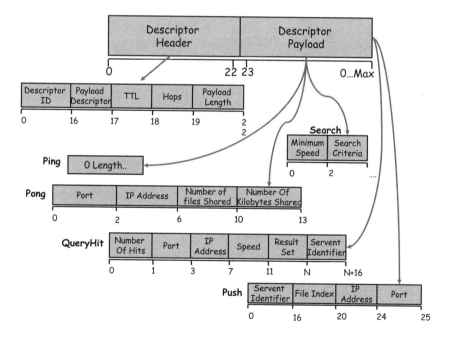

Fig. 6.5. An overview of the Gnutella specification and the descriptors it uses to define the protocol.

This section describes the Gnutella 0.4 protocol. This was the first description of the protocol and it is important to bear in mind that several more recent implementations have extended these descriptors to impose additional rules.

The Gnutella protocol defines the way in which servents communicate over the network. It consists of a set of descriptors (i.e., packets) for communicating data between servents, and a set of rules governing how Gnutella descriptors are exchanged. An overview of the various descriptors is shown in Fig. 6.5. This figure shows how the various descriptors relate to each other and how they are packaged up to create a Gnutella descriptor packet that is passed around the Gnutella network.

Briefly, a Gnutella descriptor consists of a header and a payload (i.e., message). The descriptor includes common attributes for any payload (e.g., id, TTL, hops, etc.). Then there are five payloads (messages) that can be described using this protocol. These are *Ping* (for announcing presence), *Pong* (for replying to ping messages), *Query* (for searching the network), *QueryHit* (for replying to search messages) and *Push* (for traversing firewalls). This structure and each payload is described in more detail in the remainder of this section.

6.4.1 Gnutella Descriptors

Gnutella descriptors consist of a message header and a payload (see Fig. 6.6, part *I*). As listed earlier, the following five descriptors are defined:

1. **Ping:** is used to announce presence on the network. A servent receiving a *Ping* descriptor can respond with a *Pong* descriptor.
2. **Pong:** is the response for a *Ping*, which includes the servent's contact details and the number of files it is sharing on the network.
3. **Query:** is the search mechanism, which contains a search string, e.g., "freeSongs". A servent matching a search request returns a *QueryHit*.
4. **QueryHit:** contains a list of matches for the *Query* along with the servent's contact details.
5. **Push:** provides a mechanism for a servent behind a firewall to share its files.

To join a Gnutella network, as illustrated in Section 6.3.2, a servent opens a TCP/IP connection to a peer already on the network and issues the following command (ASCII encoded):

```
GNUTELLA CONNECT/<protocol version string>\\n\\n
```

where <protocol version string> is the version of the specification (e.g. "0.4"). To accept a connection, a servent responds with:

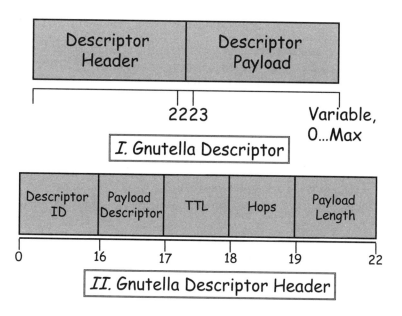

Fig. 6.6. The format of the Gnutella descriptor (I) and its header (II).

GNUTELLA OK\\n\\n

Otherwise, it is assumed that the connection is refused, perhaps because:

1. the servent has enough connections already
2. incompatible version number.

Once a servent has joined the network Gnutella *descriptors* (i.e., messages) are used to make requests and to issue responses.

Each descriptor has a *Descriptor Header*, which is described in the next section.

6.4.2 Gnutella Descriptor Header

The Gnutella descriptor header is given in Fig. 6.6, part *II* and consists of:

1. **Descriptor ID:** a unique identifier for the descriptor on (a 16-byte string).
2. **Payload Descriptor:** contains the type of payload i.e. 0x00 = *Ping*, 0x01 = *Pong*, 0x40 = *Push*, 0x80 = *Query*, 0x81 = *QueryHit*.
3. **Time to Live:** represents the number of hops this descriptor will be forwarded. Each servent decrements the TTL before passing it on. When the TTL equals 0, the descriptor is not forwarded. The TTL is the only

mechanism for expiring descriptors on the network and therefore, abuse of this field will lead to unnecessary network traffic and poor network performance.

4. **Hops:** keeps count of the number of times (i.e., hops) the descriptor has been forwarded. When the number of hops equals the initial TTL value specified, then the current TTL count equals 0.
5. **Payload Length:** is the size (in bytes) of the associated payload: i.e., the next descriptor header is located exactly *Payload Length* bytes from the end of this header. This is the only mechanism for locating Gnutella descriptors in communication streams[1] and consequently, servents should drop connections to reset if any errors occur.

The other section of a Gnutella descriptor is its payload, which can be one of five different types, mentioned previously. These are described in detail in the next five sections.

6.4.3 Gnutella Payload: Ping

Ping payloads contain no information as they are simply used to announce a peer's presence on the network. The header contains the necessary information (i.e., the UID is used) for the peers to be able to detect *Pong* replies from other peers. They will receive the reply because *Pong* descriptors always travel along the same path as their corresponding *Ping* messages and are identifiable by the initiating *Ping* UID. Further, more than one *Pong* descriptor can be sent in response to a *Ping* descriptor. This allows certain caching servers to reply with many servents' addresses in response to a *Ping*.

A *Ping* is therefore simply represented by a header whose *Payload_Descriptor* field is 0x00 and whose *Payload_Length* field is 0x00000000.

6.4.4 Gnutella Payload: Pong

A *Pong* descriptor (see Fig. 6.7) contains the address of the replying Gnutella servent and the quantity of data it is sharing. It defines four fields:

1. **Port:** is the responding servent's IP port for incoming connections
2. **IP Address:** is the responding servent's address (little endian)
3. **Number of Files Shared:** specifies the number of files the servent is sharing
4. **Number of Kilobytes Shared:** is the number of kilobytes the servent is sharing.

---

[1] All fields in this structure are in *big-endian* byte order (unless otherwise stated) and IP addresses are in IPv4 format

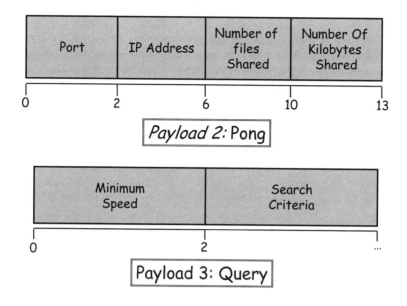

Fig. 6.7. The *Pong* descriptor, payload 2 and the *Query* descriptor, payload 3.

6.4.5 Gnutella Payload: Query

The *Query* descriptor (see Fig. 6.7) is Gnutella's search message format. It is passed to connected servents to enquire if they have the given file and has the following two fields:

1. **Minimum Speed:** the minimum connectivity speed (in kb/second) of a responding servent. Servents not passing this criteria should not respond to the message.
2. **Search Criteria:** contains the search string, which can be at most *Payload_Length* (minus 2 for *Minimum Speed* field) bytes long. This field is terminated by a *null* character (0x00).

6.4.6 Gnutella Payload: QueryHit

A servent receiving a *Query* descriptor will respond with a *QueryHit* (see Fig. 6.8, payload 4) if a match is found in its local file set. The *QueryHit* descriptor that is sent from a **responding host** defines the following fields:

1. **Number of Hits:** is the number of matches in this result set.
2. **Port:** is the port used for connecting for file transfer.
3. **IP Address:** is the IP address of the host (little-endian format).

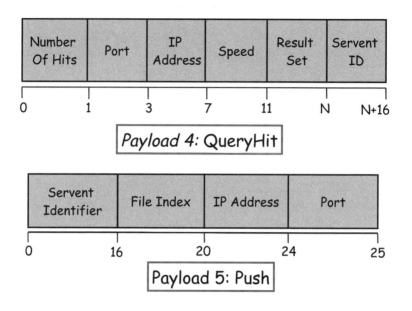

Fig. 6.8. The *QueryHit* descriptor, payload 4 and the *Push* descriptor, payload 5.

4. **Speed:** is the speed (in kb/second) of the host's connection.
5. **Result Set:** is the set of *Numberof_Hits* hits, where each hit contains:
   a) **File Index:** is a unique identifier for this file. This is up to the host to decide and is used for file retrieval, either directly or by using the *Push* mechanism, if required.
   b) **File Size:** is the file size (in bytes).
   c) **File Name:** is the name of the file matched (double-null terminated, i.e. 0x0000).
6. **Servent Identifier:** is the UID for this servent, typically calculated using some function of this servent's network address, used in the *Push* operation, if needed.

Using the same identification mechanism as the *Ping* and *Pong* messages, the *QueryHit* descriptors contain the same *Descriptor_Id* as the corresponding *Query* descriptor and since *QueryHit* descriptors may only be sent along the same path that carried the *Query* descriptor, this ensures that only those servents that routed the *Query* descriptor will see the *QueryHit* descriptor.

6.4.7 Gnutella Payload: Push

Push (see Fig. 6.8, payload 5) provides the mechanism to allow a servent hiding behind a firewall to serve files on a Gnutella network. This is illustrated below using a typical *Push* scenario:

1. A servent (A) issues a search request.
2. Servent B is contacted (via several intermediaries) and matches the search request.
3. B responds with a *QueryHit* descriptor. Imagine here that this servent is behind a firewall and consequently cannot accept incoming connections.
4. Servent A receives the *QueryHit* returned from B because it checks the *Descriptor_Id* to see if it matches the one it issued in its *Query* descriptor.
5. Servent A sends a *Push* request to servent B. The *Push* descriptor is sent along the same path as its corresponding *QueryHit*, which ensures that servent B will see it. This is achieved by a simple routing algorithm that makes a peer drop a *Push* descriptor which does not match any *QueryHit* descriptors they have seen.
6. Servent B receives this request (by matching the *Descriptor_Id*) and attempts to create a new TCP/IP connection to servent A by using the *IP Address* and *Port* fields of the *Push* descriptor; i.e., servents that cannot accept incoming connections can normally create outgoing ones.
7. A direct connection is established and the file is downloaded. If a direct connection cannot be created, then it is likely that servent A is also behind a firewall and consequently, a file transfer cannot take place.

The *Push* descriptor defines four fields. To simplify things, servents A and B from the above scenario are used to depict the originator and responder to the search request in the following description of the *Push* descriptor's internal fields:

1. **Servent Identifier:** is the UID for the servent B and is set by A by using the *Servent_Identifier* for the corresponding *QueryHit*. This UID is in fact B's UID.
2. **File Index:** is set to the value of one of the *File_Index* fields from the *QueryHit* response to specify the file to be pushed.
3. **IP Address:** is the IP address of servent A, i.e., the host where the file should be pushed (little-endian format).
4. **Port:** is the port of servent A for the connection of the push.

6.5 File Downloads

In brief, after the query hits are received by the servent, it establish a direct connection in order to download one of the files in the *QueryHit* descriptor's *Result Set*. The download request is carried out using the HTTP protocol, through an HTTP GET request with the following message format:

```
GET /get/<File Index>/<File Name>/ HTTP/1.0\\r\\n
Connection: Keep-Alive\\r\\n
Range: bytes=0-\\r\\n
User-Agent: Gnutella\\r\\n
\\r\\n
```

where *File Index* and *File Name* are the index and name for one of the files
in the *Result Set*. For example, if the *Result Set* from a *QueryHit* descriptor
contained the entries given in Fig. 6.9, then a download request would contain
the following:

```
GET /get/1234/coolsong.mp3/ HTTP/1.0\\r\\n
Connection: Keep-Alive\\r\\n
Range: bytes=0-\\r\\n
User-Agent: Gnutella \\r\\n
\\r\\n
```

File Index	1234
File Size	5678910
File Name	coolsong.mp3\x00\x00

Fig. 6.9. An example of a result set from a QueryHit Descriptor.

The servent receiving this request replies with the following *HTTP OK* message:

```
HTTP 200 OK\\r\\n
Server: Gnutella\\r\\n
Content-type: application/binary\\r\\n
Content-length: 5678910\\r\\n
\\r\\n
```

This response is followed by the actual data, which is read according to the
number of bytes specified in the *Content-length* field as illustrated. To assist
with transient connectivity, the Gnutella protocol also provides support for the
HTTP *range* parameter, which enables an interrupted transfer to be resumed
at a later point.

Gnutella Clients		
Windows	**Linux/Unix**	**Macintosh**
BearShare		
Gnucleus	Gnewtellium	
Morpheus	Gtk-Gnutella	
Shareaza	Mutella	LimeWire
Swapper	Qtella	Phex
XoloX	LimeWire	
LimeWire	Phex	
Phex		

Fig. 6.10. A list of Gnutella implementations for various platforms.

6.6 Gnutella Implementations

Figure 6.10 gives a list of some examples of Gnutella-based applications, broken down into three different operating systems, which are available (or have been available) on the internet for file sharing. Some other client implementations are listed in Appendix A.

6.7 More Information

There are a number of good articles and papers on the Internet that give concise overviews of Gnutella. One in particular can be found on the Limewire site [49]. Another [50], has a number of papers relating to Gnutella including various studies that have been and indeed still are being carried out.

6.8 Conclusion

In this chapter, Gnutella has been described. Gnutella is a search protocol that allows peers to search a network of peers without the need for any centralized control. In Gnutella, every node is both a client and a server and is referred to as a *servent*. Servents join the network using one of several techniques, e.g., the Web, IRC, GnuCache, and once joined, can discover other peers through Gnutella's discovery mechanism using *Ping/Pong* descriptors.

The Gnutella protocol defines the way servents communicate over the network. It defines a set of Gnutella descriptors and a set of rules governing their interaction. Gnutella descriptors consist of a descriptor header and a payload. The header contains a descriptor's unique identifier and its corresponding payload contains one of the following types, e.g., *Ping, Pong, Query, Query-Hit* and *Push*, which are used for peer discovery, searching and for traversing firewalls within the Gnutella decentralized network.

7

Scalability

P2P has led to a recent renewal of interest in decentralized systems. Although the underlying Internet itself is the largest decentralized computer system in the world, most systems have employed a completely centralized topology in the 1990s through the massive growth of the Web.

With the emergence of P2P in early 2000, there has been a shift into employing the use of radically decentralized architectures, such as Gnutella [6]. In practice however, extreme architectural choices in either direction are seldom the way to build a usable system. Most current P2P file-sharing software, for example, use a hybrid of the two approaches.

In this chapter, we look at the ways in which peers are organized within ad-hoc, pervasive, multi-hop networks. Social networks are introduced and compared against their P2P counterparts. A summary of the typical topologies for P2P networks is given and then an analysis is undertaken using Gnutella as a test-case example, describing the evolution of the Gnutella system into using a hybrid topology.

7.1 Social Networks

Before we analyse P2P networks, let's first take a look at a unique social experiment conducted in 1967 by Harvard professor Stanley Milgram [154], with some notes from [62]. He performed a social-networking experiment within the United States to find out how many *social hops* it would take for messages to traverse through the population, which was at the time, around 200 million people.

He posted 160 letters to randomly chosen people living in Omaha, Nebraska and asked them to try to pass these letters to a stockbroker he knew working in Boston, Massachusetts (see Fig. 7.1). The rules were that they could only pass the letter to intermediaries known to them on a first-name basis. Such intermediaries should be chosen intelligently so that they might bring the letter closer to the stockbroker. For example, this decision could

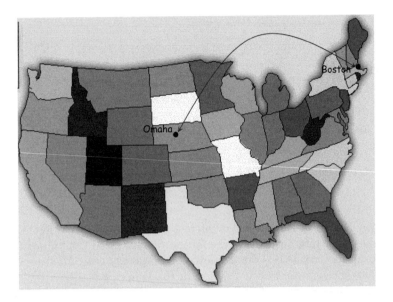

Fig. 7.1. The Milgrim social-networking experiment, illustrating the distance on a map of the states that he posted the 160 letters.

be because they may know someone who is geographically closer to Boston; e.g., they may know someone in Illinois, or that they may know someone who may know someone who lives near Boston. The friend given the letter would continue in this fashion, passing it on to another friend, and so on until the letter reached a friend of the stockbroker who could give it to him personally. At each stage of the journey the intermediaries noted their details on the package.

In the end, 42 letters made it through to the stockbroker. The interesting fact was that the average number of hops (i.e., through intermediaries) each letter passed through was 5.5. The Milgram experiment demonstrated concretely for the first time what has become popularly known as the small-world effect, something we'd say when we bump into a friend from our home town on some remote beach in the middle of nowhere, using the expression, "its a small world, isn't it!" with the infamous retort "Yes, but I wouldn't like to paint it!".

This experiment was designed to explore the properties of social networks and it gave evidence that the social network of the United States could be indeed connected with a path-length (number of hops) of around 6. This number is surprisingly low compared to the population at the time. Does this mean it takes less than 6 hops to traverse 200 million people? If so, can't we achieve the same organization in computer networks? And if so, can we not simply model these on social networks as they work so well?

It turns out that although social circles are highly clustered, some acquaintances in the group will have more wide-ranging connections and these connections form a bridge between social clusters that are geographically far away from each other. This *bridging* plays a critical role in bringing the entire network closer together. For example, in the Milgram experiment, a quarter of all letters reaching the stockbroker passed through a single person, who was the local shopkeeper. In all, half of the letters pass through just three people, who acted as gateways or hubs between the source and the wider world. A small number of bridges therefore can dramatically reduce the number of hops.

7.2 P2P Networks

P2P networks have a number of similarities to social networks. People would be peers and the intermediaries in Milgram's experiment would be known as gateways, hubs, bridges or rendezvous nodes in P2P networks. The number of intermediaries used to pass the letter from the source to the destination would be the *number of hops* in a P2P network. The similarities go on and on. In many senses, P2P networks are more like social networks than other types of computer networks as they are often self-organizing, ad hoc, they employ clustering techniques based on prior interactions (like we form relationships), and have decentralized discovery and communication, which arguably are analogous to the way we have formed neighbourhoods, villages, towns, cities, etc.

7.2.1 Performance in P2P Networks

So, how do we organize P2P networks in such a way as to get optimum performance? Well, performance in P2P networks is non-deterministic. A P2P network is often constructed in an ad hoc fashion and due to its nature and transient availability of its cooperating peers, it is therefore impossible to stabilise the network for optimal performance. However, this does not mean though that we should give up, it simply means we have to devise complicated robust algorithms that make the best of this situation. Therefore, performance in P2P networks cannot be measured precisely; it rather involves taking empirical measurements such as:

- How long does it take to search for a particular file?
- How much bandwidth will the query consume?
- How many hops will it take for my package to get to a peer on the far side of the network?
- If I add/remove a peer to/from the network will the network still be fault tolerant?

- Does the network scale as we add more peers? Such networks can rapidly expand from a few hundred peers to several thousand or even millions.

The answers to these questions have a direct impact on the success and usability of a system. Remember that P2P networks operate in unreliable environments where peers are continuously connecting and disconnecting. Resources may suddenly become unavailable for a variety of reasons: e.g., users may disconnect from the network because they may have decided that they do not want to participate any more. Further, there are more random failures, e.g., cable and DSL failures, power outages, hackers and attacks, as personal machines are much more vulnerable than dedicated servers. In such an environment therefore, there need to be algorithms which can cope with this continuous restructuring of the network core. P2P systems need to treat failures as normal occurrences, not freak exceptions and therefore P2P networks must be designed in a way that promotes redundancy with the trade-off of a degradation of performance.

There are three main factors that make P2P networks more sensitive to performance issues compared to other types of network [62]; these are:

1. **Communication:** An obvious fundamental necessity of any P2P network. Most users connect through dial-up, cable or DSL and so their connection speed is the main bottleneck. However, this problem is amplified by the highly parallel, multi-hop nature of a P2P network where it often takes a number of hops for a packet to reach its destination. Therefore other users' connection speeds also create a bottleneck; i.e., if one peer on your multi-hop request is running a 56K modem then this slows things down en route. Network traffic minimization and load balancing therefore are important considerations to overall performance.

2. **Searching:** There is no central server in P2P networks so many more peers are involved in the search process, which typically occurs over several parallel network hops. Each hop of such a search adds to the total bandwidth load and therefore the time to set up a connection becomes a critical factor. Combine this with the inherently unreliable nature of the individual peers and delivery time starts to grow alarmingly; e.g., if a peer is unreachable, TCP/IP can take up to several minutes to time out the connection.

3. **Load-Balancing Peers:** In theory, true decentralized P2P networks consist entirely of *equal peers*, meaning that each peer potentially shares as much as it consumes. However, in real-world implementation, such network ideals are skewed by usage patterns. For example, studies have indicated that around 70 percent of Gnutella users share no files at all [37]. Too many free riders will degrade the performance of the network for others and therefore care must be taken to factor in the correct proportion so that measures can be taken to optimize the current topology, not assume a static and perhaps unrealistic one.

The next section outlines a number of the topologies employed by a variety of distributed systems including the scalable P2P file-sharing applications.

7.3 Peer Topologies

This section is based on an on-line article [66] and covers a number of different types of topology that a P2P network can use. Fundamentally, the debate between centralized and decentralized systems is about topology, that is, how the nodes in the system are connected. For P2P networks, the topology is considered in terms of the information flow of the network. Nodes in the graph are the peers and links (edges) between peers indicate a regular sharing of information. For simplicity, edges here are considered undirected. Below, four common topologies are described and then three hybrid topologies are discussed. These are:

1. Centralized
2. Ring
3. Hierarchical
4. Decentralized
5. Centralized/Ring
6. Centralized/Centralized
7. Centralized/Decentralized

These topologies are described in the following seven sections.

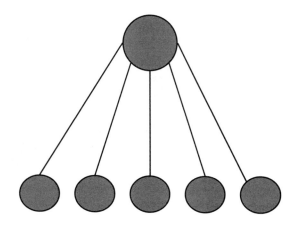

Fig. 7.2. A centralized topology.

7.3.1 Centralized

Centralized client/server systems (see Fig. 7.2) are by far the most common form of topology. Communication is completely centralized with many clients connecting directly to a single server, which is illustrated in detail in Section 1.3.3. Examples of centralized systems include Web servers, databases, SETI@Home, etc.

7.3.2 Ring

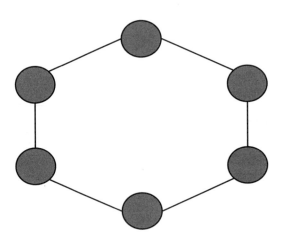

Fig. 7.3. A ring topology.

A ring topology is a physical closed loop consisting of point-to-point links and is a common method for scaling centralized services (see Fig. 7.3) to act as a distributed server. Communication between the servers coordinates the sharing of the system state. This establishes a group of nodes that provide identical function to a single server but incorporate redundancy and load-balancing capabilities. Typically, ring systems consist of machines that are on the same intranet and which are owned by a single organization.

7.3.3 Hierarchical

Hierarchical topologies have a tree-like structure and provide an extremely fast way of searching through information that is organized in a consistent fashion. For example, in a binary tree, every node's left sub-tree has values less than the node's value, and every right sub-tree has values greater, which partitions the search space into well-defined sub-segments for searching.

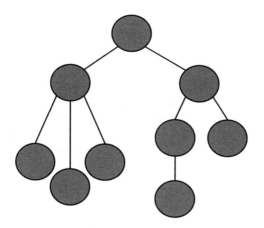

Fig. 7.4. A hierarchical topology.

The most well-known hierarchical system (see Fig. 7.4) is DNS, where authority flows from the root name servers to the server for the registered name and often down to third-level servers. Usenet is another large hierarchical system, using a tree-like structure to copy articles between servers. Here, the underlying protocols are symmetric but in practice, news articles propagate along tree-like paths with a relatively small set of hosts acting as the backbone.

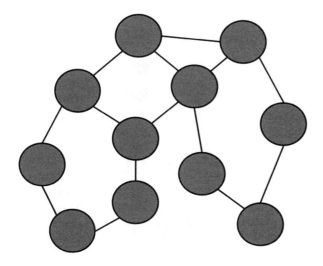

Fig. 7.5. A decentralized topology.

7.3.4 Decentralized

In a completely decentralized system (see Fig. 7.5), there is no single point of control. Peers communicate symmetrically and have equal roles. Gnutella is a good example and has been described in detail elsewhere in this book (see Chapter 6). Pure decentralized networks are extremely fault tolerant against random peer failures but this comes at a price, which is the bandwidth required to search such a network. Later in this chapter, we will see several studies that indicate this (see Section 7.7). For example, in pure Gnutella networks, a quarter of the overall network bandwidth is consumed by searching alone.

7.4 Hybrid Topologies

Distributed systems typically combine multiple topologies and are therefore generally more complicated than the simple cases listed above. When systems combine two or more topologies, they are referred to as a hybrid topology. Peers typically switch roles and act as gateways between the combined topologies. For example, within a centralized-decentralized topology described in detail below a peer is part of a decentralized network of super-peers as one role and acts similar to a simple Gnutella peer within this environment but also acts as a centralized look-up servers for the sub-network that it is responsible for.

7.4.1 Centralized/Ring

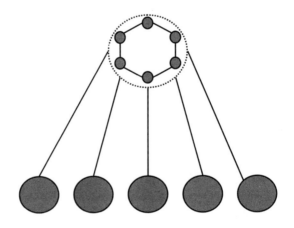

Fig. 7.6. A centralized/ring topology.

Robust Web servers often have a ring of servers for load balancing and redundancy (see Fig. 7.6). This topology is a description of a ring that also includes the client connections; i.e., this is a centralized system where the server is itself a ring. The result is the simplicity of a centralized system (from the client's point of view) with the robustness of a ring.

7.4.2 Centralized/Centralized

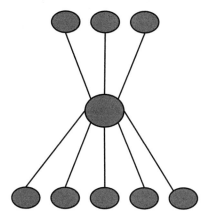

Fig. 7.7. A centralized/centralized topology.

Here, there is a central point of control but often the behind-the-scenes capabilities are distributed across one or more other servers (see Fig. 7.7). In Web applications, for example, when a Web browser contacts a server to issue a request, the Web server would contact a number of other nodes in order to satisfy that request. The Web server may be contacting a distributed database of Web links, for example (as in the Google case), or interacting with a parallel cluster of dedicated machines used to perform some scientific calculation. Stacking multiple centralized systems in this way is the core of n-tier application frameworks.

7.4.3 Centralized/Decentralized

As illustrated in Fig. 7.8, the centralized/decentralized topology consists of a two-tiered structure, where a number of centralized systems are connected in a decentralized fashion. Therefore, at the higher level, you have a structure and behaviour similar to Gnutella, that is, a highly fault-tolerant decentralized set

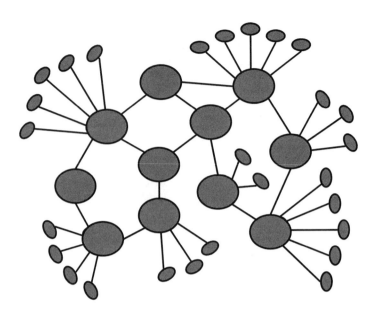

Fig. 7.8. A centralized/decentralized topology.

of peers that provide information to their lower-level collections of centrally organized peers.

The fault tolerance of the upper layer is highly dependent on the number of nodes present, but in structure, such networks are rather reminiscent of social networks, where many people typically use a a gateway (remember the shopkeeper?) in order to connect to far-flung communities i.e. the centralized/decentralized topology implements the small-world effect demonstrated by Milgrim.

It turns out that centralized/decentralized topologies scale remarkably well and have been therefore adopted by a number of popular P2P file-sharing systems. For example, the FastTrack file-sharing system used by KaZaA and Morpheus, which can connect hundreds of thousands of peers, use this topology.

Within file-sharing lingo, the decentralized peers are referred to as super-nodes or Gnutella reflector nodes. Super-nodes act as caching servers to connected clients and perform a similar operation to Napster servers. So, rather than propagating the query across the entire set of nodes, the super-peer will check its own database to see if it knows the whereabouts of the requested file and if so, it returns that address to the client, just like Napster. If not, it performs a Gnutella-type broadcast across the decentralized set of super-peers to propagate this request across the network. This means that a client can search an entire network without consuming a vast amount of bandwidth.

Jxta rendezvous nodes perform a similar type of service within Jxta networks.

7.5 The Convergence of Napster and Gnutella

It is interesting to note that both Gnutella and Napster converged towards a centralized/decentralized topology, even though they came from completely different sides of the coin. Gnutella started its life as a decentralized system and Napster started its life as a centralized search architecture, with brokered communications. However, Gnutella inserted super-peers and Napter duplicated its centralized search engines for scalability, both resulting in a similar design topology, as illustrated in Fig. 7.9.

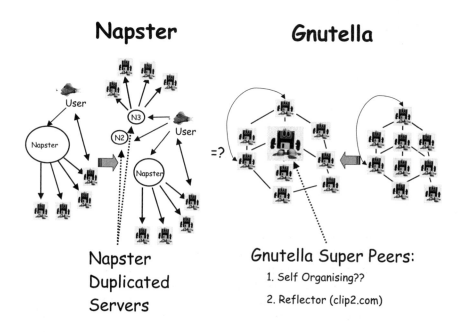

Fig. 7.9. The convergence of Naptser and Gnutella.

Consider both scenarios more closely:

- Gnutella is a completely decentralized search which operates on the premise that all peers are equal. In practice however, users operate at different levels. One user may only have several files to share, whilst others might be sharing several thousand. Therefore, in a completely self-organizing way, Gnutella tends to converge into a hybrid structure. Clip2.com [3] recognised this early on and developed a program that they call the *Gnutella Reflector*. This is a proxy and index service designed to make Gnutella more scalable that can also make outside connections to gather other information, as described.

- Napster, on the other hand started its life as a brokered system, centralizing the search but decentralizing the communication (downloading of the MP3 file). Napster however, started to replicate its main server as the user base grew, thereby creating many Napster servers that served fewer clients. This, in effect, has exactly the same result as the Gnutella reflector nodes but instead, they extended the centralized approach into a decentralized arena and not vice-versa.

The key difference here, as illustrated in Fig. 7.9, is that within a decentralized system, such as Gnutella, the formation of the Gnutella super-peers is self-organizing and scales proportionately and dynamically with the size of the network. The actual algorithm for achieving this is typically based on a combination of user preferences and communication resource considerations.

However, in a centralized/brokered approach, the servers have to be explicitly added by hand and therefore cannot scale dynamically with the network, without using some extra management software capable of monitoring the current usage. In essence though, the Gnutella reflector nodes are mini-Napster servers. They maintain an index of files from peers currently connected. When a query is issued, the reflector does not retransmit it; rather, it answers the query from its own memory.

7.6 A Southern Side-Step

During the writing of this book, I decided to get away to somewhere quiet and so I packed my bags and took a three week writing trip to Sicily. Interestingly (and unsurprisingly) one night, I was in a pub and they adopted a rather bizarre serving scheme.... Basically, a customer had to walk to one server by a till at the centre of this long bar, order his drink, then walk back to his barstool and pass this receipt onto the bartender who would bring him his drink. I thought this was very strange, as they turned an inherently decentralized service into a centralized one!! Why, I thought to myself, could I not simply pay the bartender directly?

Anyway, after a few drinks the bar got rather packed and I soon realised that this scheme in fact was working rather well. This kind of disturbed me because there I was, writing this book about decentralized systems and these Sicilians have completed circumvented the idea! so perhaps this is all wrong....

Sometime later though I was saved by the realisation of two facts, namely: the Italians, in general, don't drink so much, and I predicted that this could never work, for example, in Britain...; but most importantly, I then realised that they were not running a centralized system at all. They were in fact running a brokered system; i.e., they centralized discovery (i.e. and therefore payment) but the service of pouring drinks was still decentralized; hence the scalability.

Furthermore, I did notice that during the night every time the cashier wandered off for a cigarette, not only was there a non-trivial accumulating number of patrons waiting but also, the bartenders finished serving their current order and then stood around doing absolutely nothing; that is, the whole system came to a halt. Hence I conclude that the Waxies in Catania has in fact, the same taxonomy as Napster: centralized discovery and therefore with intermittent availability (with no redundancy). However, due to its decentralized communication, services that have been discovered (and paid for here) can still be concluded as normal. Of course, we are talking about payment and beer but as social perspectives go, there are much worse analogies!

7.7 Gnutella Analysis

The centralized/decentralized architecture is the most popular architecture used within today's P2P file-sharing applications. This section gives a background into some empirical studies that support this type of topology by analysing the behaviour of users and connectivity on a Gnutella network. But first, let's recap the core Gnutella model and how far this scales.

Gnutella uses a simple broadcast model to conduct queries, which does not utilize the small-world effect. Each peer tries to maintain a small number of connections (around 3 or 4). Gnutella's topology is in fact a 3- or 4-D Cayley tree [68].

Searching in Gnutella involves broadcasting a Query message to all connected peers. Each connected peer will send it to its connected peers (say 3) and so on. This search will run for a specific number of hops, typically 7. If the number of connected peers, $c = 3$ and the hops, $h = 7$ then the total number of peers searched (s) in a fully connected network will be:

```
s = c + c2 +c3 + ..
s = 3 + 9 + 27 + 81 + 243 + 729 + 2187 = 3279 Nodes
```

In practice, the network often converges somewhere between 3 and 4 connections per node giving around 10,000 nodes each peer can search (assuming full connectivity). In the following sections, a number of studies show how such a Gnutella network performs and evolves.

7.7.1 Gnutella Free Riding

In the article [37], they considered two types of free riding in an analysis of the Gnutella network: peers free riding that only download files for themselves

without ever providing files for download for others; and users that have unde-
sirable content, i.e., they might be sharing files but the files may be corrupted
and therefore lead to unnecessary network traffic.

They found that, in one experiment, that 22,084 of the 33,335 peers in the
network (or approximately 66%) of the peers share no files, and that 24,347 or
73% share 10 or fewer files. The data also showed that the top 1% (333 hosts)
represent approximately 37% of the total files shared. This quickly escalates
to the top 20% (6,667 hosts) sharing 98% of the files. This experiment shows
that even without Gnutella reflector nodes, the Gnutella network naturally
converges into a centralized/decentralized topology with the top 20% of nodes
acting as super-peers or reflectors.

7.7.2 Equal Peers?

Why can't there be a network full of equal peers? Well, there are a number of
reasons including: users have a variety of different spec'd machines with different capabilities; users connect via different mechanisms, and hence different
speeds; and each user has different interests. For example, one user may have
collected a huge number of files, and although she may be willing to share
these files, other users may not be interested in them at all. So, even though
they are a good contributor in theory, they are not effective in the network as
a whole, and therefore will simply be ignored.

Further, Clip2.com [2] performed an analysis of Gnutella based on measurements over a month. They noted an apparent scalability barrier when
query rates went above 10 per second. Why? Well, a typical Gnutella query
message is around 560 bits long and queries make up approximately a quarter
of traffic. A quick calculation therefore, given that Gnutella peers are connected to average of 3 remote peers, gives us 560 *10 * 3 = 16,800 bits per
second. Now, if this is a quarter of the traffic then the total traffic is 16,800 x
4 = 67,200 bits per second. Now, a 56K link cannot keep up with this amount
of traffic and therefore one node connected in the incorrect place can grind
the whole network to a halt. It is for this reason that one of the main goals
for the organization of a P2P network is to place slower nodes at the edges of
the network.

7.7.3 Power-Law Networks

A study of the topology of the Gnutella network was undertaken [69] over a
period of several months, and it reported two interesting findings:

- **Power-Law Structure:** the Gnutella network shares the benefits and
  drawbacks of a power-law structure [153];
- **Virtual Overlay:** the Gnutella network topology does not match well
  with the underlying Internet topology leading to inefficient use of network
  bandwidth.

A power-law structure is when a network organizes itself so that most nodes have a few links and a small number of nodes have many (i.e., like super-peers). This is equivalent to the centralized-decentralized topology described above. The article points out that the power-law networks have been found to show an unexpected degree of robustness when facing random node failures. Consequently, the ability of the network to communicate is unaffected by high failure rates. However, such error tolerance comes at a high price. For example, such networks are more vulnerable to attacks than completely decentralized networks, e.g., by selectively removing a few of the critical super-nodes, one can inflict massive damage on the structure and function of the network as a whole.

In the paper, the author suggested two directions for improvement. He suggested that an agent could monitor the network and intervene by asking servents to drop/add links to keep the topology optimal. Such agents would have knowledge of the underlying network and therefore, be able to create a better virtual overlay for the Gnutella network. The second suggestion is to replace the Gnutella flooding mechanism with a smarter routing and group communication mechanism.

7.8 Further Reading

Minar [66] creates a taxonomy for analysing various network topologies in his second article. Gunther [67] compares various topologies for scalability issues for networks up to two million peers. He found that the 20-dimensional hypercube performed the best. Also, Hong [62] provides an excellent overview for scalability issues within P2P networks and provides two case studies for Freenet (see Chapter 9) and Gnutella.

There are many recent developments in new virtual network overlays, creating new topologies for P2P computing. Some examples of these are Pastry [44] and Chord [45].

7.9 Conclusion

This chapter gave a background into some of the problems facing the scalability of P2P networks. Due to their extremely dynamic nature, standard network topologies do not work very well and therefore, more elaborate topologies are needed to offer scalability and robustness against random peer failures.

The most popular topology use in recent file-sharing applications is the centralized-decentralized model that employs the same characteristics as a power-law network. This topology is similar to social and biological networks, where most nodes have a few links and a small number of nodes have many, serving as gateways to other networks. Such a topology in Gnutella can be implemented by using super-peers or reflector nodes.

8

Security

This chapter covers the basic elements of security in a distributed system. It illustrates the various ways that a third party can gain access to data and gives an overview of some of the design issues involved in building a distributed security system.

Cryptography is introduced, then cryptographic techniques for symmetric and asymmetric encryption/decryption are given, along with the role of one-way hash functions. An example of the use of some of these techniques is provided through an example of how one digitally signs a document, e.g., email. Both asymmetric and symmetric secure channels are discussed, along with scenarios for their use. Finally, the notion of sand boxing is introduced and illustrated through the description of the Java security-manager implementation.

This chapter appears here in this book because it provides a gateway for the middleware and applications that will follow, which use various security techniques and frameworks. For example, Freenet (in Chapter 9) uses many of these techniques extensively for creating keys for the Freenet network, which are used, not only for privacy issues, but to actually map from the data content to network location. Further, Jxta (Chapter 10) and Grid computing (Chapter 4) also provide security infrastructures and address authentication issues.

This chapter is based on many on-line papers and articles and an excellent overview of distributed-systems security infrastructures, given by Tanenbaum and van Steen [1].

8.1 Introduction

Security has to be pervasive throughout a system. A single design flaw in the security will render the entire security system useless and therefore great care must be taken in considering the many design choices for the particular system at hand. Security is related to the notion of dependability and a dependable system must be available, reliable, safe and maintainable. Therefore, to address the security of a dependable system, we must provide:

- **Confidentiality:** where authorized access is a necessity
- **Integrity:** where alterations are only performed by authorized parties, e.g., if we send data from one place to another, we must provide techniques for ensuring that the data has not been modified along the route

Before we look at the various techniques that can be used to address these issues, let's look at the possible security threats. In brief, there are four types of security threat to computer systems:

1. **Interception:** involves an unauthorized party gaining access to a service or data, e.g., when someone is eavesdropping into a private conversation. Alternatively, interception could also involve somebody making an illegal copy of a file.
2. **Interruption:** happens when a service (or data) becomes unavailable, unusable, destroyed, etc. There are numerous examples: when a file is lost or corrupted, or denial of service through host failure or service attacks.
3. **Modification:** involves modifying the contents of data or a service without authorization. Therefore, data may become invalid or a service may return a different result than what is expected; e.g., you could rebind a Web service to an alternate implementation or modify database entries.
4. **Fabrication:** involves generating data or an activity that wouldn't normally exist, e.g., adding a password into a password file or database.

A company first needs to define a *Security Policy*. This is a set of rules defining which actions entities, e.g., users, administrators, services, etc., are allowed to take. Once a security policy has been defined, it is possible to define which security mechanisms can be used in order to enforce these criteria. There are four types:

1. **Encryption:** is fundamental to security and involves encoding (encrypting) data into something an attacker cannot understand (i.e., it implements confidentiality).
2. **Authentication:** is used to verify the claimed identity of a user. There are many types of authentication mechanisms, e.g., passwords, digital certificates, etc.
3. **Authorization:** involves checking that a user has the correct permission to perform a particular operation. Typically, authorization is performed after authentication; e.g., in UNIX, even though you have logged on (i.e., authenticated), you still may not have access to certain resources; i.e., you will not be able to write a file in any directory other than your own.
4. **Auditing:** is a passive security measure which tracks or logs the clients that log in and use the system. Auditing can be used to find out who and how a user accessed a particular resource. Auditing is useful in finding out where in the system the security breach happened, which can be used to

fix the problem for the future. Further, often if an attacker knows there is such a system in place this is a good deterrent.

8.2 Design Issues

There are a number of design issues that need to be considered when designing a general-purpose security system. In this section, descriptions of three issues are given [1]:

- **Focus of Data Control:** specifies the level (or position) where the protection for the data or services is provided.
- **Layering of Security:** concentrates on where in the security stack (i.e., within the OSI model) the security focus will be.
- **Simplicity:** focuses on the need for simplicity for any security system. If the security system is not simple to understand, then users will not trust it.

These three issues are described in the following sections.

8.2.1 Focus of Data Control

There are three points where data (or services) can be protected within a distributed system; see Fig. 8.1. These are at the:

1. **Data Level:** to protect the data directly from wrong or invalid operations (see Fig. 8.1). For example, integrity checks could be implemented within a database each time data is accessed or modified. Another, more familiar example to Java programmers, is array-bounds checking, which verifies the legality every time an array item is accessed. If the operation is legal then access is granted, otherwise an exception is thrown at runtime.
2. **Method Level:** restricts which operations can be applied to the data and by whom. In object-oriented terms, this is equivalent to a set of *accessor* methods on an object, which dictate the types of operations (e.g., setX, getY, etc.) that can be performed on the class's internal data (which could be set private). You may also restrict the access to a database using predefined interfaces. Then, within a method's implementation various types of checks can be performed to ensure the validity of the operation.
3. **User Level:** focuses on the users of the system; i.e., only selected users can have access to the application/data/service regardless of what operations they want to perform. A user role is defined for each user. For example, on Windows XP, there are two 'user roles': a *Computer Administrator* or *Limited*. A computer administrator can install programs and hardware, make system-wide changes, access and read files, and create and delete user accounts whereas a *Limited* user can only change her own settings, e.g., picture and create, change or remove her own password and files.

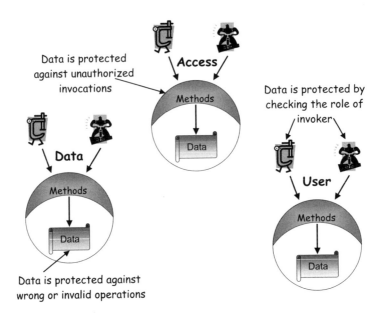

Data is protected
against unauthorized
invocations

Access

Methods

Data

Data is protected by
checking the role of
invoker

Data

Methods

Data

User

Methods

Data

Data is protected against
wrong or invalid operations

Fig. 8.1. The three approaches for protecting data: at the data, access, or user level. The diagram shows the consequences of each action.

8.2.2 Layering of Security Mechanisms

An important design issue for implementing secure systems is to decide at which *level* the security mechanisms should be placed. The *level* positions the security mechanisms within the logical organization of system components, as illustrated in Fig. 8.2. Shown here are the following broad layers: applications, middleware, operating system services, operating system kernel and communications, which illustrate an important separation of general-purpose services from communication.

Further, it is important to relate this to the notion of trust. A system can be secure but whether a customer trusts it is another matter. Therefore, a crucial factor is to make sure that a client trusts the layer you decided on but further, that he also trusts the layer(s) on which these security services are built.

For example, say Tim on machine A wanted to send a message to Gareth on machine B. If Tim is worried that his confidential message will get interrupted then he must choose a secure service for doing this. Say, he chooses secure FTP to perform this operation; then he must trust that secure FTP performs the operation it says it does. However, since secure FTP uses SSL (secure sockets layer, secure communication via sockets) then Tim needs to trust that SSL is also secure. If he does not then he may choose another form of secure

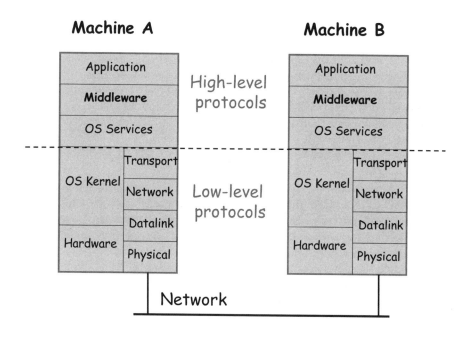

Fig. 8.2. The logical organization of a distributed system into several layers.

communication, such as public keys. As a designer of a security system all these factors are important in deciding at which level to place the security mechanisms.

Dependencies between services regarding trust define a Trusted Computer Base (TCB). TCB is the stack of security mechanisms that are needed to enforce a security policy. For example, a security policy implemented at the middleware level relies on the security of the underlying operating systems. If the underlying infrastructure is adequate then the TCB could include the local operating systems at various hosts. Globus [28], for example, defines a set of security polices at the middleware level by defining a set of rules for a virtual organization (see Chapter 4), i.e., a collection of individuals/machines. It uses a single sign-on mechanism through the use of *mutual authentication* using X.509 certificates [72] and leaves the local administration to deal with the local security levels.

Finally, another example is the Reduced Interfaces for Secure System Components (RISC) approach. Here, any security-critical server is placed on a separate machine isolated from end-user systems using low-level secure network interfaces. Clients and their applications can access the server only through the secure network interfaces. For example, in my department, the Triana [29] Web server was implemented in this way. This Web server had the capability of creating user accounts and the purchasing and downloading of software. Each user's password and information is kept private. On the actual server therefore, every means of communication is turned off except that it runs an SSH (Secure Shell) server. Furthermore, only other one machine in the department can be used to access this server by using the SSH command. If data is needed to be uploaded to the server then the administrator needs to SSH to the machine and then FTP back to the machine from which they want to download the data.

8.2.3 Simplicity

Simplicity is a key component of any software architecture and therefore, the fewer security mechanisms the better. Users tend to trust systems that are easily understood and trusted to work. If users do not understand the mechanisms then how can they truly trust them?

Simplicity contributes to the trust that end-users will put into the application and, more importantly, will contribute to convincing the designers that the system has no security holes. The more complicated the system, the harder it is to debug.

Unfortunately, it often is the case that security is an afterthought within the application-development life cycle. Therefore, the designer of the security system must develop security mechanisms around an existing complicated application. This makes it difficult to keep things simple and consequently, difficult to trust.

8.3 Cryptography

8.3.1 Basics of Cryptography

Cryptography is fundamental to security in distributed systems. It involves encrypting a message (i.e., scrambling it) before it is sent (so that it remains private) and decrypting it upon arrival before it is read. Encryption and decryption are accomplished by using cryptographic keys as their parameters. All cryptographic systems have the following two core properties:

- the algorithm is publicly known
- and the key is kept private.

The algorithms are written in such a way that it is mathematically intractable to calculate the key from any encrypted text. This ensures the simplicity of cryptography from a user's standpoint because all she needs to provide is a key and the rest is hidden under a well-known trusted algorithm. Keys typically consist of a single number, e.g., a long.

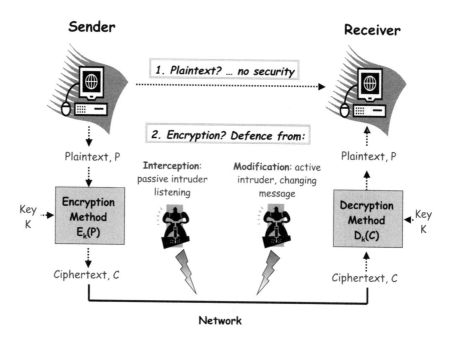

Fig. 8.3. Either a user uses plaintext (no protection) or he can use encryption. This diagram illustrates the basic cryptographic techniques and which protection these give.

So, if a user wishes to send a message to another user, she could choose to send this message as it is. However, this message would not be protected at all and could be liable for infringement using any of the mechanisms described in Section 8.1. For example, the message can be intercepted passively (i.e., eavesdropped, or actively by changing the contents of the original text of the message. Using cryptography provides defence from such security threats.

Figure 8.3 shows the basic idea behind cryptography. Here, the original form of the message is called plaintext and the encrypted form is referred to as cyphertext. The input plaintext (P) is transformed into the ciphertext (C) by using an encryption method (E) based on a given key (K); i.e., $C = E_k(P)$. The plaintext is then calculated from the ciphertext by using $P = D_k(C)$. Cryptography enables us to defend from two types of attacks (see Fig. 8.3):

1. **Interception:** would be extremely difficult. Although the user may be able to intercept (i.e., read) the message he will only see unintelligible scrambled data. He would need to obtain access to the key in order to unlock its contents.

2. **Modification:** is even more difficult since the user would not only have to intercept the message (and decrypt it) but he would then have to modify it and encrypt it again so the receiver thinks it has come from the original sender. To do this the modifier would have to know the key and the algorithm used for encryption.

8.3.2 Types of Encryption

A *cryptosystem* is used for the encryption and decryption of data, and has two fundamental approaches, whilst hash functions are one-way mapping of data to keys. Therefore there are three main categories for encryption:

1. Secret Key (symmetric cryptosystem)
   - single key is used to encrypt and decrypt information
2. Public/Private Key (asymmetric cryptosystem)
   - two keys are used: one for encryption (public key) and one for decryption (private key)
3. One-Way Function (hash function)
   - Information is encrypted to produce a "digest" of the original information that can be used later to prove its authenticity.

8.3.3 Symmetric Cryptosystem

Here, the same key is used for encryption and decryption. Keys can be created in a number of ways: e.g., they can be generated once and used over and over again or they can be generated for each session (using session keys in Section 8.5.1). A good example of a symmetric cryptosystem is the Data Encryption Standard (DES).

The Data Encryption Standard [71] is a widely used method of data encryption using a private (secret) key that was judged so difficult to break by the U.S. government that it was restricted for exportation to other countries. There are 72,000,000,000,000,000 (72 quadrillion) or more possible encryption keys that can be used. For each given message, the key is chosen at random from among this massive range of keys. Like other private key cryptographic methods, both the sender and the receiver must know and use the same private key.

DES applies a 56-bit key to each 64-bit block of data. The process can run in several modes and involves 16 rounds or operations. Although this is considered "strong" encryption, many companies use *triple DES*, which applies three keys in succession. This is not to say that a DES-encrypted message cannot be "broken".

Early in 1997, Rivest-Shamir-Adleman, owners of another encryption approach (RSA [74]), offered a $10,000 reward for breaking a DES message. A cooperative effort on the Internet of over 14,000 computer users trying out various keys finally deciphered the message, discovering the key after running through only 18 quadrillion of the 72 quadrillion possible keys! Few messages sent today with DES encryption are likely to be subject to this kind of code-breaking effort. Other known symmetrical algorithms are:

- DESX (XORed input), GDES (Generalized DES), RDES (Randomized DES): all 168 bit key
- RC2, RC4, RC5: variable length up to 2048 bits
- IDEA is the basis of PGP: 128 bit key
- Blowfish: variable length up to 448 bits

8.3.4 Asymmetric Cryptosystem

In asymmetric cryptosystems (better known as public-key systems), the keys for encryption and decryption are different but together form a unique pair. These two keys are related, but in theory, knowing one key will not help you figure out the other. This key pair is termed the *private key* and the *public key*. The private key is known only to the sender and can also be password protected for enhanced security. The public key, however, can be widely known. Public-private keys can be used in many different ways.

Public-key encryption essentially allows a user to identify themselves. They are used to create digital signatures (see Section 8.4), a far more effective version of our hand written counterpart. They can also be used to encrypt a message for sending to a specific person (using their public key) since only that person can read it (using their private key) and vice-versa. A good example of using public-key cryptography is for mutual authentication, described in Section 4.7.2.

One popular example of a public-key system is RSA, named after the inventors Rivest, Shamir and Adleman [74]. The security of RSA is based on the difficulty of factoring large numbers that are the product of two prime numbers. This factoring problem has been studied for hundreds of years and still appears to be intractable. For this reason, people are confident of RSA's security, and it has become fundamental to information security. RSA systems are also easy to use and therefore easy for executives, managers and other decision-makers, who do not have a technical or mathematical background, to understand. RSA is widely used today in many of the encryption applications and protocols in use on the Internet, including:

- Pretty Good Privacy (PGP)
- the Secure Sockets Layer (SSL)
- S/MIME, Secure Electronic Transactions (SET)
- Secure Shell (SSH)
- X. 509 V.3 certificates as used in Jxta, Globus/OGSA
- RSA is also included in major World Wide Web browsers such as Netscape and Microsoft Internet Explorer. RSA uses modular arithmetic and elementary number theory to do certain computations. It is based on the fact

that it is extremely difficult to find the prime factors of large numbers. An overview of the algorithm is given in the appendix B.

8.3.5 Hash Functions

A *hash function* is a mapping of a message from any size input message to a fixed length *hash key*, which is typically far smaller than the original message. A *cryptographically strong* hash key must have the following properties:

- It must be **non-reversible**: You must not be able to construct the original message from the hash key
- It must be **sensitive to input changes**: It must change significantly with any small change in the input message, even if this change occurs in a single bit. This is also known as the *avalanche effect*; that is, a small change in the input creates a large change in the output.
- It should be **collision resistant**: It should be impractical to find two messages with the same hash key.

Formally, a hash function H takes a message m of arbitrary length as input and produces a bit string h having a fixed bit-length as output.

    h = H(m)

A hash is similar to the extra bits added to a packet in order to perform error correction. Hash functions are one-way functions, meaning that it is unfeasible to find the input m that corresponds to a known output h. This is obvious when you consider the size of the input and output of a hash function. The output is always the same size (e.g., 128-bit) but the input can be of any size (e.g., 16 MByte).

MD5 is a good example of a hash function. It was developed by Professor Ronald L. Rivest of MIT. The MD5 algorithm takes as input a message of arbitrary length and produces as output a 128-bit "fingerprint" or "message digest" of the input [75]. It is conjectured that it is computationally unfeasible to produce two different input messages that map to the same output message digest, or key.

Hash functions are typically used within digital-signature algorithms, where a large input file is mapped (and more important, compressed) to create the basis for the signature (see next section). Another example of a hash-function algorithm is the SHA-1 [136] secured hash, used extensively in Chapter 9. SHA-1 keys are non-reversible, collision-resistant and have a a good *avalanche effect*. Non-reversibility is a property of hash functions, whilst collision resistant implies that two different input files will not create the same key, and the avalanche effect means that two almost identical input files will create vastly different hash keys. SHA-1 mappings take in one or more blocks of 512 bits (64 bytes) and create a single 160-bit hash key.

Hash functions also provide a mechanism to verify data integrity, and are much more reliable than checksum and many other commonly used methods.

8.4 Signing Messages with a Digital Signature

Asymmetric cryptosystems allow users to *digitally sign messages*, which allows a user to establish his/her identity. A hash function is used to create and verify a digital signature. Hash functions enable the software to create digital signatures that operate on smaller and more predictable amounts of data, but still maintain the integrity of the original message content. Therefore, hash keys provide an extremely concise form of the input data and therefore are extremely efficient to sign digitally. Figure 8.4 illustrates the signing process.

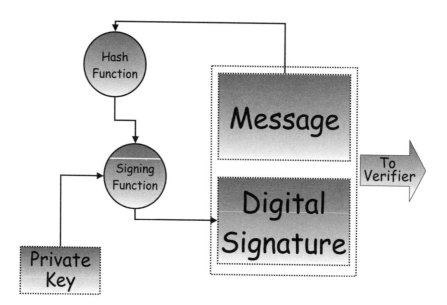

Fig. 8.4. Illustrates how a message is signed using asymmetric cryptosystems.

The signer first delimits precisely what is to be signed within the *message* element, i.e., a message, document or data. A hash function is then applied to this message, which results in a hash code (e.g., a 160-bit SHA-1) unique to the message content. This hash result is then transformed into a digital signature using the signer's private key (i.e., it is encrypted). The resulting digital signature is therefore unique to both the message and the private key of the user that created it. The digital signature is typically attached to its message, either by storing it within a specific format (e.g., X.509 certificate), or transmitted along with the message.

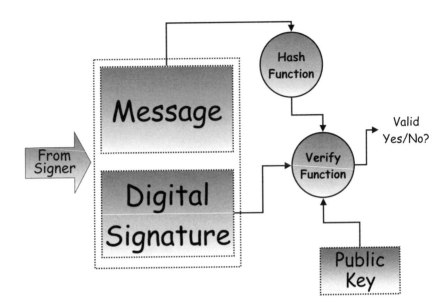

Fig. 8.5. Shows how a user verifies another user's signature.

When a user wishes to verify a digital signature (see Fig. 8.5), he/she computes a new hash from the original message using the same hash function as the one used to create the digital signature. The user now can first check whether the key was signed using the signer's private key by using the signer's public key to decrypt the message. If this succeeds then the user can verify whether this newly computed hash result matches the hash result extracted from the digital signature. If they match then the verification is complete.

Verification therefore indicates that the digital signature was created using the signer's private key (i.e., he/she is the only person with access to this key) and that the message was not altered since it was signed (because hash collisions are considered mathematically improbable). There exist a number of different mathematical formulas and procedures, but all share this overall operational pattern.

8.5 Secure Channels

The issue of protecting communication between two participants (i.e., a client and a server) can be thought of in terms of setting up a secure channel. There are two methods of encrypting the traffic, described above:

1. Symmetric Key
2. Public/Private Key.

The following technologies are examples of secure channels:

- **Secure Socket Layer:** is a standard for encrypted client/server communication between network devices. A network protocol, SSL runs on top of TCP/IP. SSL utilizes several standard network security techniques including public keys, symmetric keys, and certificates. Web sites commonly use SSL to guard private information such as credit card numbers.
- **Transport Layer Security (TLS):** [70] is a protocol that ensures privacy between communicating applications and their users on the Internet. When a server and client communicate, TLS ensures that no third party may eavesdrop or tamper with any message. TLS is the successor to the Secure Sockets Layer.

8.5.1 Secure Channels Using Symmetric Keys

There are two ways of creating keys for secure channels using symmetric keys:

- shared secret keys
- session key.

Shared secret keys are generated once and secretly passed to the individuals. This can be achieved in a number of ways. For example, they could use another method of providing a secure channel, e.g., by using public keys, they could telephone each other to decide on the key or even post it to each other. An example of a system that uses this technique is Kerberos.

Session keys, on the other hand, have to be dynamically created at run time. One method involves one of the communicators to generate a key and to send it via a secure channel to the other participant. This is rather cumbersome and incurs much communication overhead for each secure channel to be created. An alternative method involves dynamically creating the keys at run time. This can be accomplished by an elegant and widely accepted method called the Diffie-Hellman key exchange. This is used in many widely used algorithms such as TLS.

Suppose Tim and Gareth want to share a key; then the protocol works according to the algorithm in Fig. 8.6. Using this algorithm ensures that both Tim and Gareth (and only those two), will have the shared secret key $g^{xy} \bmod n$. Note that neither of them needs to make his private number ($\mathbf{x}$ and $\mathbf{y}$, respectively) known to the other.

8.5.2 Secure Channels Using Public/Private Keys

Consider the following situation where secure communication is needed:

1. Both choose 2 large numbers, *n* and *g* *(public)*
   - subject to certain mathematical properties
2. Tim chooses secret large random number = **x**
3. Gareth chooses secret large random number = *y*
4. Tim computes *(g^x) mod n (public)*
   - virtually impossible to compute *x* from g^x *mod n*
5. Gareth computes g^y *mod n (public)*
6. They *exchange* public keys *(g^x) mod n* and *(g^y) mod n*
7. Gareth computes *((g^x) mod n)^y mod n = g^{xy} mod n*
8. Then, Tim computes *((g^y) mod n)^x mod n = g^{xy} mod n*

Both now have the **shared secret key** g^{xy} *mod n*

Fig. 8.6. The Diffie-Hellman key exchange algorithm.

Tim has just sold Gareth a data projector for £750 through a chat room and by using email as their only communication channel. Gareth finally sends Tim a message confirming that he will buy the projector for £750. In addition to authentication there are another two issues:

- Gareth needs to be assured that Tim will not change the sum of £750 specified in his message to something higher.
- Tim needs to be assured that Gareth cannot deny ever having sent the message (if he starts to have second thoughts).

One way to accomplish this is by using the following mechanism using RSA keys.

1. Gareth encrypts the message using his private key.
2. Gareth also encrypts the message (for privacy) using Tim's public key.
3. Tim can first decrypt the key using his private key then he can use Gareth's public key to decrypt the original message from Gareth.

If Tim accepts that Gareth's public key is in fact his key then this can only mean that the message came from Gareth. Furthermore, Gareth knows that Tim has received the message containing the original message because only Tim can open the message as he is the only person who has access to his private key.

8.6 Secure Mobile Code: Creating a Sandbox

Traditionally, you had to trust software before you ran it. You achieved security by being careful only to use software from trusted sources, and by regularly scanning for viruses just to make sure things were safe. Once software obtains access to your system, it has full rein and if it is malicious, it could inflict a great deal of damage as there is little protection, other than certain authorization measures. So, in the traditional security scheme, you tried to prevent malicious code from ever gaining access to your computer in the first place.

The sandbox security model makes it easier to work with software that comes from sources you don't fully trust. Instead of security being established by requiring you to prevent any code you don't trust from ever making its way onto your computer, the sandbox model lets you welcome code from any source. A sandbox is a technique by which a downloaded program is executed in such a way that each of its instructions can be fully controlled. We will take a look at this here by describing the Java Sandbox [12].

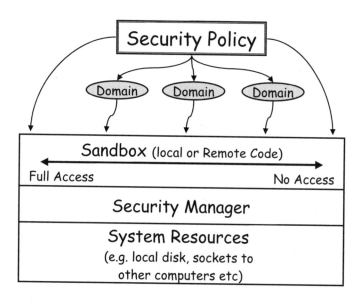

Fig. 8.7. The Java Sandbox, which is implemented using a security manager.

The Java Sandbox provides a very restricted environment in which to run un-trusted code obtained from the open network. In this sandbox model local code can be trusted to have full access to vital system resources, such as the file system, but downloaded remote code (an applet, for example) is not trusted and can therefore have access only to the limited resources provided inside the sandbox (unless it is signed). For example, an applet prohibits:

- Reading or writing to the local disk
- Making a network connection to any host, except the host from which the applet came
- Creating a new process
- Loading a new dynamic library and directly calling a native method.

By making it impossible for downloaded code to perform certain actions, Java's security model protects the user from the threat of hostile code. A *security manager* (see Fig. 8.7) is responsible for determining which resources can be accessed. All code, regardless of whether it is local or remote, can be subject to a *security policy* enforced by the security manager. The security policy defines the set of permissions available for code from various signers or locations and can be configured by a user or a system administrator. Each permission specifies a permitted access to a particular resource, such as read and write access to a specified file or directory or connect access to a given host and port.

The runtime system organizes code into individual domains, each of which encloses a set of classes whose instances are granted the same set of permissions. A domain can be configured to be equivalent to the sandbox, so applets can still be run in a restricted environment if the user or the administrator so chooses. Applications are run unrestricted by default but can optionally be subject to a security policy. A *signed applet* is treated like local code, with full access to resources, if the public key used to verify the signature is trusted.

The Java sandbox model could potentially be used to implement a secure CPU-sharing infrastructure across a P2P environment and extend the SETI@Home idea to create a generalized heterogeneous CPU-sharing environment for Java codes.

8.7 Conclusion

In this chapter, we covered the basics of security in a distributed system. The different types of security breach were discussed, followed by a description of the design issues involved in building a distributed security system.

Cryptography, fundamental to security in distributed systems, was discussed for both the symmetric and asymmetric cases. Hash functions were discussed and combined with asymmetric cryptography techniques to illustrate how a message can be digitally signed.

The concept of a secure channel was introduced, that is, the issue of protecting communication between two participants (i.e., a client and a server). A secure channel can be set up using public-key pairs or by using symmetric keys, e.g., shared secret keys or session keys. Finally, Java sandboxing was discussed for protecting the resources to which mobile code may potentially have access.

9

Freenet

This chapter is dedicated to the Freenet distributed information storage system. Freenet was chosen to be included because it gives an excellent example of how many of the techniques discussed so far in this book can be adapted and used in a practical and innovative system. For example, Freenet works within a P2P environment (Chapter 2) and addresses the inherently untrustworthy and unreliable participants within such a network. Freenet is self-organizing and incorporates a learning algorithm that allows the network to adapt its routing behaviour based on prior interactions. This algorithm is interestingly similar to social networking and achieves a power-law (centralized-decentralized) structure (discussed in Chapter 7) in a self-organizing manner. Such a technique offers a different perspective on how to efficiently scale P2P networks (e.g., Gnutella in Chapter 6) to hundred of thousands of nodes.

Freenet was designed from the ground up to provide extensive protection from hostile attack, from both inside the network and out by addressing key information privacy issues. Freenet therefore implements various security strategies that maintain privacy for all participants, regardless of their particular role. The individual security techniques that are used collectively in Freenet were discussed in Chapter 8.

This chapter is concise but it provides a relevant real-world application that integrates many of the technologies described thus far. For a more detailed overview of Freenet see [58], [59] and [61].

9.1 Introduction

Freenet is a decentralized system for storing and retrieving files within a massively distributed network. Each Freenet participant provides some network storage space and acts as a *servent* (i.e., both clients and servers as in Gnutella), both providing storage and requesting it. Freenet differs in philosophy to Gnutella as it gives P2P participants write access to the distributed file system. Gnutella is a protocol for searching distributed networks and cannot be used to propagate files onto the network. Freenet, on the other hand allows users to store and retrieve files but does not focus on searching the network. Therefore, to a user, Freenet can be seen as an extension of one's file system that provides one with more storage space, whereas Gnutella allows a user to search and download other users' files and therefore provides an extension to the information space.

9.2 Freenet Routing

The key novel feature of Freenet is how it self-organizes its routing behaviour. The network learns to route better by adapting local routing tables based on prior experience of successful file retrievals. In this section, the basic mechanisms are described for achieving this self-organizing behaviour. The same algorithm is used for file storage and retrieval, and the network actually learns according to usage patterns across the network's participants. For example, files that are retrieved often will generate more references across the network and therefore can be located quickly and will not expire (i.e., get deleted). Files that are not requested regularly can expire because peers can collectively decide to delete them. The next three sections describe the storage, retrieval and requesting of files, followed by a section on comparing this approach with other techniques

9.2.1 Populating the Freenet Network

When a file is added to the Freenet network, it is assigned a **file key** (see Section 9.3). Each node keeps a local *routing table* that contains a list of such keys that are stored on neighbouring peers as illustrated in Fig. 9.1. The actual storage location for a file is calculated by comparing such keys at each peer hop to other keys in a peer's routing table in order to find the peer with the closest match (see Fig. 9.1). The winning peer, who has the closest key, is passed the file to store. This process continues for the specified TTL (see Section 6.2).

Freenet peers can make intelligent decisions about where they think the data may be. The keys in individual routing tables either identify a file **or** a region in the key space for which they are responsible. Therefore, when a peer receives a request, it redirects it to the neighbouring peer that has the **closest key** to the one supplied. In this way, peers become responsible for regions of the key subspace between themselves and their neighbouring peers that contain similar keys. The more nodes that join the network, the finer the granularity of the key space.

Using this technique, similar keys get placed in similar parts of the network, but (as we will find out in the next section) although such keys are derived from a file's contents or description, comparisons in the key space are non-related. This ensures that files get evenly distributed throughout the

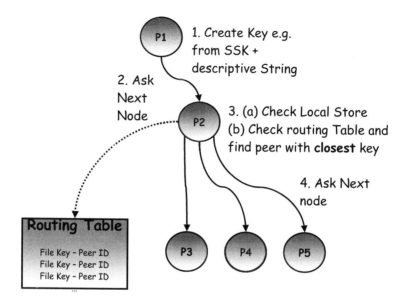

Fig. 9.1. Each peer within Freenet keeps a local routing table that stores file keys of connected peers. These are used to intelligently route the file storage or retrieval request.

network. The actual storage location for the file is determined by a number of factors and files can be replicated across several peers, depending on their local constraints, e.g., storage space, etc. The actual location(s) for the file is kept hidden from the user, which is achieved by employing a combination of random peer behaviour and multiple levels of encryption at each hop as the data traverses the network.

9.2.2 Self-Organizing Adaptive Behaviour in Freenet

When a file is retrieved from Freenet, it uses the same mechanism as for storage. Freenet peers adaptively update their routing tables when they successfully locate a file somewhere upstream on the network. Therefore, when a peer forwards the request to a peer that can retrieve the data, then the address of the upstream peer that contains it is included in the reply. The peer then updates its local routing table to include the peer that has the more direct route to the file. The peer can also nominate to store the data depending on current storage limitations. When a similar request is issued again, the peer routes the request more effectively. In this way, peers adapt to usage patterns; i.e., they learn, and they automatically replicate or delete files based on behaviour of the users within the system.

Using this mechanism, it has been shown [62] that the Freenet network converges to a centralized-decentralized model, where only a small number of nodes have large routing tables and most have small ones. This centralized-decentralized model has been shown to scale to millions of peers in other systems, such as Gnutella implementations, e.g., LimeWire [51].

This natural dynamic nature employed by Freenet to update its knowledge is analogous to the way humans reinforce decisions based on prior experiences. Remember the Milgrim experiment in Section 7.1? Milgrim noted that 25% of all requests went through the same person (the local shopkeeper). The people in this experiment used their experience of the local inhabitants to attempt to forward the letter to the best person who could help it reach its destination. Now, the local shopkeeper was a good choice because he knew a number of out-of-town people and therefore could help the letter get closer to its destination. If this experiment were repeated using the same people, then surely the word would spread quickly within Omaha that the shopkeeper is a good place to forward the letter to and subsequently, the success rate and efficiency would improve.

Another analogy, given by the Freenet authors, is deciding that since your friend George answered a question about France then the next time around perhaps he would be a good choice to ask a question about Belgium.

9.2.3 Requesting Files

When a Freenet peer receives a request for a file, it first checks its own store. If it has the file then it answers appropriately. If not, it forwards the request to a peer in its routing table with the closest key to the one requested (see Section 9.3 for more information on how key correlation is measured). This continues in this fashion until either the file is found or all possible avenues have been exhausted within a given radius of the requesting peer, i.e., within a TTL. Within Freenet, if a request fails, then the user has the option of choosing a higher TTL and sending the request again. Freenet also supports mix-net routing algorithms to be applied before normal routing to offer better security since the TTL can give clues about where in the chain the request is. Mix-net routing essentially repositions the start of the chain away from the requester.

Figure 9.2 shows a typical request sequence within Freenet. Here, the request initiates from peer A. Peer A asks its neighbour (peer B) if it has the requested file. B does not, so it looks in its routing table and locates the best-bet peer with the closest key, which happens to be peer F. F looks in its internal store and also does not have it, and further, it has no access to other peers. At this stage therefore, it returns a *request failed* message back to the requestor (i.e., B).

B does have further options and therefore forwards the request to the peer with the closest key (peer D). D looks in its internal store, does not find the file and so forwards the request to peer C. C doesn't have the file, so forwards

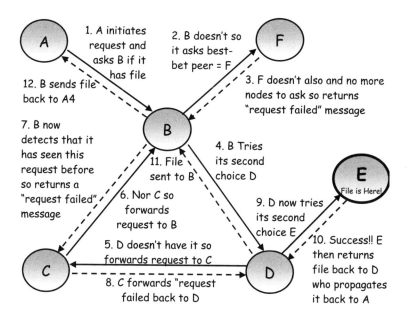

Fig. 9.2. A request sequence within Freenet.

the request to its closest neighbour (B). At this stage, B notices that it has seen this request and sends it back to the sending node, C, which in turn sends it back to peer D.

Peer D now explores further options and forwards the request to node E. Node E looks in its internal store and finds the requested file and so forwards this file back to the originator by hopping through all intermediaries. The intermediary peers update their routing tables accordingly and also each peer can choose to cache the file locally depending on the distance it is from the originator and local considerations.

A mixture of local caching and routing table updating is how the Freenet network *learns* to provide more effective routing. Such routing therefore, is based on the popularity of the requested files. As more requests are processed, the network becomes better trained. The result is a dynamically formed hierarchical routing table that clusters similar keys, which helps to minimize the number of hops to the data. This is an interesting model, reminiscent of the ways certain artificial neural networks update their weights between connections in order to learn particular patterns.

9.2.4 Similarities with Other Peer Organization Techniques

Routing in Freenet is highly dynamic and is a departure from techniques employed by other systems discussed in previous chapters. For example, in

Gnutella a user searches the network by broadcasting its request to every node within a given TTL. Napster, on the other hand, uses a central database that contains the locations of all files on the network. Gnutella, in its basic form, is inefficient and Napster, also in its simplest form, is simply not scalable and is subject to attack due the the centralization of its file indexing. As discussed in Section 7.8 however, both Napster and Gnutella matured into using multiple caching servers in order to be able to scale the network.

Such caching services form the basic building block of the Freenet network since each peer contains a routing table, similar in principle to Gnutella super peers or Napster indexes. The key difference is that Freenet peers do not store locations of files at all, rather they contain file keys that indicate the direction in the key space where the file is *likely* to be stored.

The routing algorithm used in Freenet has been analysed [62] and a number of improvements are currently being integrated within Freenet's *Next Generation Routing* algorithm [60]. For example, the current algorithm does not distinguish between slow nodes at the edges of the network and fast nodes which are fault tolerant and perhaps connected by T1 or similar links.

9.3 Freenet Keys

All files within Freenet get assigned with a globally unique identifier (GUID) that uniquely identifies the file. The assigned GUID is used in both the storage and retrieval of the file and forms the basis for the comparisons used within the routing algorithm.

Freenet uses a combination of *direct* and *indirect* references to files using three distinct types of GUID keys that ensure data integrity, authentication and privacy. The keys are computed using a combination of asymmetric cryptographic techniques and hash functions. All hash functions are computed using using SHA-1 secure hashes, which are described in Section 8.3.5. Freenet defines three keys:

1. **Keyword-Signed Keys (KSK):** are the simplest of Freenet keys that are derived directly from a descriptive string that the user chooses for the file.
2. **Signed-Subspace Keys (SSK):** are intended for higher-level human use, for example, to define ownership, or to make pointers to a file or a collection of files.
3. **Content-Hash Keys (CHK):** are used for low-level data storage and are obtained by hashing the contents of the data to be stored.

The three are analogous to files, directories and *inodes* on a conventional file system. For example, the KSK allows you to name a file, just as you would with a conventional file and this name is used to store and retrieve the file. However, by only using KSKs, you limit yourself to a flat file system; i.e., it is similar to putting all of your files in one directory.

SSKs give a subspace that can act as a container for files. This is similar to the way we use directories on a conventional file system except that SSKs are used, in practice, along with the file name, giving the absolute path of the file. In practice SSHs are used instead of KSK to expand the user namespace.

CHKs are straight hashed versions of the file itself. They identify the contents of the file and serve as a unique pointer to the file. Similarly, there is an inode for each file and a file is uniquely identified by the file system on which it resides and its inode number on that system.

9.3.1 Keyword-Signed Keys

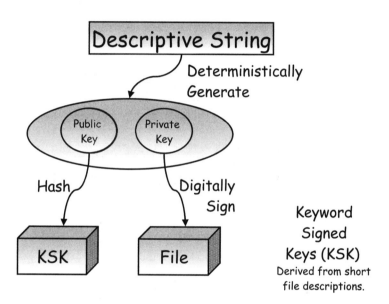

Fig. 9.3. KSK keys are derived directly from a descriptive string for a file.

A Keyword-Signed Key is the simplest type of file key, which is computed directly from the descriptive string that a user chooses for his/her file. The descriptive string is used to **deterministically** create a public/private key pair. The public half is hashed to give the KSK and the private key is used to sign the actual file (see Fig. 9.3). This provides a minimal integrity check, since the user can check whether the retrieved file matches its file key; i.e., from the public key, a user can compute the KSK and also check the signature for the file itself. Files are also encrypted using this descriptive string.

To retrieve the file using the KSK, the user only needs to provide the descriptive string, since he can easily regenerate the rest of the keys because they are deterministically generated from this string. However, such keys form a flat global namespace, analogous to creating a file system without any directories. The SSK keys in the next section address this issue.

9.3.2 Signed Subspace Keys

An SSK enables a personal namespace to be set up. The namespace can be used in a number of ways; for example, to store a file, to store multiple files, to store a file that is split into multiple sections or to point to other namespaces. In this way, complex multiple-level structures can be created, similar to directories on a file system. For example, you could create a subspace called *books* and make this a container for other SSKs (e.g., *fiction* and *non-fiction*), which could, in turn, be a container for a list of author SSKs, followed by a list of files containing descriptions of each book.

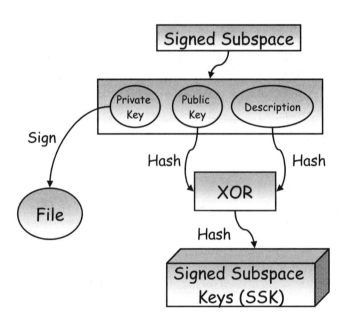

Fig. 9.4. Signed subspace keys (SSK) incorporate a description and a namespace for files.

SSKs are created as follows. First, the user randomly generates an asymmetric key pair (public/private key) for the subspace. She keeps the private key private but the public key is made available to other users. This key pair uniquely identifies the subspace and is highly unlikely to clash with other subspace keys.

To insert a file into the subspace, the user provides a descriptive string for the file. Then, as illustrated in Fig. 9.4, the public key and the file description are hashed independently, XORed together, then hashed again to give the SSK for that file. The private key is then used to sign the file, to ensure the authenticity of the file when it is retrieved. Since SSKs are generated using hash functions, they are also one-way functions so in order to reconstruct the SSK, you need the inputs to the function, which are the public key for the subspace and the descriptive string for the file. From this, you can recalculate the SSK and locate the file within the system.

However, to store files in a subspace, a user needs to be able to sign the actual file with the subspace's private key in order to be able to generate the correct digital signature. Therefore, subspaces are set up so that anyone can read from them but only the subspace owner can write; analogous to the way we add permissions to directories in UNIX file systems.

9.3.3 Content Hash Keys

Content-Hash Keys are computed directly from the file's contents using SHA-1 secure hashes (see Section 8.3.5) and hence are called content-hash keys. A CHK gives each file a unique hash key for each file based on the contents of that file (since SHA-1 collisions are considered nearly impossible). This is useful in many contexts, e.g., when updating or splitting files.

For example, in a conventional file system, we label files using file names and directories. If we change the contents of a file and press the save button, the file gets overwritten with the new contents and the previous version is lost forever. However, in Freenet, using CHKs this is impossible because, if you change the contents of the file, a different CHK will be generated and consequently, it will get stored in a different part of the network. Therefore, both *versions* of the file will remain accessible.

CHKs are generally used in conjunction with SSKs to create indirect files. Indirect files are created within a two stage process. First, the user inserts the file using the CHK. He then creates an SSK by pointing to the CHK rather than to the file itself. Therefore, for retrieval, the user first obtains the CHK from the SSK subspace and then retrieves the file itself using the CHK.

CHKs are computed directly from the contents of the file and this is independent of the originator. This helps to maintain privacy, if desirable. Also, CHKs help with versioning of files. As mentioned, if a file is modified slightly then a new CHK will be generated for that file. This ensures that old copies of the file will not get overwritten but further, if two identical files are inserted from different participants, then the same GUID will be generated and therefore be considered equivalent. This helps avoid unnecessary duplication and alongside the SSK can ensure appropriate file authentication.

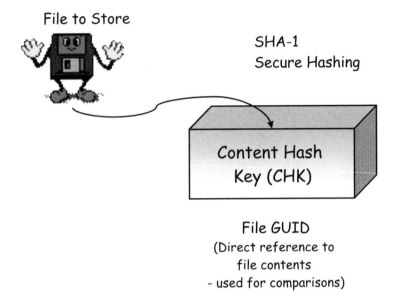

File to Store

SHA-1
Secure Hashing

Content Hash
Key (CHK)

File GUID
(Direct reference to
file contents
- used for comparisons)

Fig. 9.5. The construction of a content hash key is simply a secure hash of the contents of the file.

9.3.4 Clustering Keys

Keys are clustered by comparing their GUID values which are created in various ways, as described in the three previous sections. However, since they are constructed using hash keys that have a good *avalanche effect* (see Section 8.3.5) then key comparisons are completely unrelated to the similarities of their input. For example, if we are using CHKs and comparing two almost identical input files, their hash values will be completely different.

This non correlation of Freenet hash comparisons is unimportant and does not adversely affect the convergence and efficiency of the network. In fact, it somewhat helps the network because it ensures that files get evenly distributed across the entire network as a quasi-random set of keys will be produced. Clustering files within the GUID space results in unbiased decisions about where the files are actually located.

This property is in practice very useful since setting up such a Freenet network will normally involve a particular type of data storage and consequently, there may be a number of files with similar content being stored on the network. If these files were correlated directly to determine where they would be stored on the network, then such files would converge to a particular network segment, resulting in a partitioning of data storage with an uneven distribution across the resource. However, using hash functions produces quasi-random representations of the data which are typically spread across the spectrum and therefore enable a more even distribution across the mass data storage network.

Such a distribution has been shown [62] to demonstrate good scaling and fault-tolerant characteristics and, in fact, converge to a power-law (centralized/decentralized) structure (see [153] and Section 7.7.3) that exhibits all the advantages of *small-world* networks. Freenet therefore has been shown to scale effectively to hundreds of thousands of nodes.

9.4 Joining the Network

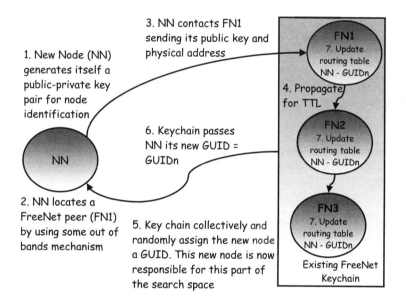

Fig. 9.6. A scenario about how a new node joins the Freenet network and gets assigned a GUID that identifies for which proportion of the CHK key space it will be responsible.

This section briefly describes how a node joins the Freenet network, which is illustrated in Fig. 9.6. Initially, the new peer creates itself a public-private key pair (step 1) that is not only used to identify the peer but also to sign its current physical address reference for security; peers can keep their identities even though their physical addresses may differ.

Nodes then locate a node in the Freenet network (Step 2). This is achieved in a similar fashion to the way Gnutella peers locate a node within the network (see Section 6.3.1), either by using an IRC, Web site or lists through some server. The new node sends its public key and physical address to the existing Freenet node it has discovered (FN1, step 3). FN1 now makes a note of NN's identity and forwards this information to other connected peers in a random fashion by taking entries from its routing table. This continues in this fashion for the specified TTL.

Once the TTL expires, all nodes in the keychain collectively assign the new node a GUID, which assigns the new node a part of the key space for which it will be responsible. This new GUID is calculated using a cryptographic protocol for shared random number generation, which is designed to prevent any one participant from biasing the result. The new node is then passed this new GUID (GUIDn in step 6) and each peer updates its local routing tables accordingly.

9.5 Conclusion

This chapter gave a brief overview of the Freenet distributed information storage systems, with the aim of providing a concrete example of how the many techniques so far described in this book can be integrated into a single system. Freenet is designed to work within a P2P network and is fault tolerant to both random peer failures and breaches of security.

It employs an adaptive routing algorithm which updates the information cached at each peer according to its previous experience of successful queries or data inserts. The mechanism by which a peer routes queries is based on comparisons in the key-space domain, which are all calculated using a combination of hash functions and asymmetric cryptography techniques. Such keys are therefore unrelated to the input (i.e., file descriptions or file content) and therefore create a key space in a random fashion that has been shown to utilize the entire network and create a desired power-law distribution of peer connections across the peers, which can scale to hundreds of thousands of nodes.

There are three types of keys, which are calculated from: the file description for keyword-signed keys; a subspace and the file description for signed-subspace keys; and directly from hashing the contents of the file for the content-hash keys. The construction of these keys illustrates the practical use of the security mechanisms described earlier in this book.

10

Jxta

The Jxta[1] middleware is a set of open, generalized peer-to-peer protocols that allow any connected device (cell phone to PDA, PC to server) on the network to communicate and collaborate. Jxta is an open-source project that is developed by a number of contributors and as such, it is still evolving. For the most recent Jxta Technology Specification, see [15].

The goal of project Jxta is to develop and standardize basic building blocks and services to enable developers to build and deploy interoperable P2P services and applications. The Jxta project intends to address this problem by providing a simple and generic P2P platform to host any kind of network services. The term Jxta is short for juxtapose, as in side by side. It is a recognition that P2P is juxtaposed to client/server or Web-based computing, which is today's traditional distributed-computing model. Jxta provides a common set of open protocols[2] and an open-source reference implementation for developing P2P applications.

10.1 Background: Why Was Project Jxta Started?

Project Jxta was originally conceived by Sun Microsystems, Inc. and designed with the participation of a small number of experts from academic institutions and industry. This team identified a number of shortcomings in many existing P2P systems and set up project Jxta in order to address these. The three main objectives were to achieve interoperability, platform independence and ubiquity.

---

[1] I use the lower-case version of Jxta to be consistent with other terms used in this book; that is, Jxta is not an acronym so I do not spell it as one.

[2] The Jxta protocols are open and generalized but they are not standardized.

10.1.1 Interoperability

Jxta notes that current P2P systems are built for delivering a single type of services, e.g.:

- Napster provides music file sharing
- Gnutella provides decentralized file sharing
- AIM provides instant messaging
- SETI@Home performs specific computations on specific data. Recently however, the BOINC project has generalized this into a standard platform for use by other applications but even in this case it is specific to the CPU sharing class of applications.

Each software vendor tends to create specific code for each of these services, which results in incompatible systems; i.e., they cannot interoperate. Consequently, there is much duplication in the effort of creating the middleware primitives commonly used by all P2P systems. Project Jxta attempts to provide a common language that all peers can use to talk to each other.

10.1.2 Platform independence

Jxta technology is designed to be independent of:

1. programming languages, e.g., C or Java
2. system platforms, e.g., Microsoft Windows and UNIX
3. networking platforms (such as TCP/IP or Bluetooth).

This set of criteria solves a number of development issues including code duplication and incompatibility. For example, many P2P systems offer services through APIs that are tied to a particular operating system using a specific networking protocol; i.e., one system might use C++ APIs on Windows over TCP/IP, whilst another uses a C API hosted on UNIX systems over TCP/IP but also requiring HTTP. A P2P developer is then forced to choose which set of APIs to use and consequently, which set of P2P customers to target. Further, if the developer wants to target both communities then he may have to develop the services twice, one for each platform (or develop a bridge system between them).

Jxta achieves programming language and platform independence through the use of the Jxta protocols being defined in a textual representation (i.e., XML) and the networking independence is achieved through the use of Jxta pipes (described in Section 10.3.3).

It should be noted that Jxta is not original in this respect. A number of distributed-systems technologies are based on exchanging XML messages, e.g., Web services. XLM represents a common format that enables applications to abstract the message format into a programming language-neutral representation. For example, a SOAP (see Chapter 13)) performs a similar operation, that is, all communications between SOAP endpoints are represented in XML. A Jxta binding or a SOAP processor converts language-specific internal representations into and out of XML, which enables various programming languages to interoperate at this textual representation level. As long as you can map into and out of text, any client or server can encode or decode the information. Therefore, XML is the key here to interoperability, not Jxta.

10.1.3 Ubiquity

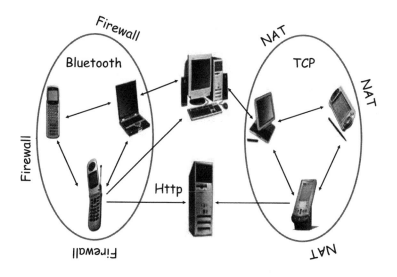

Fig. 10.1. Jxta networks are designed to work on all kinds of devices, underlying transport mechanisms and operating systems.

Another problem Jxta addresses is in the limitations of the deployment of applications to a particular set of devices either due to incompatibility issues and transport problems or that they are too complicated for particular devices due to size limitations. Jxta technology is designed to be implementable on "every device with a digital heartbeat" [15]. For example, devices that could join a Jxta network include:

1. PDAs
2. phones
3. sensors
4. consumer electronics

5. network routers
6. appliances
7. desktop computers
8. data-center servers
9. storage systems.

For example, currently many P2P systems tend to choose Microsoft Windows as their target deployment platform (unsurprisingly since this is the largest installed base and therefore the fastest path to profit) resulting in many Wintel-specific dependencies. Even though the earliest demonstration of P2P capabilities are on Wintel machines it is very likely that the greatest proliferation of P2P technology will occur at the two ends of the spectrum, e.g., large systems in the enterprise and consumer-oriented small systems. Current Jxta implementations include:

- Jxta for the Java 2 Platform Standard Edition (J2SE); the reference implementation
- Jxta (JXME) for the Java 2 Platform Micro Edition (J2ME); for MIDP-1.0 compliant devices such as cell phones, PDAs and controllers
- Jxta for Personal JavaTM technology; for devices such as PDAs and Webpads
- Jxta for C and other languages such as PERL, Python and Ruby.

This is conceptualised in Fig. 10.1, which shows a number of interconnected devices, using a number of different transport protocols (e.g., HTTP, TCP/IP, Bluetooth, etc.) and operating systems.

The most mature implementation is currently in Java but other versions exist. See the Web site [15] for more information. To date, most other implementations (e.g., C++/C) only have implemented a small subsection of the Jxta protocols and can only be used as *edge peers*. An edge peer is a peer that cannot function as anything more than a simple Jxta peer; i.e., it cannot be a *Rendezvous* or *Relay*, for example. Here, we will base our discussion on the Java Jxta version.

10.2 Jxta Overview

Project Jxta defines a set of six protocols that can be used to construct P2P systems using a centralized, brokered or decentralized approach but its main aim is to facilitate the creation of decentralized systems. In this section, we describe these protocols and other components of a Jxta application.

10.2.1 The Jxta Architecture

The Jxta protocols standardize the manner in which peers:

- Discover each other
- Self-organize into peer groups
- Advertise and discover network services
- Communicate with each other
- Monitor each other.

The Jxta protocols do not require the use of any particular programming language or operating system; network transport or topology; or authentication, security or encryption model. The Jxta protocols therefore allow heterogeneous devices with completely different software stacks to interoperate.

Figure 10.2 shows that the common layering structure defined by Jxta is broken down into three layers:

1. **Jxta Core:** at the lower level is the core layer that deals with peer establishment, communication management (such as routing) and other low-level "plumbing".
2. **Jxta Services:** second, there is a service layer that deals with higher-level concepts, such as indexing, searching and file sharing. These services make heavy use of the plumbing features provided by the core but further, can be commonly used as components in P2P systems.
3. **Jxta Applications:** at the upper level, there is an applications layer, such as file sharing, auctioning and storage systems.

Some features (e.g., security) exist throughout the P2P system (although in different forms). Jxta technology is designed to provide a thin layer on top of which services and applications are built using powerful primitives.

Briefly, the Jxta protocols are: the *Peer Resolver Protocol* (PRP) is the mechanism by which a peer can send a query to one or more peers, and receive a response (or multiple responses) to the query. The *Peer Discovery Protocol* (PDP) is the mechanism by which a peer can advertise its own resources, and discover the resources from other peers (peer groups, services, pipes and additional peers). The *Peer Information Protocol* (PIP) is the mechanism by which a peer may obtain status information about other peers, such as state, uptime, traffic load and capabilities. The *Pipe Binding Protocol* (PBP) is used to connect pipes between peers. The *Endpoint Routing Protocol* (ERP) is used to route Jxta messages. Finally, the *Rendezvous Protocol* (RVP) is the mechanism by which peers can subscribe or be a subscriber to a propagation service. The Jxta protocols are described in more detail in Section 10.4.

10.2.2 Jxta Peers

A peer is any networked device that implements one or more of the Jxta protocols (see Fig. 10.3). Each peer operates independently and asynchronously from all other peers, and is uniquely identified by a *Peer ID* (identifiers, like in Gnutella). Peers publish one or more network interfaces (advertisements)

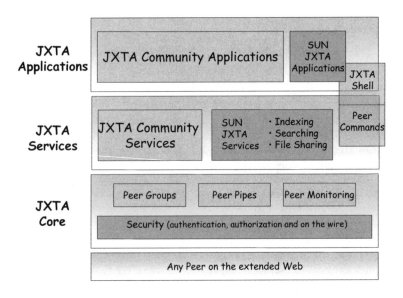

Fig. 10.2. The Jxta software architecture.

for use with the Jxta protocols, which are passed around the network in datagrams (messages). Peers can form transient or persistent relationships (peer groups). Each published interface is advertised as a peer endpoint, which is used to establish direct point-to-point (but not fixed) connections between two peers (pipes). These are discussed in more detail in the rest of this section.

A Jxta peer therefore is any entity that can speak the protocols required of a peer. This is akin to the Internet, where an Internet node is any entity that can speak the suite of IP protocols. As such, a peer can manifest in the form of a processor, a process, a machine or a user. Importantly, a peer does not need to understand all the six protocols as a peer can still perform at a reduced level if it does not support a protocol.

A Jxta peer, just like a Gnutella servent, can be a client and a server. Furthermore, Jxta peers can act as rendezvous nodes, which are meeting places (or lookup servers) for other Jxta nodes.

10.2.3 Identifiers

Jxta uses UUID, a 128-bit datum to refer to an entity (see Fig. 10.3), e.g., a peer, an advertisement, a service, etc.; remember Gnutella used the same mechanism to identify messages, albeit in a cruder form. It is easy to guarantee that each entity has a unique UUID within a local runtime environment, but

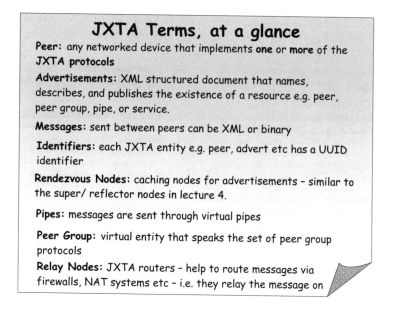

Fig. 10.3. Brief definitions for a number of the key Jxta terms.

because any global state is not assumed, there is no absolute way to provide a guarantee of uniqueness across an entire community that may consist of millions of peers. Jxta address this by binding the UUID to other information such as a name and a network address.

10.2.4 Advertisements

An advertisement is an XML structured document that names, describes, and publishes the existence of a resource, such as a peer, a peer group, a pipe, or a service (see Fig. 10.3). Jxta technology defines a basic set of advertisements but more advertisement subtypes can be formed from these basic types using XML schemas, or more typically by using the particular language binding, e.g., in Java, you would subclass the *Advertisement* class.

10.2.5 Messages

A message is an object that is sent between Jxta peers that can be represented in either XML or binary format (see Fig. 10.3). The Java binding uses the binary format to encapsulate the message payload. Services can use the most appropriate format for that transport. A service that requires a compact representation, for example, for sending scientific data, can use the binary representation, while other services can use XML.

A Jxta message is the basic unit of data exchange between peers. Messages are sent and received using the *Pipe Service* and routed using the *Endpoint Service*. Typically, applications interface with the *Pipe Service* directly and the routing is hidden behind the scenes.

A message is a set of name/value pairs represented as an XML document. The content can be an arbitrary type. The Jxta protocols are specified as a set of messages exchanged between peers. Each software platform binding describes how a message is converted to and from a native data structure such as a Java object or a C structure.

10.2.6 Modules

Jxta modules are an abstraction used to represent any piece of "code" used to implement a behaviour in a Jxta network (see Fig. 10.3). The module abstraction does not specify what this "code" is: it can be a Java class, a Java jar, a dynamic library DLL, a set of XML messages, or a script. The implementation of the module behavior is left to module implementers. For example, modules can be used to represent different implementations of a network service on different operating system platforms in a similar fashion to Web service implementations (see Chapter 3).

10.3 Jxta Network Overlay

Conceptually, Jxta consists of a collection of peers which interact and are organized in a number of ways. The organization of Jxta peers is independent of the underlying physical devices and connectivity (see Fig. 10.4). Here, it can be seen that Jxta peers are arranged within a virtual overlay which sits on top of the physical devices, as mentioned in Chapter 1. Peers are not required to have direct point-to-point network connections between each only (through the use of pipes) and they can discover each other on the network to form transient or persistent relationships called peer groups. These concepts are described in the following two sections.

10.3.1 Peer Groups

A peer group is a virtual entity that speaks the set of peer group protocols (see Fig. 10.3). Typically, a peer group is a collection of cooperating peers providing a common set of services; e.g., you could have a file sharing peer group, a CPU sharing peer group (see Fig. 10.5). Therefore, peer groups are typically formed and self-organized based upon the mutual interest of peers and therefore provide a scoping environment for the group. Peer group boundaries define the search scope when searching for a group's content.

Peer groups can also be used to create a monitoring environment, monitoring a set of peers for any special purpose (heartbeat, traffic introspection,

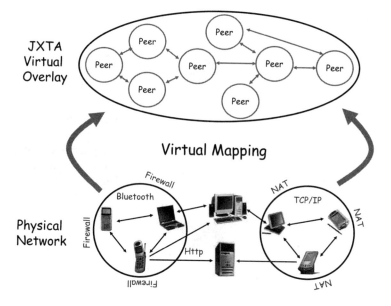

Fig. 10.4. The virtual network overlay used within Jxta providing the applications with a virtual view of the physical underlying network.

accountability, etc.). Peer groups can be password protected and implement local security policies if secure groups are desired. There is one special group, called the *World Peer Group* (the default peer group a peer joins) that includes all Jxta peers (see Chapter 12).

10.3.2 Rendezvous Nodes

To compensate for the absence of a central service (such as a domain name server), a Jxta network uses rendezvous peers. Rendezvous peers are volunteers that have agreed to act as a meeting point (or a caching server) for other peers. Rendezvous peers often maintain a permanent (early bound) IP address, so that other peers can contact them to check the current bindings of dynamic (late bound) peer endpoints. Rendezvous peers may also keep a record of other rendezvous peers. Therefore, if you know a rendezvous point and your friend also knows a rendezvous point, and the two rendezvous points know each other (directly or through other rendezvous points), you and your friend can find and reach each other, as illustrated in Fig. 10.5.

Rendezvous nodes can be used to automatically configure intranets by using multicast but they can be configured as permanent unicast servers also. Rendezvous points are similar in concept to Gnutella super-peers in that they

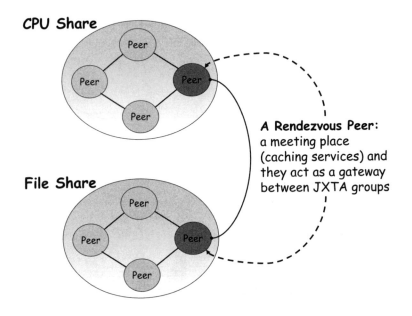

CPU Share

File Share

A Rendezvous Peer:
a meeting place
(caching services) and
they act as a gateway
between JXTA groups

Fig. 10.5. A Jxta group and the relationship between Jxta groups through the use
of rendezvous nodes.

cache the peer advertisements (which can be anything including files) that
peers use to publish the services they offer. Rendezvous nodes therefore, are
an integral part of scalability in Jxta. There can be many rendezvous nodes
per group (as there are super peers within a Gnutella network) and allow the
network to implement a centralized /decentralized network structure. Applications do not have to worry about these low-level details. Peers just send
search messages to the rendezvous points they know and the Jxta network
will do what's necessary by itself.

10.3.3 Pipes

Jxta peers use pipes to send messages to each other (see Fig. 10.3). Pipes
are an asynchronous and unidirectional message transfer mechanism used for
service communication. Pipes support the transfer of any object, including
binary code, data strings and Java technology-based objects.

The pipe endpoints (see Fig. 10.6) are referred to as the input pipe (the
receiving end) and the output pipe (the sending end). Messages flow from the
output pipe into the input pipes.

Pipes are virtual communication channels and may connect peers that do
not have a direct physical link. In the example given in the upper section of

Fig. 10.6, *Peer 1* has created a virtual Jxta pipe between itself and *Peer 2*. The actual physical route however that this connection travels is through a firewall, via a desktop (*Peer 3*) and a server (*Peer 4*). The number of intermediaries used to communicate a message is known as the number of *hops*.

Further, at each hop of this network a different transport protocol may be used as pipes are independent of any particular communication mechanism. To date, there are three implementations: HTTP, TCP and Bluetooth. Pipes dynamically switch at runtime depending on what is available for use. In some sense, a pipe can be viewed as an abstract, named message queue that supports a number of abstract operations such as create, open, close, delete, send and receive. Pipes offer two modes of communication, point-to-point and propagate, as seen in the lower part of Fig. 10.6.

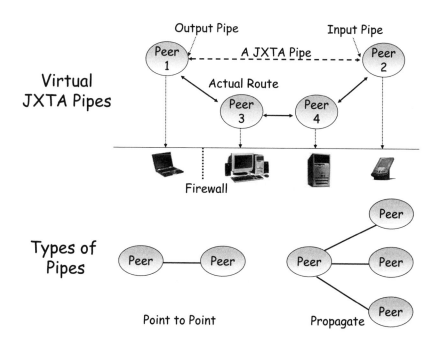

Fig. 10.6. A Jxta pipe is not a fixed one-to-one connection. It can traverse through multiple hops and networks before the message reaches its destination. Also, the two types of Jxta pipes, point-to-point and propagate are shown.

A point-to-point pipe connects exactly two pipe endpoints: an input pipe on one peer receives messages sent from the output pipe of another peer. A propagate pipe connects one output pipe to multiple input pipes. The Jxta core also provides secure unicast pipes, a secure variant of the point-to-point pipe that provides a secure communication channel.

10.3.4 Relay Nodes

A Jxta relay peer is a kind of Jxta router for Jxta messages (see Fig. 10.3). There are many examples of why these are needed. They can be used to help traverse firewalls or to help micro-Jxta nodes. For example, the Java Jxta version for micro devices (e.g., PDAs using J2ME) simply talks to a Jxta relay (a message relaying peer), which in turn bears most of the message processing (such as XML authoring for advertisements, sending search messages across the Jxta network and so forth) and relaying burden. A J2ME-based peer, together with a Jxta relay, is functionally equivalent to a normal Jxta peer. Therefore, J2ME peers act as an edge device, sitting on the perimeter of a Jxta network.

10.4 The Jxta Protocols

The Jxta protocols are a set of six protocols that have been specifically designed for ad hoc, pervasive and multi-hop P2P networking.

Each of the JXTA protocols addresses a specific aspect of P2P networking that has been identified by the Jxta core design team. A peer can choose to implement the protocols it wishes and then rely on other peers to provide them with extra functionality. For example, a peer could rely on a set of known router peers and not need to implement the *Endpoint Routing Protocol* or a peer could elect not to be a *Rendezvous* because there may be dedicated persistently connected peers that are known to provide this functionality for their group.

The Jxta protocols are not totally independent of each other. Each layer in its protocol stack relies on its layer below to provide connectivity to other peers (see Fig. 10.7). For example, the *Peer Discovery Protocol* relies on the *Peer Resolver* and *Endpoint Routing* protocols to transport its messages to other peers. The six protocols are described briefly, in the next six sections. For more information see [83] and [15].

10.4.1 The Peer Discovery Protocol

A peer uses the *peer discovery protocol* to discover a Jxta resource. Jxta resources are described by XML advertisements, as mentioned previously. Note, that the first word, peer, is the subject and not necessarily the object. Using this protocol, peers can advertise their own resources, and discover the resources from other peers.

Jxta does not mandate exactly how discovery is done. It can be decentralized, centralized, or a hybrid of the two. There are two levels of discovery:

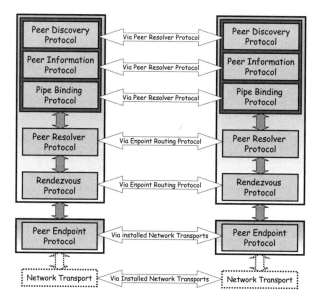

Fig. 10.7. The layering of the six Jxta protocols.

joining a Jxta network and discovering a Jxta resource within a Jxta network. Further, there are two methods of joining a Jxta network:

1. **Multicast:** which uses the multicast protocol to a local (or well known) network, i.e., as soon as a Jxta peer connects to the network, it broadcasts a presence announcement by sending a multicast packet onto a well-known port. Other peers monitor this port using multicast requests for appropriate packets and when received, make contact with the other peers.
2. **Point-to-Point, i.e., Unicast:** which is used when the peer knows the location of a Jxta peer, typically a rendezvous node (or a collection of known peers) and therefore can contact it directly. Typically, peers search for several rendezvous nodes for redundancy.

Once a peer has joined the Jxta network, it can find out about Jxta resources in several ways. For example, a peer can use cascaded discovery; that is, if a peer discovers a second peer, the first peer can view its horizon and discover other peers or rendezvous points and so on.

10.4.2 The Peer Resolver Protocol

The *peer resolver protocol* enables a peer to implement high-level search capabilities, allowing a peer to send and receive generic queries to find or search for peers, or other generic advertisements.

10.4.3 The Peer Information Protocol

This *peer information protocol* allows peers to learn about the capabilities and status of other peers, e.g., up time, load, capabilities, etc. For example, a peer could send a ping message to see if another peer is alive or query a peer's properties.

10.4.4 The Pipe Binding Protocol

The *pipe binding protocol* allows a peer to establish a virtual communication channel (i.e., a pipe) between one or more peers. It allows the binding of the two or more ends of the pipe endpoints forming the connection. Specifically, a peer binds a pipe advertisement to a pipe endpoint to create a virtual connection. See Section 10.3.3 for more information on pipes.

10.4.5 The Endpoint Routing Protocol

This *endpoint routing protocol* allows a peer to find information about the available routes for sending a message to the destination peer, which allows a message to traverse multiple hops in a flexible way. Peers implementing the endpoint routing protocol respond to queries with available route information giving a list of gateways along the route.

10.4.6 The Rendezvous Protocol

The *rendezvous protocol* allows a peer to send messages to all the listeners of the service. By default, query messages only reach peers within the same physical network. The rendezvous protocol defines how a peer can subscribe or be a subscriber to a propagation service allowing larger communities to form. A rendezvous node's scope is a peer group. The rendezvous protocol allows a peer to propagate messages to all the listeners of the service.

10.5 A Jxta Scenario: Fitting Things Together

A Jxta peer, just like a Gnutella servent, can be a client and a server. Furthermore, Jxta peers can act as rendezvous nodes, which act as meeting places (or lookup servers) for other Jxta nodes. Figure 10.8 gives a scenario of how a peer joins a Jxta network, performs a search query and locates a file for download.

The various Jxta protocols involved in the operation at each stage are described below:

1. The rendezvous node (RV) accepts connection for nodes 1 to 7 and stores their advertisements locally.

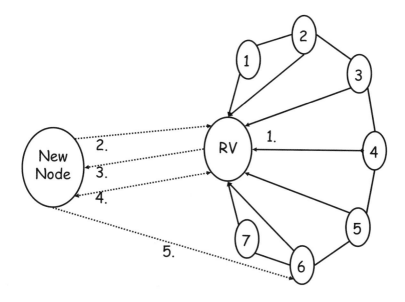

Fig. 10.8. A connection scenario for a simple file search using Jxta.

2. A *new node* then contacts the RV using a discovery mechanism, e.g., Unicast/multicast via the peer discovery protocol
3. RV authenticates the *new node* and adds the new node to the group
4. The *new node* performs a file search query by contacting the RV to search for local match or to propagate this query to all other members in the group. The file is eventually found on node 6. This uses the peer discovery protocol, the peer resolver protocol and the endpoint routing protocol.
5. The *new node* and node 6 set up and communicate directly through a Jxta pipe. This connection is virtual and may actually traverse (route) through the RV node and node 7. This step uses the pipe binding protocol, the peer resolver protocol and the endpoint routing protocol.

Note here, that peers can volunteer to become rendezvous peers. They do this when they join the Jxta network using the Jxta configurator (see Section 12.3.1).

10.6 Jxta Environment Considerations

10.6.1 Security

Jxta does not enforce specific security approaches but provides the following security primitives:

- Cryptography: hash functions (e.g., MD5), symmetric encryption algorithms (e.g., RC4) and asymmetric cryptographic algorithms (e.g., Diffie-Hellman and RSA).
- An authentication framework based on PAM (Pluggable Authentication Module).
- Password-based login scheme that can be plugged into the PAM framework.
- An access control mechanism based on peer groups; i.e., members of the group have access to the data offered by another member whereas non-members do not.
- A transport security mechanism, based on SSL/TLS.

10.6.2 NAT and Firewalls

The wide spread use of NAT and firewalls severely affects many P2P systems and hence the usability of Jxta. In particular, a peer outside a firewall or a NAT gateway cannot discover peers inside the firewall or the NAT gateway. In the absence of asking system administrators to let Jxta traffic through (e.g., by opening a specific port), Jxta provides some solutions to this problem. Specifically, Jxtat peers inside the firewall can contact a relay peer, outside the firewall, in order to advertise its services. It can then periodically contact the relay peer to retrieve messages. The relay effectively acts as a broker for the firewalled peer.

10.7 Comment

It is hard to see how Jxta protocols can compete with the mass of standardized XML technologies used in Web services and the like. Without widespread support from the community at large, the momentum will surely be difficult to sustain, or will it? Many have commented on this approach, for example, [17].

10.8 Conclusion

The Jxta protocols define how peers can locate, communicate and collaborate with other peers within multi-hop pervasive P2P networks. Jxta peers can operate on a wide range of heterogeneous devices, which can run on any programming language, computer platform or networking protocols, through the use of XML.

Jxta peers live within a virtual network overlay and are organized in peer groups. Each peer group can have one or more rendezvous nodes which act as a local propagation service for advertisements of Jxta resources (e.g., pipes, peers, services, etc.). Jxta also supports relaying which allows smaller devices with limited functionality to join the Jxta network and gives a support mechanism for traversing firewalls. A typical file-sharing scenario illustrated how these mechanisms fit together.

Part III

Middleware Deployment

In this theme, we look at some of the specifics of programming and deploying applications using distributed-object (Chapter 11), P2P (Chapter 12) and Web services (Chapter 13) middleware. Together, these represent a broad section of the domain as most distributed systems are constructed within one of these areas. Even Grid computing has adopted a Web-services based environment for exposing its functionality, which we'll see in the next theme, *"From Web Services to Future Grids."*

11

Distributed Object Deployment Using Jini

In this chapter, two specific examples illustrate the use of RMI and Jini. The focus of this chapter is not to create complicated remote Java services and therefore give a lesson in Java programming, but rather it is to provide the reader with the core framework and components needed in order to run simple RMI and Jini services. Providing complicated services at this stage simply clouds this issue of understanding the fundamentals of running remote services.

Therefore, the source is very concise but it gives all the necessary code needed in order to run and describe remote RMI and Jini services. Such code can easily be extended to provide as complicated a service as the reader desires. The complete set of examples for this chapter and others can be found at the following Web site:

http://www.cleverfish.co.uk/peerbook/

On this Web site, there is a complete set of batch files that enable the reader to set up and run the various services required in order to run these examples. Such batch files are described in detail for each example. Typically though, the reader will need to set a few variables in each case specifying things such as where JINI is installed for example, which is outlined on the Web page.

Let's first look at the RMI security which is pervasive throughout the source code in the rest of this chapter.

11.1 RMI Security

This section briefly describes the role of the security manager for remote code. This is common to both Jini and RMI and is set using the code:

```
if (System.getSecurityManager() == null) {
    System.setSecurityManager(new RMISecurityManager());
```

A security manager protects access to system resources from untrusted downloaded code running within the virtual machine (i.e., provides basic sandboxing capabilities; see Section 8.6). A security manager is needed not only by the RMI server, but also the client because it is possible that RMI could be downloading code to the client in a similar fashion to the way an *applet* works. Therefore, both *applets* and *Jini* clients have to implement a sandbox, which is a necessary restriction that ensures that all operations performed by downloaded code are passed through a security layer.

If a security manager is not set then RMI will not function because, without a security manager, RMI will not download classes for objects in remote method calls[1], e.g., parameters, return values or exceptions.

In the examples given here, we simply set the security manager to the default, which is a similar security policy to that adopted in applets; i.e., downloaded code is not allowed to access the local disk or to open sockets to third party hosts, etc. This can be overridden by either using another SecurityManager or through the use of a *policy file* to grant specific permissions (see [82] for more information).

11.2 An RMI Application

We discussed in Section 5.2 that Jini is based on the RMI technology. This section therefore provides an RMI example to outline the core transport mechanism for Jini. In the next section, this is expanded to illustrate how this fits in with Jini. You'll notice straight away how similar they are.

This example therefore provides a simple RMI application that outputs *Hello World* on a remote machine. It consists of three files:

1. **RemoteMessageInterface.java:** is the Java RMI proxy object to the remote implementation of this code. The client calls this locally.
2. **RemoteMessage.java:** is the remote implementation of the Java proxy that is run on the remote machine.
3. **LocalObject.java:** is the local client that calls the Java proxy (*RemoteMessageInterface*), which transmits this call over the network to call the function in the remote object (*RemoteMessage*).

11.2.1 The Java Proxy

The *RemoteMessageInterface* provides a simple interface that allows the user to invoke a function containing a message argument. This code is implemented on a server and invoked using the generic RMI mechanism. To extend the service, simply extend this *RemoteMessageInterface* with the methods you require and reimplement these in the server code described in the next section.

---

[1] Other than from the local class path.

The rest of the code stays exactly the same. The source code for this interface is given below:

```
public interface RemoteMessageInterface extends Remote {
    public void sendMessage(String message) throws RemoteException;
}
```

Remote RMI interfaces need to extend *java.rmi.Remote*. This interface marks our *RemoteMessageInterface* as one whose methods can be called from any virtual machine and therefore has the ability to be located remotely. Further, as a member of a remote interface, the *sendMessage(String)* method is also a remote method and as such, it must be capable of throwing a *java.rmi.RemoteException*.

RMI uses exceptions to handle remote errors, indicating that a communication failure, an internal method error in *sendMessage()* or protocol error has occurred. Remote exceptions are checked at compile time, so this has to be *thrown* from any remote method.

11.2.2 The Server

The server code implements our *RemoteMessageInterface* and therefore provides the code that *sendMessage()* will invoke on the remote machine. The source code is given below:

```
public class RemoteMessage extends UnicastRemoteObject
                    implements RemoteMessageInterface {

    public RemoteMessage() throws RemoteException {
        super();
    }

    public void sendMessage(String message) {
        System.out.println(message);
    }

    public static void main(String[] args) {
        if (System.getSecurityManager() == null) {
            System.setSecurityManager(new RMISecurityManager());
        }
        try {
            RemoteMessageInterface rmi = new RemoteMessage();
            String name = "//"
              + InetAddress.getLocalHost().getHostName()
                            + "/RemoteMessageInterface";
            Naming.rebind(name, rmi);
            System.out.println("Remote Message bound");
        } catch (RemoteException e) {
            System.err.println("RemoteMessage exception: "
```

```
                              + e.getMessage());
                    }
            }
    }
```

This class implements the *RemoteMessageInterface* to provide the remote *sendMessage()* method implementation, which outputs the given
string on the remote machine. This class also extends the class
java.rmi.server.UnicastRemoteObject, which is a convenience RMI class that
can be used as a super class for remote object implementations. This class basically supplies appropriate remote implementations for the *java.lang.Object*
methods (e.g., equals, hashCode, toString) along with extra constructors and
static methods used to export a remote object and make it available (via the
RMI registry) to remote clients.

Note though that a remote object implementation does not have to extend
UnicastRemoteObject. However, if it does not then it must supply an appropriate implementation of the *java.lang.Object* methods; otherwise the code
will not compile. It must also provide exporting functions (or link to the ones
in *UnicastRemoteObject*).

The **main()** method provides the main RMI mechanism for setting up
and registering this object with the local RMI registry.

First, as in any remote Java implementation, you must set the security
manager for that remote machine (see the RMI Security in Section 11.1 for
details). Next, we create an instance of the *RemoteMessage* and cast it as
a *RemoteMessageInterface* (which it implements) so that remote clients can
access this through our defined proxy interface (via the RMI Registry) and
not the implementation.

```
        RemoteMessageInterface rmi = new RemoteMessage();
```

The RMI registry is a basic remote object name service, which allows remote
clients to gain references to a remote object by using its class name. The
java.rmi.Naming interface is used for binding, registering, or looking up remote objects. The *RemoteMessage* class creates a name for itself and registers
this in the RMI registry using the following code:

```
        String name = "//" + InetAddress.getLocalHost().getHostName()
                                        + "/RemoteMessageInterface";
        Naming.rebind(name, rmi);
```

This name includes the host where the registry is located and a name that
identifies the remote object in the registry. The *getLocalHost()* function dynamically obtains the local host name, which works well for our server class
defined here (for clients, see 11.2.3). For more information about how such
names are created, see the *RMI Trail* of the *Java Tutorial* [82].

This is added to the RMI registry by using *rebind* with the name and reference to the object associated with this name (i.e., our *RemoteMessage* object,

rmi) as arguments. During this process, any *RemoteExceptions* generated are caught by the corresponding *try* and *catch* block.

11.2.3 The Client

The client code gets access to the remote object (via the *RemoteMessageInterface*) and invokes the *sendMessage* funtion. The mechanism of how this is accomplished is given in Fig. 11.1 and is described along with the source code given below:

```
public class LocalObject {
    public static void main(String args[]) {
        if (System.getSecurityManager() == null) {
            System.setSecurityManager(new RMISecurityManager());
        }
        try {
            String name = "//"
              + InetAddress.getLocalHost().getHostName() +
                            "/RemoteMessageInterface";
            RemoteMessageInterface rmi =
              (RemoteMessageInterface)Naming.lookup(name);
            rmi.sendMessage("Hello Remote Machine!!!");
        } catch (Exception e) {
            System.err.println("LocalObject exception: "
              + e.getMessage());
            e.printStackTrace();
        }
    }
}
```

At first, the client sets a security manager (see the RMI Security in Section 11.1 for details). Now, since our RMI server program (*RemoteMessage*) has registered itself with the remote RMI registry using its implemented remote interface, *RemoteMessageInterface* (see Fig. 11.1), the client can now use the *rmi.Naming* interface to look up the reference to the remote object (see step 2, in Fig. 11.1). This is achieved using the following code:

```
String name = "//" + InetAddress.getLocalHost().getHostName() +
                "/RemoteMessageInterface";
RemoteMessageInterface rmi =
  (RemoteMessageInterface)Naming.lookup(name);
```

This code is identical to the server because this example is configured to run the client and the server on **ONE** machine. Although this is not distributed in the network sense, the principles are exactly the same. It is easy to reconfigure the code to insert an IP address of a remote RMI machine if desired. To do this, the formation of the name will have to be changed to point to the remote machine directly, for example:

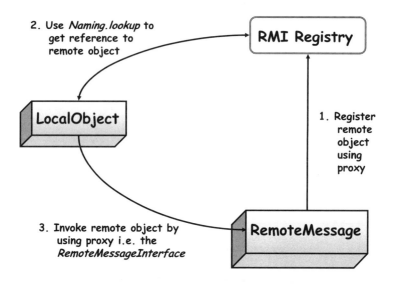

Fig. 11.1. An overview of how the client gets access to the remote object using RMI.

```
String name = "//" + "spectra.astro.cf.ac.uk"
  + "/RemoteMessageInterface";
```

or better still, pass this as a command line argument to your program:

```
String name = "//" + args[0] + "/RemoteMessageInterface";
```

Once a reference to the remote interface has been looked up, the client can invoke the remote method (see step 3 in Fig. 11.1) as if it were a local method call, by using:

```
rmi.sendMessage("Hello Remote Machine!!!");
```

The next section explains what RMI services you need to run and how you execute this RMI example.

11.2.4 Setting up the Environment

With any RMI program, you must start an *RMI Registry* on the machine that is running the remote service, using the command:

```
> rmiregistry
```

Note that before you start the rmiregistry, you must make sure no CLASS-PATH is set; i.e., unset the CLASSPATH environment variable. See the Java Tutorial for a detailed explanation [82]) but briefly, if the rmiregistry can find your local stub classes, it will forget that the loaded stub class can be loaded from your server's code base and subsequently, the client will not be able to locate and load the stub class or other server-side classes.

There is a convenience batch file for running rmiregistry (runRegistry.bat) on the Web site. There are also batch files for: compiling and creating the local *stubs* file (*build.bat*); for setting the *java.policy* file (sets all permissions granted) and running the RMI Service, RemoteMessage (*runRemote.bat*); and for setting the *java.policy* file and running the RMI client, LocalObject (*runLocal.bat*).

Briefly, to run your service, you can use the batch file or run using the following command:

```
java -Djava.rmi.server.codebase=file:/./classes
    -Djava.rmi.server.hostname=localhost
        -Djava.security.policy=./java.policy
            -classpath ./classes
                    RemoteMessage
```

and to run the client, you would use a similar command:

```
java -Djava.rmi.server.codebase=file:/.classes/
    -Djava.security.policy=java.policy
        -classpath classes
                LocalObject
```

and now, on to Jini....

11.3 A Jini Application

This section illustrates how to create a Jini remote service and how a client might access that service. The actual service, as in the RMI example above, is very simple. In this example, the remote service method takes no parameters but returns a *String* in order to retrieve a message from the remote service.

Again, to extend these interfaces in order to make a more advanced Jini service is trivial and application specific. For a Java programmer, the framework of how you go about creating and deploying Jini services can be the majority of the learning step.

Specifically, this example returns a "Hello World" string from the remote computer. The client uses the Jini lookup service to locate the "Hello World" service and obtains a Java Proxy (essentially an RMI stub). It makes a call on this object which remotely executes the specific function in the server code. As in RMI, you need to implement three files: one interface (or proxy), one client and one server. As you will see, the actual source code is very similar to RMI. The files are:

1. **MyService.java:** is the Jini service which implements the *MyServiceInterface.*
2. **MyServiceInterface.java:** is the interface to the Jini service, i.e., the Java proxy.
3. **MyClient.java:** is the local client that calls the Java proxy (*MyServiceInterface*), which RMI transmits over the network to call the function in the remote object (i.e., *MyService*).

11.3.1 The Remote Interface

As with RMI, we start off with the Jini proxy interface for the remote object. Like RMI, the Jini proxy contains the functionality that the remote object will provide. The code for this interface is given in the following listing:

```
public interface MyServiceInterface extends Remote {
    public String sayHello () throws RemoteException;
}
```

As you can see, the only method our remote implementation has to implement is the *sayHello()* function which returns a *String*.

11.3.2 The Server

The remote *MyService* class implements the *MyServiceInterface* interface and provides the necessary calls in order to publish its service to the Jini lookup server, using the Jini *Join* protocol (see Section 5.4.2. The source code is given below:

```
public class MyService extends UnicastRemoteObject
                            implements MyServiceInterface {

    public MyService () throws RemoteException {
        super ();
    }

    public String sayHello () throws RemoteException  {
        System.out.println ("MyService: sayHello() called");
        return ("Hello World from MyService!");
    }

    public static void main (String[] args) {
        MyServiceInterface myServer;
        LookupLocator lookup;
        ServiceRegistrar registrar;
        ServiceItem serviceItem;

        try {
```

```
        System.setSecurityManager (new RMISecurityManager());

        myService = new MyService ();

        Entry[] attr = new Entry[1];
        attr[0] = new Name("HelloWorldService");
        serviceItem = new ServiceItem(null, myService, attr);

        lookup = new LookupLocator ("jini://localhost");
        registrar = lookup.getRegistrar();

        registrar.register(serviceItem, Lease.FOREVER);

        System.out.println("Service Ready ...");
      } catch (Exception e) {
          System.out.println("MyService.main: Exception " + e);
      }
    }
  }
```

As in RMI, all Jini services should subclass the server-side RMI implementation class (*java.rmi.server.UnicastRemoteObject*) unless they wish to reimplement these underlying calls themselves. The first operation of the *main* method, as in RMI, sets the security manager to the default RMI manager, since our transport is RMI. We then create an instance of our Jini service, *MyService* that implements the *MyServiceInterface* proxy interface.

In order to add this Jini service we need to *register* it with the lookup service. The *register* function expects a *ServiceItem* object and a lease duration (see Section 5.4.2). A *ServiceItem* object has the following parameters:

```
ServiceItem(ServiceID id, Object service, Entry attrSets)
```

where:

- **id:** is a universally unique identifier for registered services (128-bit value). Service IDs are intended to be generated only by lookup services, not by clients.
- **service:** is the object implementing the Jini Service, i.e., a **MyService** instance.
- **attrSets:** are attributes for service represented by a list of objects.

In our example, we use the following code to populate the attribute array to describe this server. This is used to identify this service when it is registered with the lookup service:

```
        Entry[] attr = new Entry[1];
        attr[0] = new Name("HelloWorldService");
        serviceItem = new ServiceItem(null, myServer, attr);
```

Note here that the attribute used for lookup is the Jini *Name* class and we set its contents to "HelloWorldService". The service could be advertised, however, using a number of mechanisms, for example, by using the *Java proxy* name. The service item is created by ignoring the ID, using our *MyService* instance and the set of attributes that describe this service. Note that this description is much more sophisticated than in the RMI example as Jini provides much more sophisticated capabilities for searching for services.

Once we have our service item created, we can locate the lookup server and populate it with our service. This is achieved by using the Jini *LookupLocator* class as follows:

```
lookup = new LookupLocator ("jini://localhost");
registrar = lookup.getRegistrar();
registrar.register(serviceItem, Lease.FOREVER);
```

The *LookupLocator* expects you to pass it a resource that is running a Jini lookup server address. Jini uses its own protocol for this purpose, i.e., "jini://". Following the protocol is the name of the computer hosting the lookup service. We specify this as the *localhost*, i.e., this machine. The LUS could easily be stored elsewhere and specified here in the same way.

Therefore, for this example, we are using the *Unicast Discovery* mechanism to find our lookup server. When we have a reference to the lookup server, we can then get the registrar object and publish our service using the register method. Here, we register our Jini service and allow the Jini LUS to lease it forever. The service is now deployed and waiting for use.

11.3.3 The Client

```
public class MyClient {
    public static void main (String[] args) {
        Entry[] aeAttributes;
        LookupLocator lookup;
        ServiceRegistrar registrar;
        ServiceTemplate template;
        MyServerInterface myServerInterface;

        try {
            System.setSecurityManager (new RMISecurityManager ());

            lookup = new LookupLocator ("jini://localhost");
            registrar = lookup.getRegistrar();

            aeAttributes = new Entry[1];
            aeAttributes[0] = new Name ("HelloWorldService");
            template = new ServiceTemplate (null, null, aeAttributes);
            myServerInterface =
                (MyServerInterface)registrar.lookup(template);
```

```
            System.out.println ("Calling sayHello()->"
                    + myServerInterface.sayHello () + "<-");
        } catch (Exception e) {
            System.out.println ("MyClient.main() exception: " + e);
        }
    }
}
```

The client code, as in the other examples, sets the security manager to access remote objects. It then discovers the Jini lookup service by creating a *LookupLocator* object in the same way as with the service:

```
    lookup = new LookupLocator ("jini://localhost");
```

After obtaining the lookup service's *ServiceRegistrar* object, it performs a search to find the service that has the attribute name of "HelloWorldService". This is accomplished in the same way as the service publishes the description of the service except that rather than creating a *ServiceItem* object, the client creates a *ServiceTemplate* object as follows:

```
    aeAttributes = new Entry[1];
    aeAttributes[0] = new Name ("HelloWorldService");
    template = new ServiceTemplate (null, null, aeAttributes);
    myServerInterface = (MyServerInterface)registrar.lookup(template);
```

A *ServiceTemplate* has the following parameters:

```
public ServiceTemplate(ServiceID serviceID,
                java.lang.Class[] serviceTypes,
                      Entry[] attrSetTemplates)
```

where:

- **serviceID:** service ID to match, or null
- **serviceTypes:** service types (i.e., Java Classes that the service implements) to match, or null
- **attrSetTemplates:** attribute set templates to match, or null.

Here, we use the attributes to search for all services that identify themselves with the "HelloWorldService" tag. The Jini lookup protocol is invoked by the *lookup* method on the *ServiceRegistrar* object. It service returns the Jini *proxy* object to the service, which gives the client direct access to the remote Jini service.

This is an extremely simple example but forms the basis of programming with Jini. It can be easily expanded to implement any Jini service you desire.

11.4 Running Jini Applications

To run Jini applications, you can use the Jini starter kit [79] but in fact, to run the example given here you actually only need five Jini Jar files from this kit:

1. jini-core.jar, core Jini functionality
2. jini-ext.jar, Jini lookup functionality (from client)
3. reggie.jar, Jini lookup service
4. reggie-dl.jar, Jini lookup service
5. tools.jar, HTTP server.

Of course, you'll also need the Java Runtime Environment (JRE) [12]. You then start three services:

1. **an HTTP server:** for accessing the remote class files
2. **RMID Daemon:** which starts on machines where you want to host the remote Java objects
3. **Reggie:** the default Jini lookup server.

These are described in more detail in the following 3 sections.

11.4.1 HTTP Server

To run the example, you need to start an HTTP server for communicating data files between the Jini client/service and the Jini lookup service. There is a default implementation in the *tools.jar* jar file supplied with Jini. You execute it as follows:

```
java -jar -classpath %JINI_CLASSPATH%
      %JINIHOME%\lib\tools.jar -port 8081 -dir
          %JINIHOME%\lib -verbose
```

11.4.2 RMID Daemon

The next step is to start an RMI daemon for executing remote code (if the Jini service is actually remote). This can be achieved by using the following command:

```
rmid -J-Dsun.rmi.activation.execPolicy=none
```

Also, you can use the following *rmid* command-line option to enable logging for debugging purposes:

```
-J-Djava.rmi.server.logCalls=true
```

11.4.3 The Jini Lookup Service

There is a default implementation of a Jini lookup service, called Reggie. This can be executed by using the following command:

```
java -jar -classpath %JINI_CLASSPATH%
  -Djava.security.policy=%JINIHOME%/example/lookup/policy.all
    %JINIHOME%/lib/reggie.jar
      http://localhost:8081/reggie-dl.jar
        %JINIHOME%/example/lookup/policy.all
          reggie_log public
```

The parameters here specify the various lookup policies and jar files needed. The details are beyond the scope of this book but you can find more information at [80] or the Jini Web site [78].

11.4.4 Running the Service

To run the service, you'll need to add the Jini Jar files (listed in Section 11.4) to the Java CLASSPATH, set the security policy and set the codebase to the address of the HTTP server that you started in Section 11.4.1. Therefore to run the service (which obviously needs to be started first), you would type in:

```
java -classpath %JINI_CLASSPATH%;./classes
    -Djava.security.policy=policy.all
        -Djava.rmi.server.codebase=http://localhost:8080/
          MyService
```

and to run the client the following command would be issued:

```
java -classpath %JINI_CLASSPATH%;./classes
    -Djava.security.policy=policy.all
        -Djava.rmi.server.codebase=http://localhost:8080/
          MyClient
```

Note that, as in the RMI example, the Web site listed at the beginning of this chapter has a number of batch files to help you run these examples. These are:

1. **Compile.bat:** which compiles the example and creates the local stubs file.
2. **Setup.bat:** which sets up the local environment. This file MUST be edited to configure your platform correctly; i.e., you must insert the location of the JRE (RUNTIME_JAR in the example below).
3. **HTTP-1.bat:** which runs the HTTP server for the transportation of the Java code on the Jini network. This must be run first.
4. **RMID-2.bat:** is the RMI registry that keeps track of the RMI objects, currently available on the remote machine.
5. **REGGIE-3.bat:** is a Jini lookup server.

6. **runService.bat:** is a batch file that uses the *policy.all* file to set up the security model (all permissions are granted in this example). It then runs the RMI service, emphRemoteMessage.

7. **runClient.bat:** also uses the *policy.all* file to set up the security model for the client and then runs the RMI client, *LocaLObject*.

```
set RUNTIME_JAR=c:\java\jdk1.4\jre\lib\rt.jar set
JINIHOME=.
set JINI_CLASSPATH=.;%RUNTIME_JAR%;
        %JINIHOME%\lib\jini-core.jar;
           %JINIHOME%\lib\jini-ext.jar;
              %JINIHOME%\lib\reggie.jar;
                 %JINIHOME%\lib\reggie-dl.jar;
                    %JINIHOME%\lib\tools.jar
```

11.5 Conclusion

In this chapter, two examples were used to illustrate how one would use the Remote Method Invocation (RMI) and Jini frameworks for distributing Java objects. Both examples consist of very simple source code and services that illustrate the core building blocks necessary for applications working within these environments.

RMI and Jini are alike, except that Jini has much more comprehensive searching capabilities, which can be used to locate objects in a much more distributed and scalable fashion. Jini also integrates other mechanisms essential for writing robust distributed object-based applications, e.g., distributed event modelling and object management.

12

P2P Deployment Using Jxta

This chapter begins with three specific examples of programming using Jxta's Java binding. The code illustrates three examples ranging from simple boot-strapping code to more advanced pipe-connectivity scenarios. The purpose of these examples is twofold: to familiarise the reader with what is involved in Jxta programming; but more important, to discuss what is involved in using a P2P platform, outlining the fundamental issues that a P2P environment exhibits.

Therefore, here a number of practical issues are illustrated, such as how one deals with out-of-date advertisements and what is involved in configuring peers within a P2P environment. These are discussed and illustrated using the Jxta mechanisms and its potential solutions. Finally, peer configuration using the Jxta configurator is illustrated, focusing on the types of settings and issues it addresses. Each programming example provided here can be found on the following Web site:

http://www.cleverfish.co.uk/peerbook/

12.1 Jxta Programming: Three Examples Illustrated

There are three Jxta [15] examples illustrated in this section:

1. A simple example that starts the Jxta platform
2. An example that uses the Jxta discovery mechanism to discover Jxta peers on the network
3. Creating and using Jxta pipes.

Each of these examples is a variation of code that you can find on the Jxta Web site [15]. [1] The code listed here outlines the main methods and

---

[1] The original code was adapted from various examples, written by Mohamed Abdelaziz (jxta.org user name: hamada).

variables used but does not include comments or Java *import* commands. For a complete version of the code see this book's Web site [18]. Also, when trying these examples, it is extremely useful to use the on-line *JAVADOC* Jxta documentation wherever possible to help understand the meaning of the various Jxta calls, which can be found at:

```
http://platform.jxta.org/nonav/java/api/index.html
```

12.1.1 Starting the Jxta Platform

This simple example primarily illustrates how you can start and use the Jxta platform from a Java application.

```java
public class StartJxta {
    static PeerGroup netPeerGroup = null;
    static PeerGroupAdvertisement groupAdvertisement = null;
    private DiscoveryService discovery;
    private PipeService pipe;

    public StartJxta() { }

    public static void main(String args[]) {
        StartJxta myapp = new StartJxta();
        myapp.startJxta();
        System.exit(0);
    }

    private void startJxta() {
        try {
            netPeerGroup = PeerGroupFactory.newNetPeerGroup();
        } catch (PeerGroupException e) {
            System.out.println("FATAL: Group Creation Failure");
            e.printStackTrace();
            System.exit(1);
        }
        ..
    }
}
```

The functionality here is provided in the *startJxta* method, which is called from the main program. Here, we create a new *net peer group*, the default platform peer group. This function simplifies the method by which applications can start Jxta. The *newNetPeerGroup* method is contained in a general factory class for creating new peer groups, called *PeerGroupFactory* which extends *java.lang.Object*.

In Jxta, there are two subclasses of peer groups:

- **Platform:** which is used to represent the *World* group. This group provides minimum core services needed and every peer, when booting, automatically becomes part of this group.

- **StdPeergroup:** which is used to implement all other kinds of peer groups, which is achieved by using one of the *newNetPeerGroup* methods: the one above to create a new default net peer group, or using the *newNetPeer-Group(PeerGroup pg)* method and by defining a new *PeerGroup* object. Peer group objects allow groups to be customised to define their own set of customised services. Peer groups can be discovered via the *Discovery-Service* protocol.

If you use the newNetPeerGroup() method, a general default peer group is created. Further, if you enter the minimal information possible into the Jxta configurator (peer name, user name and password; see Section 12.3.1) then the peer will attempt to connect to the Jxta site and locate available *Rendezvous* peers. Therefore, by default, you can join the worldwide Jxta network and discover various peers running worldwide.

12.1.2 Discovery

The *DiscoverPeers* example illustrates how to use the Jxta asynchronous discovery services. Specifically, a peer is created and a *DiscoveryListener* is attached, which allows this peer to be notified when other peers have been discovered on the network. The code is as follows:

```
public class DiscoverPeers implements
          Runnable, DiscoveryListener {

    static PeerGroup netPeerGroup  = null;
    static PeerGroupAdvertisement groupAdvertisement = null;

    private DiscoveryService discovery;
    private int myqueryid;
    PeerAdvertisement padv;

    public DiscoverPeers() {}

    private void startJxta() {
        try {
            netPeerGroup = PeerGroupFactory.newNetPeerGroup();
        } catch ( PeerGroupException e) {
            System.out.println("FATAL: Group Creation Failure");
            e.printStackTrace();
            System.exit(1);
        }
        discovery = netPeerGroup.getDiscoveryService();
        discovery.addDiscoveryListener(this);
    }

    public void run() {
        try {
```

```
        discovery.getRemoteAdvertisements(null,
    DiscoveryService.PEER, null, null, 1, null);

        while (true) {
            try {
                Thread.sleep(10 * 1000);
            } catch(Exception e) {}

            System.out.println("Sending a Discovery Message");

            discovery.getRemoteAdvertisements( null,
             DiscoveryService.PEER, null, null, 15, null);
            }
        } catch(Exception e) {
            e.printStackTrace();
        }
    }

    public void discoveryEvent(DiscoveryEvent ev) {
        int adCount=0;
        DiscoveryResponseMsg res = ev.getResponse();
        Advertisement adv=null;
        Enumeration enum = res.getAdvertisements();

        if (enum != null ) {
            while (enum.hasMoreElements()) {
                ++adCount;
                adv = (Advertisement) enum.nextElement();
                String name="NOT A PEER ADVERT";
                if (adv instanceof PeerAdvertisement)
                    name = ((PeerAdvertisement)adv).getName();
                System.out.println ("Advert ["
                        + adCount + "]  from peer : "+ name);
            }
        }
    }

    static public void main(String args[]) {
        DiscoverPeers myapp  = new DiscoverPeers();
        myapp.startJxta();
        myapp.run();
    }
```

As in any Jxta program, we first start the Jxta platform (see Section 12.1.1). We then obtain a reference to the Jxta discovery service by using the *netPeerGroup.getDiscoveryService* method.

The Jxta *DiscoveryService* class provides an asynchronous mechanism for discovering peer, group and other general Jxta *Advertisements*, e.g., pipes, services, etc. In this example, we use the discovery service to provide an asynchronous callback notifications of peer advertisements. There are two methods that provide this functionality:

- **run:** to implement the asynchronous callback, we need to multi-thread the class. This class therefore implements the *Runnable* interface, which requires a run method that includes the code that is to be threaded. For more information on multi-threading using Java, please see the Java Tutorial [82].
- **discoveryEvent:** is the method that must be implemented by any class that implements the *DiscoveryListener* interface. The process of attaching a discovery listener is achieved by the *addDiscoveryListener* method on the discovery server class, shown above. This results in creating a *callback* mechanism which invokes the discoveryEvent method every time a new peer is discovered on the network.

The run method creates a separate thread that runs an infinite loop. Within this loop, the *getRemoteAdvertisements* method of the discovery service is called at one second intervals:

```
public int getRemoteAdvertisements(
    java.lang.String peerid,
        int type, java.lang.String attribute,
            java.lang.String value,
                int threshold,
                    DiscoveryListener listener)
```

The parameters for the *getRemoteAdvertisements* are as follows:

- **peerid:** the ID of a peer, specifying *null* results in a propagation to all of this group rather than discovering an individual peer.
- **type:** the type of advert we are trying to discover (a *PEER*, a *GROUP* or an generic advert (*ADV*)). In this example, we specify that we only want to discover peers. This can be used to dynamically find other peers as and when they log onto the Jxta network.
- **attribute:** specifies an attribute that you search for, e.g., "CPU Sharer". This enables a user to narrow the search. Specifying *null* here means find anything.
- **value:** is used to specify a value for the attribute parameter, e.g., *Pentium* for our *CPU Sharer* attribute. Wildcards can be used, e.g., *Pent** would return any adverts for Pentium-based processors.
- **threshold:** specifies the upper limit for the number of responses you want to receive.
- **listener:** specifies the listener that will be notified when adverts have been found. In this example, we specify this using the *addDiscoveryListener* method and therefore we set this value to *null*, i.e., none.

In this example therefore, remote advertisements will be imported every second. Once local, the asynchronous callback will call the *discoveryEvent* method when new peers join the network. Once received, we can read the advert as follows:

- The *getResponse* method returns the response associated with the event encapsulated within a *DiscoveryResponseMsg* object.
- The *DiscoveryResponseMsg* object contains the advertisements which can be retrieved by its *getAdvertisements* method. This returns a Java *Enumeration* of *Advertisement* objects.
- *Advertisements* are XML documents that contain Jxta adverts in a platform-neutral manner and can represent peers, peer groups, services, pipes or other Jxta resources. The Java implementation of Jxta adverts provides a suite of objects for each specific advert. Therefore, the Java *instanceof* instruction can be used to determine the specific type of advert.
- If the instance of emphAdvertisment is a *PeerAdvertisement* then the code above extracts the name of the peer that issued the advert, otherwise a default string "NOT A PEER ADVERT" is assigned to the the *name* variable.
- The *name* variable is printed out, either containing the name of the peer or the default message if this advert originated from something other than a peer.

12.1.3 Creating Pipes

This a two-part example primarily to illustrate how to create an *InputPipe* and *OutputPipeListener* to send and receive messages.

1. **PipeListener.java:** a Jxta application that creates an *input pipe* and waits forever for messages to arrive.
2. **PipeExample.java:** an *OutputPipeListener* is created, which attempts to resolve the supplied *InputPipe*. When it has been resolved, a message is sent through the pipe.

This example is analogous to the socket client and server implementation. The input pipe is like a socket server and the output pipe is similar to a socket sender.

There are two ways of creating a pipe advert in JXTA. Either you can create a dynamic advertisement that produces a different UUID for each pipe or you can generate an advert once and use this advert for advertising a generic pipe. By taking the latter approach, you save a lot of confusion with advert versioning which is discussed in Section 12.3.4.

In this example, a pipe advert (*pipexample.adv*) is created first (using a simple Jxta application; see Web site for more details), which looks something like the following:

```
<!DOCTYPE jxta:PipeAdvertisement>
```

```
<jxta:PipeAdvertisement xmlns:jxta="http://jxta.org">
    <Id>
        urn:jxta:uuid-59616261646162614A757874614D504725184
                        FBC4E5D498AA0919F662E40028B04
    </Id>
    <Type>
        JxtaUnicast
    </Type>
    <Name>
        PipeExample
    </Name>
</jxta:PipeAdvertisement>
```

Note here that first, all Jxta adverts are XML based (to provide the programming language independence) and second, that each advert has its own universally unique identifier. This UUID is crucial for several reasons, e.g., to avoid looping when routing messages.

The code for the the pipe receiver is as follows:

```java
public class PipeListener implements PipeMsgListener {
    static PeerGroup netPeerGroup = null;
    private final static String SenderMessage = "PipeListenerMsg";
    private PipeService pipe;
    private PipeAdvertisement pipeAdv;
    private InputPipe pipeIn = null;

    public static void main(String args[]) {
        PipeListener myapp = new PipeListener();
        myapp.startJxta();
        myapp.run();
    }

    private void startJxta() {
        try {
            netPeerGroup = PeerGroupFactory.newNetPeerGroup();
        } catch (PeerGroupException e) {
            System.exit(1);
        }

        pipe = netPeerGroup.getPipeService();
        try {
            FileInputStream is = new FileInputStream("pipexample.adv");
            pipeAdv = (PipeAdvertisement)
                    AdvertisementFactory.newAdvertisement(
                        MimeMediaType.XMLUTF8, is);
            is.close();
        } catch (Exception e) {
            System.out.println("failed to read/parse pipe advertisement");
            System.exit(-1);
```

```
        }
    }

    public void run() {
            try {
                    pipeIn = pipe.createInputPipe(pipeAdv, this);
            } catch (Exception e) {
                    return;
            }
            if (pipeIn == null) System.exit(-1);
            System.out.println("Waiting for messages on input pipe");
    }

        public void pipeMsgEvent(PipeMsgEvent event ) {
            Message msg=null;
            try {
                msg = event.getMessage();
                if (msg == null) {
                    return;
                }
            } catch (Exception e) {
                    return;
            }

            MessageElement msgElement =
                msg.getMessageElement(null, SenderMessage);

            if (msgElement.toString() != null)
                System.out.println("Message: "+ msgElement.toString());
        }
    }
```

The pipe listener code is the more complex and contains the following aspects:

1. The *startJxta* method starts the Jxta platform, as discussed previously, and gets a reference to the pipe service, via the *netPeerGroup.getPipeService* method.
2. The *pipexample.adv* file is then loaded and converted into a *PipeAdvertisement* object by creating a new advert via the *AdvertisementFactory.newAdvertisement* method. This method specifies the format, i.e., *MimeMediaType.XMLUTF8* for the XML text file.
3. The *run* method is run within a separate thread to create the input pipe by using the the *createInputPipe* method of the pipe service. The arguments take the *PipeAdvertisement* object created and the *PipeMsgListener* interface that provides the asynchronous callback of *PipeMsgEvent* events through the *pipeMsgEvent* method. Our *PipeListener* class implements this interface and therefore registers itself to receive the pipe adverts.

4. Within the *pipeMsgEvent* method, the messages are extracted via the *getMessage* method on the *PipeMsgEvent* events, which are encapsulated within the Jxta *Message* object.
5. The message can be retrieved from the *Message* object using its *getMessageElement* method that returns a *MessageElement* by providing the message *id* inserted at construction. A *MessageElement* can then, in turn, be converted to a string using the standard *toString* Java method.

The pipe sender is implemented as follows:

```
public class PipeExample implements Runnable, OutputPipeListener {
    static PeerGroup netPeerGroup = null;
    private final static String SenderMessage = "PipeListenerMsg";
    private PipeService pipe;
    private PipeAdvertisement pipeAdv;

    public static void main( String args[] ) {
        PipeExample myapp = new PipeExample();
        myapp.startJxta();
        myapp.run();
    }

    private void startJxta() {
        try {
            netPeerGroup = PeerGroupFactory.newNetPeerGroup();
        } catch ( PeerGroupException e ) { System.exit( -1 ); }
        pipe = netPeerGroup.getPipeService();

        try {
            FileInputStream is = new
                        FileInputStream( "pipexample.adv" );
            pipeAdv = (PipeAdvertisement)
                    AdvertisementFactory.newAdvertisement(
                MimeMediaType.XMLUTF8, is );
            is.close();
        } catch ( Exception e ) {
            System.exit( -1 );  } }
    }

    public synchronized void run() {
        try {
            pipe.createOutputPipe( pipeAdv, this );}
        } catch ( IOException e ) {
            System.exit( -1 );
        }
    }

    public void outputPipeEvent( OutputPipeEvent event ) {
        OutputPipe op = event.getOutputPipe();
```

```
        Message msg = null;

        try {
            msg = new Message();
            msg.addMessageElement(null,
                new StringMessageElement(SenderMessage, "hello", null));
            op.send( msg );
        } catch ( IOException e ) {
            System.exit( -1 );
        }
        op.close();
    }
```

As with the *PipeListener* class, the *PipeExample* starts the Jxta platform and loads in the advert (in *startJxta*), using the pipe service.

In a separate thread, to illustrate the output pipe creation, it creates an output pipe and attaches this class as a listener for such events, via the *Output-PipeListener* interface. When the pipe has been created it notifies all listeners (i.e., our *PipeExample* class) and calls the *outputPipeEvent* method.

The *outputPipeEvent* method then creates a new message by passing a *StringMessageElement*, which attaches an *id* (i.e., the *SenderMessage* string) and a simple "hello" message, to the *Message*'s *addMessageElement* method. This message is sent using the *OutputPipe send* method.

12.2 Running Jxta Applications

To run Jxta applications, you need the Jar files for the core platform, which are available at the Web site listed above[2], or for the most recent version, look here:

    Jar Files: http://download.jxta.org/stablebuilds/

then include the core jar files for the Jxta platform in your class path. These are:

- jxta.jar
- log4j.jar
- jxtasecurity.jar
- cryptix32.jar
- cryptix-asn1.jar
- minimalBC.jar
- and jxtaptls.jar.

---

[2] The Jxta version used for the examples provided here is 1.x. The current version of Jxta may differ in syntax and the number/names of Jar files required for running, but the basic principal is the same.

12.3 P2P Environment: The Jxta Approach

This section illustrates how Jxta configures a peer with a P2P environment. There are a number of issues here to deal with including the inherent transient availability of peers and how one may go about representing a number of peers on one machine. Jxta provides a solution to this but these issues outline inherent problems that any P2P middleware needs to be able to address. Therefore this section, through the use of Jxta, outlines some of these.

12.3.1 Peer Configuration Using Jxta

This first issue within a P2P environment is how to configure a local peer. This has a number of connotations because there may be a number of peers running on the same machine, and therefore each peer needs to be individually identifiable within this environment. In other systems, services are hosted within a container that provides a hosting environment for outside access; e.g., OGSA services can be hosted within a J2EE container.

In Jxta, however, they have chosen to allow peers to be self-configurable and independent of any external hosting environment. Instead they use a configuration application per peer that allows it to set specific parameters about how it is hosted and what operations it can perform.

This approach can be more flexible but also has more individual administrative overhead than allowing a hosting environment to make these decisions for you. Within a true P2P environment therefore, a number of extra parameters that are extremely specific to individual peers have to be specified.

For example, within the Web services/OGSA world, services do not suddenly decide to become a lookup service, whereas, within Jxta, this is not only possible (via Rendezvous) but for some applications it may be essential (e.g., in ad hoc wireless sensor networks where a peer may change its role depending on its battery strength).

These specific settings for a peer are accomplished through the use of the *Jxta configurator* application. Since a Jxta peer can operate as a client, a server and a Rendezvous (Jxta's lookup mechanism) at the same time, they all are run in the same way and configure and bootstrap themselves.

With the Jxta configurator application therefore, you can specify to which port the peer listens, where Rendezvous Peers are, whether this peer will be operating as a Rendezvous and also which username and password you will be using to access the network.

At the time of writing, the Jxta configurator consisted of four screens that allowed the various peer settings to be configured. For detailed on-line information, please see the latest documents on the Jxta Web site [84] and [85]. The first screen is shown in Fig. 12.1.

The *Peer Name* can be set to whatever you want. If you are behind a firewall, then you need to specify your proxy server.

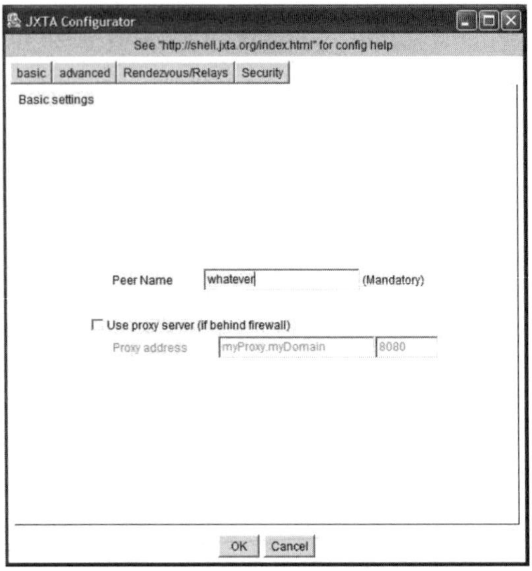

Fig. 12.1. Jxta configurator: screen 1.

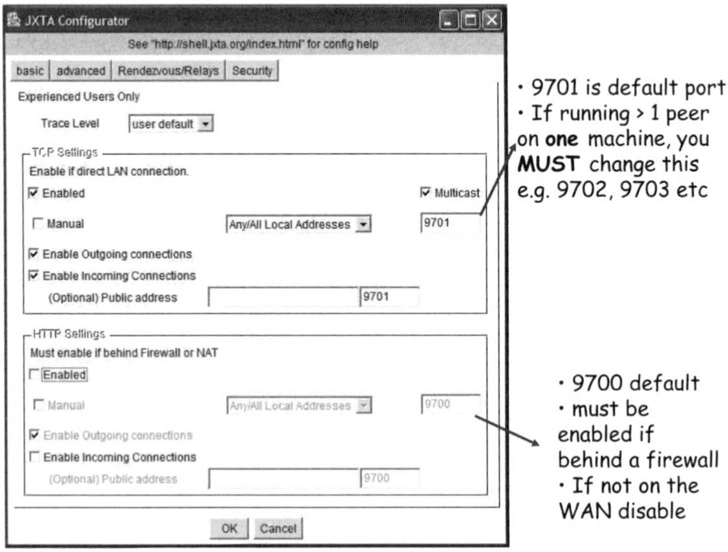

Fig. 12.2. Jxta configurator: screen 2.

The Advanced Settings (see Fig. 12.2) screen is used to set parameters about the environment in which the peer is running:

1. **TCP Settings:** by default, TCP is enabled on the default network interface (port 9701). When TCP is enabled, each instance of a Jxta platform is bound to a specific TCP port number of a given peer. If you select manual configuration an additional box "always manual" will be displayed. If you check this box, the configurator screen will be displayed to prompt the user to manually select the network interface for TCP each time a Jxta peer is booted (e.g., useful for nodes using DHCP where the IP address can change). A peer may have multiple network interfaces and so you can select which network interface should be used from the pull-down menu to the right. You can also change the port used for TCP (multiple instances of the Jxta platform can be run on a single peer by using different TCP port numbers). Finally, if the Jxta peer is located behind NAT, you may need to specify the public NAT address for this node.

2. **HTTP Settings:** by default, HTTP is enabled on the default network interface (port 9700). HTTP must be enabled if the Jxta peer is located behind a firewall or NAT. If you want to use a different network interface for HTTP, use the pull-down menu to select the desired network interface (IP address). You can also set port for for HTTP manually as with TCP/IP. If you're running Jxta on an intranet (i.e., with no Internet connection) then this should be disabled.

The Rendezvous/Router settings panel enables you to specify rendezvous and HTTP relay settings. By default, the Jxta peer does not act as a rendezvous node or a relay. A peer can opt to act as a Rendezvous here and perform a similar function to super-peers, described in Section 7.4.3. HTTP relaying is not required unless the peer is connected behind a firewall.

Finally, the last screen (see Fig. 12.4) allows you to enter your user name and password for this peer on the Jxta network, which allows you to protect your settings.

12.3.2 Peer Configuration Management Within Jxta

The *configurator* application creates a local configuration file and identity directory and the Jxta platform creates a directory for caching advertisements locally. The directory structure created by a Jxta peer is shown in Fig. 12.5.

When the Jxta *Configurator* (see Section 12.3.1) is run, it creates a *.jxta* directory (see Fig. 12.5). As shown in this screen shot, this directory contains three significant sections:

1. *The PlatformConfig file:* stores all of the current configuration settings that you specify using the Configurator, e.g., TCP/IP port used, whether this peer is a Rendezvous or a relay, etc.

2. *The cm Directory:* stores the cached adverts that this peer discovers.

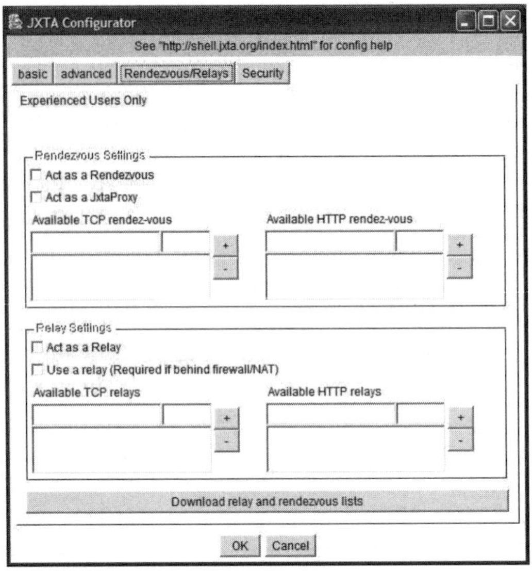

Fig. 12.3. Jxta configurator: screen 3.

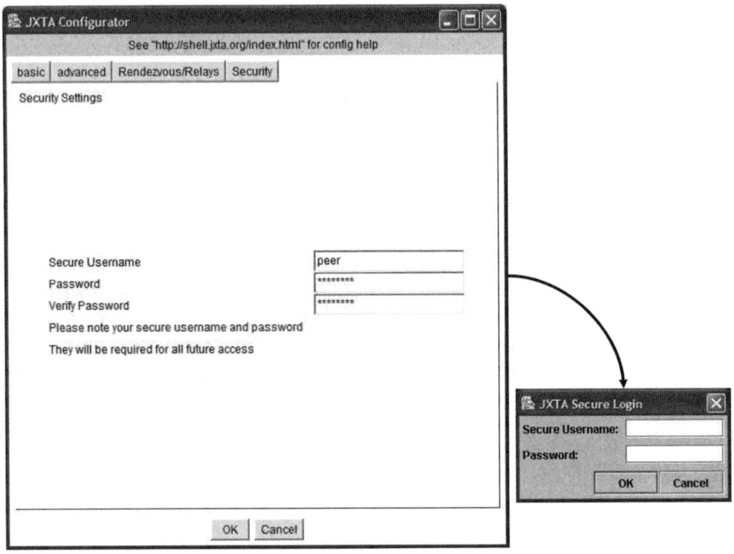

Fig. 12.4. Jxta configurator: screen 4.

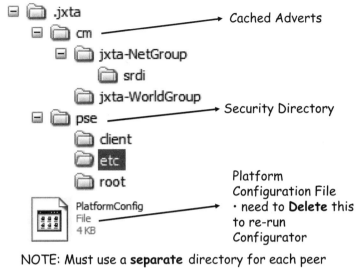

NOTE: Must use a **separate** directory for each peer
you run on the system !

Fig. 12.5. A screen shot of the directories that the Jxta platform creates when it is *bootstrapped*.

3. *The pse Directory:* contains security information, e.g., username and password are stored in the pse subdirectory.

Configuration information is stored in the current directory in the *PlatformConfig file*, which is used every time the peer runs. If you would like to re-run the auto-configuration tool, a file named *reconf* needs to be created in the current directory (or you can remove the *PlatformConfig* file).

When running multiple peers on one machine (e.g., you may do this for the pipe example described in Section 12.1.3, for PipeListener and PipeExample), the different Jxta applications (i.e., peers) will need to be run in *different* directories. This is necessary because each peer needs to use an different TCP port for its communication and the reliance on the cached directory structure for the configurator means that you must separate these for each peer. Otherwise, the configurator will use the previously cached settings and the second peer created would not be able to bind to the same port.

For example, for the pipe example, the default is 9701 so set the *PipeListener* to use this port and run the *PipeExample* using port 9702.

12.3.3 Running The Examples

To run these Jxta applications, you must put the Jxta Jar files in your class-path. These are listed in Section 12.2.

12.3.4 Jxta and P2P Advert Availability

When you are running a Jxta peer, both the availability of adverts and out-of-date adverts can seem extremely confusing. In this section, we examine some of the issues involved with adverts in such transient environments. Adverts may be unavailable for several reasons: e.g., the UDP connection may fail or a peer may be temporarily unavailable or has disconnected, etc. Further, out-of-date adverts can also linger around the Rendezvous caches long after the peers that advertised them have disappeared. Such issues have to be addressed by any distributed system that has transient connections.

For example, consider the following two scenarios:

1. *Intranet File Sharing Application:* Here, a company creates a simple Jxta file sharing application that has a number of persistent servers that contain files that multiple (and transient) users wish to access on a daily basis.
2. *A Chat Application:* here, the same company has implemented a decentralized chat application (i.e., similar functionality to ICQ). Here all users are transient; i.e., they are continually logging on and off.

In the first case, a peer joins the network and will want to discover files in which it may be interested. Each advert it discovers contains the file name and location, with respect to the unique peer ID, on the Jxta network. Therefore, when it logs off, it will certainly want to remember its cached adverts from previous runs because files on the network will be continually available on the set of persistent peers.

Therefore, here, the *cm* directory should *not* be flushed, as the cache will remain persistent and will efficiently allow each peer to bootstrap and immediately be aware of all previously accessed files on the network. Therefore, in this case the peer itself acts as a local cache (i.e., like a super-peer) for the files in which it is interested.

In the second case however, peers can advertise themselves in a number of ways, e.g., as a chat service or a pipe[3]. When a peer joins the network, there is a high probability that the previously cached adverts are mostly out of date. For example, other peers may have logged off and then logged back onto

---

[3] In some ways, the use of a Jxta service can be somewhat redundant because in most cases it can be represented as a pipe. A service provides a labelling mechanism (i.e., a chat service) along with a pipe (for connection to that chat service). However, a pipe can itself be advertised as a chat pipe and therefore we do not have to use the Jxta service framework at all. The difference is only semantic.

the network. It is important therefore here to realise that every new advert, no matter how it is advertised, is unique, due to the unique identifiers being assigned to the advert.

Therefore, when the peer logs back onto the network and reloads its cache, these adverts may well be out of date, and not resolve to a living peer. Even though the peer may advertise itself using a unique name, it will create a new advert each time it logs on, but each advert can be discovered using this unique string. This leads to several adverts being discovered for each peer, but only one will be valid.

12.3.5 Expiration of Adverts

Apart from the existence of invalid adverts, there are reasons why you may not want to expire adverts that are perceived to be no longer available. For example, a node might have been temporarily disconnected from the network but is still available because it has temporarily gone out of range of the wireless network signal. When such a node returns then its advert (and functionality) will be available again.

The highly transient nature of the peers within such a network makes it impossible to retain a current set of valid adverts and therefore, it is important to account for this type of failure. This situation of out-of-date adverts is amplified with the introduction of Rendezvous points which are themselves caching services.

There will always be a trade-off because any accurate management of valid adverts will surely result in an extremely high overhead of a fine-grained temporal quantization of checking and updating cached adverts. The update quantization time would have to be so frequent (i.e., several times a second for example) that the network would be completely flooded with update requests and render it completely useless.

Furthermore, such a mechanism could never be completely fault tolerant free because even if the problem of current availability of adverts were solved, it would be impossible to tackle the transient connectivity of the peers that they were advertising. For example, by the time a peer has retrieved this advert, the service provider for the advert may have left the network making the advert temporarily (or even permanently) unavailable.

Using systems like Jxta and gaining such experience really amplify the points raised in the P2P environments chapter (see Chapter 2). Within P2P or transient networks, **it is far easier to deal with failure in a P2P network than it is to eliminate it.**

Invalid adverts can be highly confusing when using Jxta for the first time. For example, when you are testing your program, you may have forgotten to flush adverts from a previous run and discover these instead of the new adverts just advertised. In this case, your program may intermittently fail and seem to exhibit somewhat inconsistent behaviour, i.e., since sometimes it could work and other times not, depending on the ordering of the cached adverts.

12.4 Conclusion

In this chapter, three simple Jxta applications were illustrated to give the reader a feel for what the Jxta programming environment is like. Due to the P2P environment Jxta is designed to work within, there are a number of configuration and inevitable failure issues with which such a system must be able to deal. To this end, each Jxta node has a configurator application to help it specify what role it is playing within the network (e.g., a peer, a Rendezvous, a relay, etc.) and how it connects to the other peers within the network.

The Jxta approach is flexible but extremely fine grained because each peer is required to manage its own settings. Other systems (e.g. Web services, see Chapter 13) deploy services within hosting environments which perform a lot of this kind of housekeeping for you. Such systems however, do lose the individual configurability, which may be important in certain deployment conditions.

The transient nature of P2P networks was illustrated later in this chapter when the issue of advert availability was addressed. Adverts in such highly dynamic networks are likely to fail sometimes because they may be out of date or the resource they are advertising may be temporarily or permanently unavailable. These issues illustrate the importance of dealing with failure as a normal occurrence in such networks.

13

Web Services Deployment

The basic building blocks for using Web services are the service-oriented architecture (SOA) and Internet protocols. Web services are based on standards and standards-based technologies, which ensure applications are compliant, thereby enabling program-to-program interoperability. Within an SOA, such services can be represented, advertised, discovered and communicated within a dynamic environment. In this chapter, the standardized Web service technologies, SOAP, WSDL and UDDI that can enable such an environment, are outlined. Further, a short overview of how such technologies can be installed and used within a popular hosting environment is given.

13.1 SOAP

The submission of SOAP v1.1 to the WC3 (by 11 vendors in May 2000)[1] and the subsequent starting of the XML Protocols Working Group were significant events in the Web services history. Since then, the software industry has entered a consolidation phase and begun to broadly adopt the use of SOAP, WSDL and UDDI. SOAP v1.2 reached recommendation status in June 2003, which is the highest recommendation of a standard that the WC3 can give.[2] To illustrate the level of support, SOAP has currently been implemented in over 60 languages on over 20 platforms.

Simple Object Access Protocol (SOAP) is a "protocol that can be used to exchange structured information in a decentralized, distributed environment" [92]. It is a simple protocol that you may use, but not necessarily need to write, which allows users exchange information in a lightweight fashion, requiring a minimal amount of overhead. It provides an XML format for sending

---

[1] UserLand, Ariba, Commerce One, Compaq, Developmentor, HP, IBM, IONA, Lotus, Microsoft and SAP

[2] However, WC3 does not call its specifications standards because it does not have the official standing of a standards organization, such as the International Organization for Standardization.

messages which is independent of programming language or computer platform. It also allows this communication to occur over HTTP, which simplifies things greatly; e.g., it helps with firewalls and simplifies communication (i.e., you don't need socket servers listening on oddly numbered ports).

13.1.1 Just Like Sending a Letter...

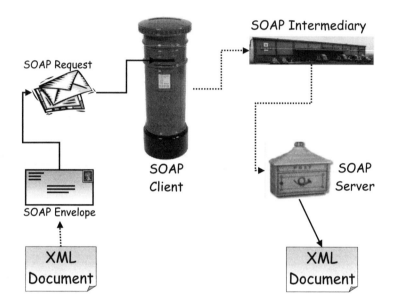

Fig. 13.1. SOAP provides an envelope for the XML message, just like a real envelope.

A SOAP message is analogous to a letter, as depicted in Fig. 13.1. First you write a letter and then put it in an envelope, which includes the receiver's address and other routing information (e.g., specifying air mail), plus a stamp representing a means of payment.

In SOAP, you write a document, just like a letter but it is written in XML. Then you pop your XML document into a SOAP envelope. The SOAP envelope contains your document (in the *body* element) along with a header that can contain optional routing and security information; it could be used to add the name or identification of the sender for example (just as real letters that are sent to the United States have to).

The SOAP envelope basically allows you to wrap everything up in a convenient format without needing to alter the XML document that is being sent, just like our paper envelope counterpart.

Once the envelope has been created, it is converted into a SOAP request and passed to a SOAP client for delivery; just like putting our letter in a post box. The SOAP client takes this message and delivers it to the destination. Such a delivery may traverse several intermediate SOAP servers before it reaches its destination, just as a letter may be transported by bus then a plane, for example. The actual route the SOAP message travels through depends on the (optional) routing information that may have been included in the message header, e.g., like specifying *Air Mail* will, *it is hoped*, make your letter fly across to its destination.

When the SOAP message reaches its destination, it is handled by a receiver, i.e., a SOAP server. The SOAP server performs extra operations than our letter box counterpart however, as it unwraps the envelope for you and passes the Web service the message via whatever means it needs.

13.1.2 Web Services Architecture with SOAP

Web services enable *service virtualization* by separating the Web service interface, which is represented by WSDL (see Section 13.2.3), from the service implementation. There could potentially exist a number of implementations for a service that, for example, could enable it to work on various computer platforms. Web services remove these underlying technicalities and users only deal with the service interface and are not aware of or interested in how the functionality is implemented.

The *glue* that binds the implementation with the interface and specifies the data format (e.g., SOAP) and protocols (e.g., HTTP) for communicating with the service is defined in a separate section in the WSDL document. Typically, you define one interface and then insert the various bindings that that interface supports.

This architecture is illustrated in Fig. 13.3, which builds on the model described in Section 3.2.2. Here, a C++ client is invoking a Web service written in Java. The figure also gives the details of the various stages and how they relate to SOAP. SOAP messages are delivered from a client to a SOAP server in the following way:

- The user prepares a message that conforms to the service interface (i.e., the WSDL). For example, the service may have several input elements and therefore the message has to be formatted appropriately in order to convey this information correctly. This typically involves building up a list of variables or strings in the client's language (e.g., C++ here) in preparation.
- The user sends this message to the Web service:
  - The client sends the request to the SOAP client, typically as a method call (in this case in C++). Programmers never really need to deal with the XML directly; there are numerous utilities that do this for you.

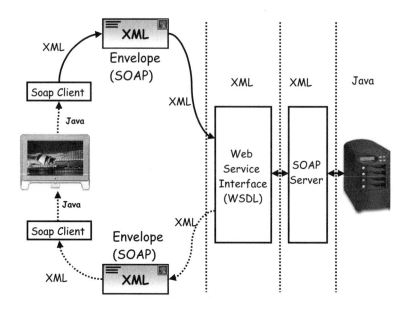

Fig. 13.2. An overview of how a message gets sent from a client to a Web service using SOAP.

–   The SOAP client takes this request and converts it into an XML message.
–   The SOAP client then puts this message into the body of a SOAP envelope and populates the other elements with optional information provided by the user.
–   The SOAP client then makes a SOAP request document, which adds things like destination and transport protocols to the SOAP message and sends this to the receiving SOAP server.
–   The SOAP server then transforms this XML message back to a language-dependent representation. For example, it could convert the XML to Java to invoke a function call within a Java class that implements the service.[3]
•   The SOAP server then uses the same mechanisms to send the response, if there is any, from the Web service back to the client.

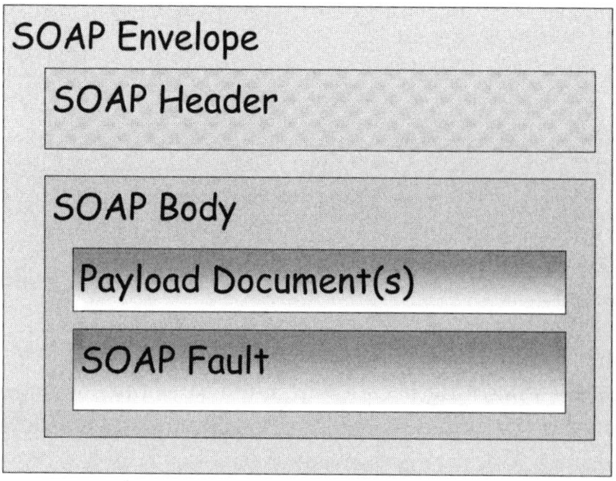

Fig. 13.3. The anatomy of a SOAP message.

13.1.3 The Anatomy of a SOAP Message

A SOAP message is an XML document containing the following elements, as shown in Fig. 13.3:

1. An *Envelope* that identifies the XML document as a SOAP message (*required*).
2. A *Header* element that contains information about the request defined in the SOAP body. For example, it might contain security, contextual or user profile information (*optional*).
3. A *Body* element that contains the actual *Payload Document*, containing the request and response in XML format (*required*).
4. A *Fault* element that provides error information that may have occurred while processing the message (*optional*).

In the example below, a request/response message for obtaining the price of a CD from a fictional CD retailer is given. In this example, we show a SOAP message with a *Header* element and a *Body* element:

```
<SOAP:Envelope
  xmlns:SOAP="http://schemas.xmlsoap.org/soap/envelope/"
  SOAP:encodingStyle="http://schemas.xmlsoap.org/soap/encoding/"

  <SOAP:Header>
    <person:mail
```

---

[3] You may have surmised by now that implementations of the Web are quite simple because the underlying infrastructure takes care of a number of housekeeping issues.

```
      xmlns:fan="//http://www.ibycds.com/">tapfan@ibycds.com
   </person:mail>
 </SOAP:Header>

 <SOAP:Body>
    <m:getCDPrice xmlns:m="http://www.islcds.com/">
        <name xsi:type="xsd:string">Smell the Glove</name>
    </m:getCDPrice>
 </SOAP:Body>
</SOAP:Envelope>
```

A SOAP *Envelope* normally requires defining two basic *namespaces* for the envelope and for the encoding, as shown. The namespace for the envelope (this is SOAP 1.1) must be included as it identifies the message as a SOAP message. Messages that do not follow this namespace declaration are considered invalid. Here, a namespace is also given for the encoding style, which represents the data used in the message.

The *Header* element is optional, but if included, must also be namespace qualified. Namespaces are analogous to Java *packages*: Java packages give a Java class a namespace in order to differentiate it from a class with the same name in a different package. Java classes are therefore grouped into packages by functionality, whereas namespaces just provide a unique context for an element. Here, the body contains information about the buyer of the CD.

The *Body* element is required and specifies the payload intended for the receiver of the message. Here it contains a procedure, called *getCDPrice*, which accepts one argument to specify the name of the CD for which you wish to obtain the price. The argument is typed as a string.

The example here provides only a brief overview. For a comprehensive description of SOAP documents, see [92] or [188].

13.2 WSDL

The Web Services Description Language (WSDL) is "an XML format for describing network services as a set of endpoints operating on messages containing either document-oriented or procedural-oriented information" [101]. WSDL describes an abstract interface for Web services while simultaneously allowing you to bind to a specific transport mechanism, such as HTTP. WSDL functions as a reusable Web service technology by abstracting the interface and providing a transport binding mechanism; i.e., the transport may change, but the payload persists. There are similar techniques employed in other technologies, e.g., Jxta pipes 10.3.3.

WSDL was developed by Microsoft, Ariba and IBM and V1.1 of the specification was accepted as a note and published on the Web site [101] and [104]. Twenty-two other companies then joined the submission (the largest number to date to support a joint submission) and therefore WSDL already has broad support.

WSDL documents can be flexibly organized by using the *import* element, which allows other files to be imported (e.g., other WSDL documents or XML schemas). When composing a WSDL document, the various sections (typically two or three) can be composed completely independently and then combined (or more important, reused) to form complete WSDL files. For example, two WSDL documents can import the same basic elements and yet include their own service elements to make the same service available at two physical addresses. WSDL documents are divided into two broad sections:

- **A Service Description:** an abstract definition for a set of operations and messages. The service description is reusable and contains information common to a certain category of services, such as message formats and port types (abstract interfaces).
- **The Implementation Details:** define how the interface maps onto the underlying concrete protocol binding and a network endpoint specification for the binding.

The following two sections give an overview of the contents of these two broad sections of a WSDL file. This is followed by giving a more in-depth anatomical description of a WSDL file, illustrating the various XML sections.

13.2.1 Service Description

Web service interfaces are defined in WSDL by using a *portType* XML element (illustrated in Section 13.2.3). The portType element in programming terms, is analogous to an object-oriented class as shown in Fig. 13.4. PortTypes consist of a collection of *operation* elements, each of which defines a specific function of the portType. In programming terms, this would be analogous to a method in a class.

Finally, within each *operation* you have associated messages, which are defined in a separate WSDL *message* element. The message element is an abstract definition of the data along with its data types and describes a one-way message, whether it is a single message request (input) or a single message response (output). It defines the name of the message and contains zero or more message part elements, which can refer to message parameters or message return values.

Each message has a type that can be specified by a schema (e.g., XSD) or can be composed arbitrarily to form complex types. Standard types can be inserted directly into the *message* section, whilst more custom types, e.g., complex types, are declared within the *types* WSDL element. The message elements are analogous to arguments passed to and from a method or function call.

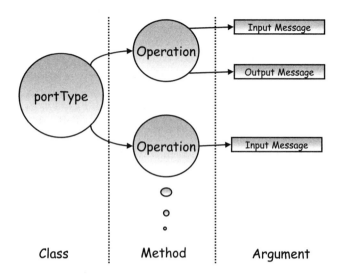

Fig. 13.4. The WSDL portType element contains operations that have input and (optionally) output arguments.

13.2.2 Implementation Details

There are three WSDL document elements that are used to bind the abstract interface to concrete endpoints:

- **Service:** is a collection or set of related endpoints (i.e., **ports**).
- **Port:** is a single endpoint that consists of a **binding** and a network address.
- **Binding:** is a protocol and data format specification for a particular port-Type.

A WSDL document defines a service as collections of network endpoints, or ports. A port is defined by associating a network address with a specific network binding or data format and different ports of a service can be located at geographically different locations. WSDL has specific binding extensions for the following protocols and message formats:

1. SOAP
2. HTTP GET/POST
3. MIME.

For example, Fig. 13.5 shows an interaction between a client and a server in a Web services scenario. In the first case, the Web service is invoked using a WSDL SOAP binding and the SOAP HTTP transport binding. The second

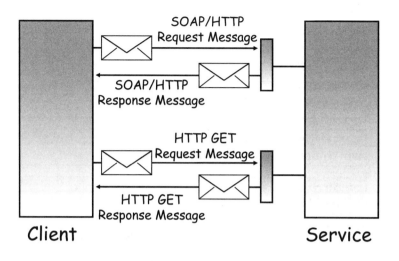

Fig. 13.5. An example of transport bindings that can be specified for WSDL.

scenario illustrates that the same Web service is invoked using the the WSDL HTTP GET/POST protocol binding.

WSDL makes a clear distinction between messages and ports. Messages define the abstract syntax and semantics of a Web service and are required. Ports, on the other hand, are concrete as they specify the network address where the Web service can be invoked. Ports are optional elements and therefore a WSDL file could contain just the abstract interface information and may not refer to any concrete implementation; i.e., WSDL files are decoupled from implementations and there can be multiple implementations of a single WSDL interface.

This design allows disparate systems to write implementations of the same abstract interface, thereby guaranteeing that the systems can talk to each other, as discussed in detail in Section 3.2.2.

13.2.3 Anatomy of a WSDL Document

In this section, an explanation of a simple WSDL file is given. For a comprehensive description, see [101].

Just as SOAP messages are encapsulated by an *Envelope* element, WSDL documents are encapsulated within an element called *definitions*. WSDL documents consist of a set of definitions, and although WSDL has seven definitions,

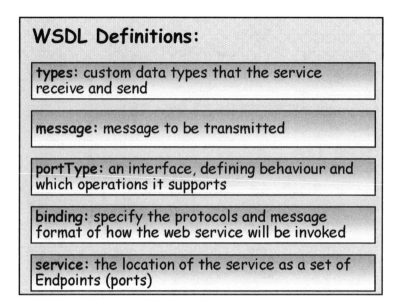

Fig. 13.6. An overview of a WSDL document.

a document is split into five main sections, illustrated in Fig. 13.6. The other two elements are *import*, described earlier and *documentation*, which can be used to provide human-readable documentation and can be included inside any WSDL element.

As part of the definitions tag itself, we first need to set up the *namespaces*, which give a context for elements:

```
<definitions name="SimpleService"
    targetNamespace="http://cleverfish.co.uk/wsdl/SimpleService.wsdl"
    xmlns="http://schemas.xmlsoap.org/wsdl/"
    xmlns:soap="http://schemas.xmlsoap.org/wsdl/soap/"
    xmlns:tns="http://cleverfish.co.uk/wsdl/SimpleService.wsdl"
    xmlns:xsd="http://www.w3.org/2001/XMLSchema">
```

In WSDL, namespaces are typically specified as a URI because URIs are unique. However, in fact, namespaces do not have to be URIs at all. For example, the first element shown above specifies a *targetNamespace* attribute. The targetNamespace is a convention of XML schema that enables the WSDL document to refer to itself. However, this address, *"http://cleverfish.co.uk/wsdl/SimpleService.wsdl"* does not actually have to exist; it's just a placeholder for the uniqueness of this document. The definitions element also specifies a default namespace (*xmlns=http://schemas.xmlsoap.org/wsdl/*), which gets attached to any element that hasn't defined one, such as the message or portType.

The *types* section is optional and depends on the complexity of the data-typing needs for the Web service. If you were defining a customer record, for example, then several typed fields would be needed, e.g., name, address, telephone number, etc, and therefore, this would have to be set up as a complex type. However, for a simple message, it could be defined using the following:

```
<message name="MyRequest">
    <part name="myRequestString" type="xsd:string"/>
</message>
<message name="MyResponse">
    <part name="myResponseString" type="xsd:string"/>
</message>
```

Here, the input and output types are defined using the simple *XSD* typing mechanism [99]. The *xsd* prefix identifies the message part as a string (xsd:string).

The portType tag defines an interface and the operations it supports, for example:

```
<portType name="RequestPortType">
    <operation name="aRequest">
        <input message="tns:MyRequest"/>
        <output message="tns:MyResponse"/>
    </operation>
</portType>
```

Here, the operation (aRequest) accepts an *input* message (MyRequest) and responds with an *output* message (MyResponse) and since we defined the types in the message definition, they are typed as strings. Note that the input and output messages to this operation are *namespace* qualified, using *tns* defined earlier.

The *binding* section of the file specifies how the portType operation will be transmitted on the wire, i.e., using any of the bindings described in Section 13.2.2. Here, we use the SOAP binding:

```
<binding name="aBinding" type="tns: RequestPortType">
<soap:binding style="document"
    transport="http://schemas.xmlsoap.org/soap/http"/>
        <operation name="aRequest">
            <soap:operation soapAction="aRequest"/>
            <input>
                <soap:body use="literal"/>
            </input>
            <output>
                <soap:body use="literal"/>
            </output>
        </operation>
```

```
</binding>
```

The binding is given a name (any) and a type, which is the portType that was defined earlier; i.e., we are specifying a binding for a portType. There can be any number of bindings for a specified portType.

SOAP is specified using the *soap:binding* element, which specifies a *style* attribute. There are two styles, either RPC-oriented or document-oriented. In the RPC case, the messages contain parameter and return values, whereas in the document style, the messages contain documents. The document style is used here.

The *transport* attribute specifies the transport binding for the SOAP protocol, e.g., HTTP in this case. The *soap:operation* element defines a SOAP action for the operations defined within the portType. Finally, for each operation a *soap:body* is specified, which defines how the message elements appear in the SOAP body element. The *use* attribute defines whether the message element is encoded using any encoding rules. Here, we chose a literal coding, i.e., no encoding rules.

The *service* definition specifies the location of the service:

```
<service name="MyService">
   <documentation>A do-not-a-lot service</documentation>
   <port binding="tns:aBinding" name="MyPort">
      <soap:address
         location="http://localhost:8080/axis/services"/>
      </port>
</service>
</definitions>
```

The *MyService* is bound to SOAP, so therefore the *soap:address* element is used to specify the URL, in this case, to the local Tomcat/Axis server running the service.

13.3 UDDI

Universal description, discovery and integration [100] is a service discovery protocol for Web services. It provides an on-line electronic registry, which serves as a kind of electronic *yellow pages* that allows applications to dynamically provide information about companies and the (Web) services that they offer. It provides a similar role to the Web service business community that a Jini lookup server does for the Jini Service community but whereas Jini is designed for the intranet, UDDI and Web services are designed for the Internet.

UDDI is a cross-industry effort driven by commercial sectors and the OASIS standards organization [167]. The UDDI standard was unveiled by Ariba, IBM, Microsoft and 33 other companies in September 2000.

The UDDI XML schema defines four core data types for business and service information each having an XML-based data structure containing mandatory and optional fields. They are called *businessEntity, businessService, bindingTemplate* and *tModel.* These core types can be used to represent three types of information:

- **White Pages:** which contain addresses, contacts, and other general information about a company or individual. So, for example, you could use this to search for a company that you already knew something about, e.g., its name or address, etc.
- **Yellow Pages:** this contains industrial classifications based on some standardized taxonomies, such as the North American Industry Classification System (NAICS) [168].
- **Green Pages:** contains technical information about Web services including references to specifications of interfaces for Web services.

Both WSDL and UDDI were designed to clearly delineate between abstract metadata and concrete implementations. In a typical usage scenario, a programmer contacts the UDDI's green pages to discover a Web service using some search mechanism. She would then extract the location of its WSDL definition from UDDI, which contains the service's abstract interface along with its network address.

For best practice techniques, there exists a document [169] that gives a detailed account of using WSDL in a UDDI registry.

13.4 Using Web Services

In this section, a brief overview is given on how to install Axis, a Web services hosting platform. A simple example Web service is given along with scripts necessary to deploy and invoke that service within the Axis environment. The notes here are brief but serve as a concise illustration of how Web services are developed and how they interact within the Web services environment.

13.4.1 Axis Installation

Apache Axis [189] is an open source implementation of a SOAP engine. It provides a framework for constructing SOAP processors, such as clients and servers, and contains implementations of such. Specifically, it has an implementation of a server that plugs into servlet engines so that Web services can be hosted using traditional Web server frameworks. It also supports WSDL (v.1.1) and creates a WSDL file for each Web service deployed using the platform. The Axis version used here (1.1) is written in Java but a C++ client-side implementation is also under development, at the time of writing.

In order to run Axis, you need to install (or have) an application server or servlet engine. Here, Jakarta Tomcat is used (version 4.1.x but not the LE version) and is executed using Java 1.4 (which has the Xerces XML parser). The following list describes the installation process:

1. Download and install Tomcat; see [190] and its various dependencies; it will be assumed that Tomcat is installed in */usr/tomcat/.*
2. Download and install Apache Axis; see [189]; in the configuration here, Axis is installed in the */usr/axis* directory.
3. In the Tomcat installation, there is a directory where Web applications are placed (*/usr/tomcat/webapps*). Copy the Axis */usr/axis/webapps/axis* here.
4. Start Tomcat (see below); it will, by default, run locally on port 8080
5. Go to the Axis home page on the server at *http://localhost:8080/axis/*. You should see a screen similar to the one displayed at the top of Fig. 13.8.
6. Press the first tag named *Validate the local installation's configuration*. This page will list the various dependencies needed for a correct installation (see Fig. 13.7). If there are problems, it will list them and provide solutions. Step through these one by one and reload this page to check that each problem has been solved.

Fig. 13.7. A happiness page for the Axis installation.

In the */usr/tomcat/webapps*) directory, there is a WEB-INF sub-directory, which contains the basic configuration information and sub-directories that contain, amongst other things, the Java libraries (in *lib* and the Web service classes to be deployed (in *classes*, see Section 13.4.2).

At this stage, some environment variables need to be set up to specify things like the Axis home directory, the library directory and the Java class-path needed for the compilation of this example. Below, a snippet from *.tcshrc* is given that shows how the various *jar* files from the */usr/tomcat/webapps/lib* directory are added to the classpath. Further, the *PATH* environment variable is updated for easy access to the start-up scripts for the Tomcat Web server:

```
setenv AXIS_HOME /usr/tomcat/webapps/axis
setenv AXIS_LIB $AXIS_HOME/WEB-INF/lib
setenv AXISCLASSPATH $AXIS_LIB/axis.jar:
$AXIS_LIB/commons-discovery.jar:
$AXIS_LIB/commons-logging.jar:
$AXIS_LIB/jaxrpc.jar:
$AXIS_LIB/saaj.jar:
$AXIS_LIB/log4j-1.2.8.jar:
$AXIS_LIB/xml-apis.jar:
$AXIS_LIB/xercesImpl.jar

setenv PATH /usr/tomcat/bin:$PATH
```

You can start the Tomcat Web server using the following script (in /usr/tomcat/bin):

```
startup.sh
```

and shut it down using the following script:

```
shutdown.sh
```

13.4.2 A Simple Web Service

Firstly, note that as with the other programming sections in this book, the source files and associated scripts can be downloaded from:

```
http://www.cleverfish.co.uk/peerbook/
```

The Web service given here provides a simple digit incrementor service. The code is trivial but provides a simple demonstration of what a Web service looks like in Java. The implementation increments a Java *Integer* but could easily be implemented in another language if hosted differently:

```
public class SilverService {
    public Object getIncrement(Object number) {
        if (number instanceof Integer)
            number = new Integer(((Integer)number).intValue()+1);
```

```
            return number;
        }
    }
```

You'll notice straight away how simple this looks, unlike other systems, e.g., Jini and Jxta, illustrated elsewhere in this book. Web services do not need to be persistent (even though OGSA-based services provide this facility) and therefore do not need any special requirements on the service side. Further, there is a strong focus on service environments, which provide behind-the-scenes mechanisms to help with the deployment details, e.g., creating the WSDL, locating the class, etc. Therefore, what is left is a very open, flexible and simple service-side implementation.

The *SilverService* class simply checks for an appropriately wrapped class, i.e., a Java *Integer*, and increments its value. The returned *Integer* object contains this incremented value. The service is not typed; i.e., the inputs and outputs are Java Objects but it would be trivial to change these to Integers if you wanted to restrict your class to such object types.

When developing Web services within Axis, the class files need to be located by the deployment tools and therefore the simplest thing to do is to make sure the compiled Java class (i.e., bytecode) is put in the */usr/tomcat/webapps/classes* directory, which is automatically added to the default *classpath*. You can provide your individual services within Java packages also, if you wish to organize your services into directories.

13.4.3 Deploying a Web Service Using Axis

To deploy a service, you need to configure an Axis Web Service Deployment Descriptor (WSDD) file to describe the service you wish to deploy:

```
<deployment xmlns="http://xml.apache.org/axis/wsdd/"
    xmlns:java="http://xml.apache.org/axis/wsdd/providers/java">

  <service name="SilverService" provider="java:RPC">
    <parameter name="className" value="SilverService"/>
    <parameter name="allowedMethods" value="*"/>
  </service>
</deployment>
```

The WSDD format contains a *deployment* XML element. This defines the "Java" namespace along with a *service* element, which actually defines the service. The *service* element may have any or all of the following:

1. a request flow
2. a pivot Handler, which is the service *provider*
3. a response flow.

In our case, the provider is "java:RPC," i.e., remote procedure caller (*RPCProvider*). The *parameter* tag specifies which class (i.e., *SilverSevice*) the provider should load and which methods in that class to call. Here, we specify that any public method on our class may be called. Alternatively, the accessible methods could be restricted by using a space or comma separated list of available method names. WSDD files are fairly reusable and typically only require minor modifications for use by other services, e.g., service name and class name.

The WSDD description is then passed to the Axis *AdminClient*, which compiles a Web service based on these parameters and deploys the Web service in the appropriate place, as follows:

```
java -cp $AXISCLASSPATH org.apache.axis.client.AdminClient
    -lhttp://localhost:8080/axis/services/AdminService deploy.wsdd
```

Alternatively, you could utilize the Axis Java Web services (JWS) deployment mechanisms by renaming (or copying) your SilverService.java implementation to */usr/tomcat/webapps/SilverService.jws*. The Apache subsystem will then automatically locate the file, compile the class and convert the SOAP calls correctly into Java invocations of the service class. However, JWS is only intended to deploy simple services.

To ensure that the Web service has been installed correctly, you can check the Web services deployed within the Axis environment using a Web browser and navigating to the *View the list of deployed Web services* option on the Axis configuration page (see upper part of Fig. 13.8). This should display something similar to the bottom screen shot, if the service has been deployed correctly.

13.4.4 Web Service Invocation

The following code provides the client-side implementation of the Web service:

```
import org.apache.axis.client.Call;
import org.apache.axis.client.Service;
import javax.xml.namespace.QName;

public class Client {
    public static void main(String [] args) {
        try {
            String endpointURL =
              "http://localhost:8080/axis/services/SilverService";

            Integer in = new Integer(10);
            Service service = new Service();
            Call call = (Call) service.createCall();

            call.setTargetEndpointAddress(
```

Fig. 13.8. The screen shot on the top shows the Axis home page, giving a list of utilities. The bottom shot shows the list of the deployed Web services, including the SilverService just deployed.

```
                new java.net.URL(endpointURL) );
        call.setOperationName(
                new QName("SilverService", "getIncrement") );

        Object ret = call.invoke( new Object[] { in } );

        System.out.println("Object = " + ret.getClass().getName());
        System.out.println("Number Returned : " + ret.toString());
    } catch (Exception e) {
        System.err.println(e.toString());
    }
  }
}
```

First, we create new Axis *Service* and *Call* objects, which store metadata about the service to invoke. We set the endpoint address URL to specify the actual location of the class. Here, our SilverService class is located in the *http://localhost:8080/axis/services/* directory. We then set the operation name, i.e., the method call that we wish to invoke on the service (i.e., get-Increment()). We can now invoke the service by passing it any Java Object or an array of Java Objects. Here, we pass it a Java *Integer* containing the value 10.

To invoke the service, the client-side implementation (Client.java) is executed, as follows:

```
java Client
```

which will produce the following output:

```
Object = java.lang.Integer
Number Returned : 11
```

13.4.5 Cleaning Up and Un-Deploying

To un-deploy the Web service, you first need to create a corresponding *WSDD undeployment* file to the previous deployment file, as follows:

```
<undeployment xmlns="http://xml.apache.org/axis/wsdd/">
 <service name="SilverService"/>
</undeployment>
```

Be careful to check the spelling of the service name. If this is incorrect then the service will not be un-deployed and no corresponding error will be provided to indicate this. The un-deployment file is passed to the *AdminClient* Axis class for processing:

```
java -cp $AXISCLASSPATH org.apache.axis.client.AdminClient
    -lhttp://localhost:8080/axis/services/AdminService undeploy.wsdd
```

Again, you can verify that the service has been correctly un-deployed by checking the list of deployed services using a Web browser as described earlier.

13.5 Conclusion

In this chapter, a concise overview of SOAP, WSDL and UDDI was given. SOAP provides an envelope for sending XML messages to specify routing details and other information without needing to modify the actual message. WSDL provides an interface definition for the Web service along with its deployment details in such a way as to decouple the interface from the implementation. This decoupling allows for the virtualization of services in that a service interface can have multiple back-end implementations. UDDI serves as a lookup server or yellow pages for Web services and can be used to retrieve the locations of a Web service's interface, based on search criteria. Finally, an example Web service implementation was given along with the steps involved in hosting it within a popular Web services hosting environment.

Part IV

From Web Services to Future Grids

In this theme, we take a look at how the Grid community is adopting and exposing its functionality as Web services, in the form of OGSA-based distributed services. OGSA services re-introduce the notion of state to a Web service so that services can be referenced or monitored and that steering applications can receive distributed notifications of state changes.

This convergence of technologies (if widely adopted by both communities) could represent a major step forward in the goal of ubiquitous deployment, which is needed to make the Grid dream a reality. This integration and related issues are discussed in Chapter 14, the final chapter of this book.

Looking at the more longer-term future, as Grid deployment increases, other technologies such as P2P will become increasingly more important to address the issues of scalability and discovery in real-world dynamic environments, which some applications are already employing. However, for this to be successful, any proposals need to undergo a standardization (or other) process or be accepted by the community at large. There is currently much effort in this direction [193] [194].

14

OGSA

The Globus toolkit (GT) is the de facto open source toolkit for Grid computing. The functionality of the GT version 3.x is exposed as a collection of virtual Open Grid Services Architecture services [21]. OGSA services, or Grid services, extend Web services, discussed in the previous two chapters, to add features that are often needed within distributed applications. Specifically, OGSA adds *state* to Web services in order to control the remote service during its lifetime. Whereas Web services are *stateless*, as noted in Section 3.4.1, OGSA-based services are *stateful*. OGSA services represent the GT's various components, e.g., GRAM, MDS, etc., described in Chapter 4, using this unified representation and can be aggregated and used within virtual organizations in a number of different ways.

However, the road to OGSA realisation has not been easy. During the two years from its conception, 2002, the infrastructure for Web services was defined through the Open Grid Services Infrastructure specification. This specification defined the extensions to WSDL needed in order to represent and enable stateful Web services. The designers of OGSI introduced the notion of a Grid service, which *extended* a basic Web service to attach a number of additions to which a Grid service must adhere. Stateful resources within OGSI were modelled as Web services that support the GridService *portType* (see Section 13.2.2), which is an extension of the WSDL portType.

This approach led to much unrest in the Web service community for several reasons discussed in Section 14.3.1 but principally because Grid services did not conform to Web service standards. For these reasons, OGSI has been surpassed by a new specification called the Web Services Resource Framework that addresses these criticisms. In the GlobusWORLD conference at the beginning of 2004, Foster [139] described Globus as "a balancing act between addressing short-term needs (software engineering and development plus supporting user needs) and long-term needs (pushing development of standards, conducting research and keeping the project on the 'bleeding edge')." He added that "Globus must be a research and a development organization."

This chapter therefore will be split into three sections. The first section will describe the OGSA architecture, the second OGSI and the third the newly adopted WSRF, upon which the Globus toolkit version 4, will be based.

14.1 OGSA

The Open Grid Services Architecture Framework is the Globus and IBM vision for the convergence of Web services and Grid computing. OGSA was presented at the GGF in February 2002 and described in the accompanying paper [21], which outlines this new architecture for distributed systems integration. The GGF has since set up an Open Grid Services working group to review and refine the architecture.

OGSA adopts the service-oriented architecture, discussed in Section 3.3 in order to expose Grid functionality as collections of service-oriented software assets. To this end, the OGSA authors define how the various Grid technologies can be implemented and applied through the use of this service-oriented approach. They noted "we view a Grid as an extensible set of **Grid services** that may be aggregated in various ways to meet the needs of VOs, which themselves can be defined in part by the services that they operate and share" [21].

In the next section, Grid services are described and put into context with the current Web services.

14.1.1 Grid Services

At the core of the OGSA specification and implementation (see Section 14.2) is a *Grid service*. A Grid service is "a Web service that provides a set of well-defined interfaces and that follows specific conventions" and more specifically it is "a (potentially transient) stateful service instance supporting reliable and secure invocation (when required), lifetime management, notification, policy management, credential management, and virtualization" [21].

Simply put, within the OGSA model, everything is represented as a Grid service, whether it is a computational resource, a storage resource, a network, an application, a database, etc. The difference between OGSA and Web services is that within OGSA, the Grid services can be managed, i.e., created, monitored, destroyed, etc. The OGSA architecture therefore allows an application to obtain references to Grid service instances that can be used to monitor a service and access its local data directly, similar in principle to the functionality provided by distributed object systems. However, all of this is achieved within XML documents that are passed between the Grid services, in the same way as Web services.

Grid services are built on Web services for a number of reasons. First, Web services support dynamic discovery and composition in heterogeneous environments by using WSDL to describe the Web service in such a way that it is independent of any specific implementation of that service (see Section 13.2.3). Second, there has been a widespread adoption of Web services technology and this helps for two reasons: first, there are a number of tools that already exist, e.g., WSDL to language convertors; and the actual uptake of the technology is vast, which helps the ubiquitous deployment needed to realise a truly global Grid (see Section 4.2). Further, Web services are built on standards-based technology, which is necessary for such widespread adoption (see Section 4.5.2).

At the core of Grid services, the focus is on the management of transient service instances. Within a Grid computing environment, services often need to be created dynamically, as and when a service is needed. As an example, let's take a look at a simple *migration* scenario. Migration involves moving the execution of a job across the network from one machine to another, perhaps because the job is not running quickly enough at present. There are several steps needed for this simple scenario, as shown in Fig. 14.1.

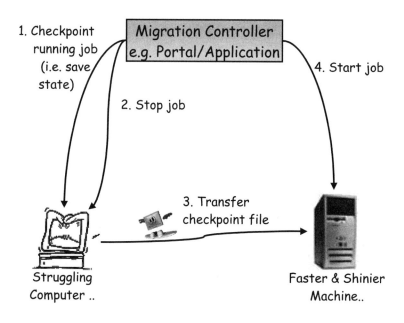

Fig. 14.1. A simple job migration scenario.

The first step is to save the current state of the job that you wish to migrate, which is called *checkpointing*. Typically, a job checkpoints by saving its state to a file. This information can be passed to another instance of the same job at a later stage in order to resume the progress. Second, the first job needs to be stopped because any further work would be redundant as it would not be *checkpointed*.

Checkpointing can be achieved in numerous ways depending on the particular scenario and the application that is controlling the migration. For example, a job could checkpoint itself and then coordinate the rest of the migration process by using the relevant services directly or a portal could manage these tasks. In this example, the migration process is controlled by a third-party migration controller, which monitors the job's progress and makes a decision on whether to migrate the job to another machine based on some quality of service requirement: e.g., perhaps the job is running too slow to complete by a given time. Such coordination could be achieved by using a communication mechanism between the controller and the job (e.g., sockets, Jxta, Jini, etc.) or it could be implemented with a Grid service directly using the stateful distributed systems mechanisms.

Once the job has been stopped the checkpoint file needs to be moved to the machine to which the job is being migrated. This would typically be achieved by using a Grid data service, e.g., GridFTP. There may already exist such a service on both machines but, if not, one may need to be dynamically started and have a lifetime for the duration of the file copy.

Once the file is in place, another Grid service, e.g., GRAM, needs to be discovered and invoked in order to submit the job to the new machine. Again, such a service may be associated with this one operation and consequently transient in nature, having a lifetime equivalent to the lifetime of the job (since GRAM monitors the job during execution). When the job starts, it reads the data from the checkpoint file and resumes execution. This example is simple but it does illustrate the types of services needed and their potential transient deployment.

14.1.2 Virtual Services

Grid services, like Web services, are *virtual services*. Virtual services are services that provide a consistent interface to diverse back-end implementations as described in Section 3.2.2. This virtualization of services is essential for overlaying services on heterogeneous collections of devices, which are inherent within a Grid. Access to the resources therefore becomes transparent, which allows the mapping of multiple logical resource instances onto the same physical resource, which is a necessity for providing state to the distributed OGSA services.

Virtual services appear in other systems described in this book. For example, Jxta can provide the same behaviour and have multiple back-end implementations of the same service interface. Jini, on the other hand deals strictly with distributing Java objects and through the use of RMI and Java proxies makes it unsuitable for service virtualization.

Within the context of the Grid, the virtual Grid services help to provide a virtual overlay across the various Grid resources, providing the ability to map common service semantic behaviour onto multiple platforms; e.g., the same service could be built for Linux, Solaris and Windows machines, and the user would not realise (or care) which platform was hosting the service.

14.1.3 OGSA Architecture

OSGA uses WSDL (see Section 13.2.3) to describe Grid services. OGSA proposed several new WSDL *portTypes* that can be used to access this added functionality, which were refined by the OGSI specification. These will be described in the next section.

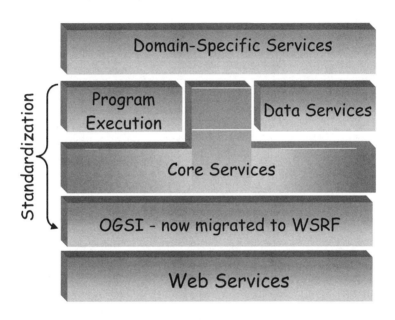

Fig. 14.2. The open Grid services architecture showing the OGSI layer that provides the infrastructure to expose OGSA services.

Figure 14.2 shows how OGSI fits in with the OGSA architecture. At the core of a Grid service is the Web service framework that enables XML messages to be sent between distributed processes. At the next level there is the OGSA infrastructure that builds on Web services to provide the stateful behaviour that a Grid service requires. Here, this is provided by OGSI but this is now specified using different syntax within the WSRF.

Even though the manner and syntax in which the OGSA services are defined has changed, this does not affect the semantic behaviour of the resulting services; i.e., both provide stateful Web services for representing network-enabled components on the Grid. This is indicated at the left-hand side of the figure, which emphasises the fact that the middle three layers of the architecture are currently going through a standardization process, i.e., still under debate.

The core Globus services are unlikely to change significantly but their external service representation may be tuned. The fact that these may be built upon OGSI or WSRF makes little difference to the outcome; it's really just syntax. The core services are outlined in Section 14.2.1 and the more advanced services build upon the core services to expose greater functionality and so on. At the top of the architecture, we have the domain-specific services that could be as specific as solving a particular problem or again represent common functionality for a subset of application domains.

14.2 OGSI

The open Grid services infrastructure is concerned with creating the standard interfaces that enable OGSA-based services. OGSA lays the foundations, whilst OGSI concentrates on the details of the interfaces that are required for OGSA. OGSI defines a component model by using extended WSDL and XML schema definitions. "OGSI is concerned primarily with creating, addressing, inspecting, and managing the lifetime of stateful Grid services" [21]. It also defines mechanisms for asynchronous notification of state change.

Specifically, the OGSI specification defines a number of WSDL extensions (some of which have analogous support in WSDL 2.0 [102]) that define the following functionality (a list of the corresponding portTypes and operations is given in Fig. 14.3):

1. **Grid Service Descriptions and Interfaces:** provides descriptions of the Grid service interface via GWSDL (Grid WSDL), an extension to the WSDL standard contain the Grid extensions. OGSI allows descriptions of the actual instance of the Grid service; e.g., the instance could potentially be stateful and transient and needs to be addressable.
2. **Service Data:** OGSI extends WSDL to allow users to gain access to a service's state information, e.g., a service's internal data; analogous to access methods on a Java object, e.g., setX(), getX(), etc. OGSI defines mechanisms that allow both querying (pull model) and subscription-based (push model) access to the data. The subscription-based access is similar to attaching a *Java Listener* to an object or subscribing to a newsgroup. Within OGSI, essentially, you subscribe to a data element and thereafter any change occurring on that element is sent to you (via notification). OGSI defines the *NotificationSource*, *NotificationSink*, and *Notification-Subscription* WSDL portTypes for this purpose.
3. **Naming and Name Resolution:** a Grid service can be dynamically created and therefore you need to obtain a reference in order to gain access to its state information. OGSI defines a two-level naming scheme for

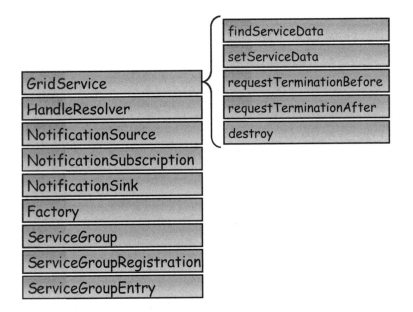

Fig. 14.3. A list of the OGSI portTypes used to define the various interfaces necessary. Also the operations defined by the Grid service portType are shown.

this purpose: a Grid Service Handle (GSH) and a Grid Service Reference (GSR). The GSH is an invariant abstract globally unique name that identifies the service instance. It is guaranteed to be unique from all other service instances but has no protocol or instance-specific information. The GSR, on the other hand, encapsulates the information required to interact with a particular service instance. For example, in a SOAP environment, the GSR will typically contain the WSDL *service* and *binding* information (see Section 13.2.3). Within one execution, you could potentially have many different GSRs if the job migrates from machine to machine but it will retain the same GSH. OGSI contains a resolver function therefore to extract the current GSR from the GSH, which is performed by the *HandleResolver* OGSI portType.

4. **Service Life Cycle:** OGSI provides factories for creating transient Grid services. The *Factory* OGSI portType is used to create a Grid service instance. The *destroy GridService* operation is used to destroy a service instance. Further, OGSI allows users to specify the lifetime of a service, i.e., when a service can or should be terminated. OGSI uses a *soft-state* approach, where services are created with a specified lifetime, using the *requestTerminationAfter* (earliest termination time) or *requestTerminationBefore* (latest termination time) OGSI *GridService* operations. The initial lifetime can be extended by request and if the time period expires

then the hosting environment is free to terminate the service instance and reclaim any resources.

5. **Fault Type:** OGSI represents service faults (or exceptions) in a common format. The fault model consists of a standard XSD type, *ogsi:FaultType* that defines two required elements: the originating service and a timestamp. It also defines several optional elements including descriptions of the fault, a fault code and extensibility elements that can be used to convey custom information.

6. **Service Groups:** OGSI allows users to represents groups of services. This is particularly useful for virtual hosting environments, which can group all services that it has created within a VO, for example. OGSI defines three portTypes for this purpose, as shown in Fig. 14.3: *ServiceGroup*, *ServiceGroupRegistration* and *ServiceGroupEntry*.

There exist around half a dozen independent implementations of the OGSI specification. In the next section, a brief overview of one such implementation, the Globus Toolkit, version 3, is given.

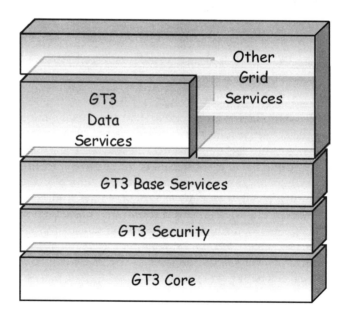

Fig. 14.4. GT3 architecture.

14.2.1 Globus Toolkit, Version 3

GT3, officially released in mid-2003, is based on the OGSI specification. All services from GT2, described in Chapter 4, have been adapted to conform to the OGSI specification. This section briefly outlines the structure and contents of this toolkit.

Figure 14.4 illustrates the architecture of the GT3 toolkit. At the lower level you have the GT3 core, which implements the core OGSI infrastructure to enable the other services to be exposed as Grid services. For example, the *GridService* core is implemented here, e.g., obtaining references and handles, the notification framework, the state management and service data, as described in Section 14.2.

The next layer implements the GT3 security layer, which adapts the mechanisms outlined in Section 4.7.2 to work within the service-oriented framework technology stack. For example, Globus has created a new secure protocol, called *httpg*, which is based around the transport layer security mechanisms, described in Section 8.5, e.g., TLS and SSL. They have also adapted the SOAP layer security based on *WS-Security* [187], *XML Encryption* [186] and *XML Signature* [185] standards. For mutual authentication, delegation, etc., X. 509 certificates are used in a similar fashion to those described in Section 4.7.2.

The next layer consists of the GT2 components translated to Grid services, e.g., MDS, GridFTP, GRAM, etc., plus the addition of new services that have been developed since GT2, e.g., a file streaming service, a reliable file transfer service and a managed-job service. See [28] for more information.

The structure of the toolkit is built to reuse functionality of the lower levels and it is anticipated that many new services will be implemented, as illustrated in Fig. 14.4, by the Globus team itself and other services created by other companies and organizations. Within GT3, an example of a higher-level service is illustrated here, for replica management of data files stored across the Grid. This service utilizes other data services already implemented in order to replicate and catalogue data. Since the release of v2.4, the Globus Web site has experienced more than 10,000 downloads per month and therefore momentum is building and many groups are already developing such services.

14.3 WSRF

In parallel with the work on OGSI through the GGF, the Web services community were working on standardizing their own components which related to aspects of the OGSI specification. In particular, WS-Addressing [103] was developed that provides a transport-neutral mechanism for representing *service endpoints* to Web services, which duplicates the work on the Grid handles and references, described in Section 14.2. Further, the OGSI specification resulted in a number of criticisms from the Web services community, which in turn, compromised Globus' goal of ubiquity. Consequently, a compromise was reached through the WSRF [25] and [184].

On the 20th January 2004, Akamai, The Globus Alliance, HP, IBM and Sonic Software announced new Web service specifications that integrated Grid and Web services standards [26]. This resulted in two proposed infrastructures, which are a repackaging and rearrangement of OGSI: the Web Services Resource Framework and Web Services Notification (WS-Notification).

In a keynote speech, Foster noted: "OGSA is a work in progress, but it's moving forward rapidly" [139]. He further acknowledged the recent "bump in the road" by the necessity to migrate OGSI to the WSRF. This effectively means that the OGSI Grid services are now considered deprecated and should therefore be converted to WSRF. Consequently, GT4 will be written according to the WSRF specification.

14.3.1 Problems with OGSI

Work on WSRF started late in the summer of 2003, following feedback on OGSI from the Web services community. The WSRF involved input from senior Web services architects, which resulted in a prompt release of the WSRF specification for public comment. The Web services community identified four main problems with the OGSI specification [183]:

- **Too Much in One Specification:** the OGSI specification defined a number of areas of functionality. Many felt that this was far too much for one specification and that a clear separation of functionality would provide a more flexible infrastructure for incremental adoption, allowing services to implement some things but not others. For example, a service may want to retain state but not implement event notification. WSRF therefore partitions the OGSI specification into six distinct areas, outlined in Section 14.3.3.
- **Incompatible with Web Services and XML Tooling:** OGSI used XML schema which were incompatible with XML tooling, e.g., JAX-RPC, and it extended the WSDL *portType* causing compatibility problems. WSRF uses standard XML schema, familiar to developers and existing tooling and annotates the *portType* definition, making it compatible with WSDL 1.0.
- **Too Object Oriented:** Within OGSI, a Grid service is a Web service that encapsulates the resources state; i.e., both the service and resource states are coupled. Therefore, current Web services would have to be extended and rewritten to create a Grid service. In WSRF, the service and the resource state are separated; see Section 14.3.2.
- **Relied on WSDL 2.0:** OGSI exploited constructs from the promised WSDL 2.0 specification, which had been delayed in coming, resulting in difficulty with existing Web services tooling. WSRF conforms to the WSDL 1.0 specification entirely.

14.3.2 Grid Services or Resources?

The basic requirement addressed by both OGSI and WSRF is the ability to create, address, inspect, discover and manage stateful resources [182]. As noted previously (in Section 14.1.1), services that conform to OGSI specifications are called Grid services. Grid services in OGSI however *extended* Web services in order to provide this extra functionality. Such an approach was deemed *heavyweight* by the Web services community and therefore WSRF uses a different approach that separates the message processor (i.e., the Web service) from the resource (i.e., the stateful instance).

The essential difference here is that OGSI uses the same construct to represent a Web service and the stateful resource, whereas WSRF uses different constructs for both. Briefly, WSRF uses the so-called *implied resource pattern* to define the relationship between the Web services interface and resources. Any service that adheres to the implied resource pattern is called a *WS-Resource* and the properties of the WS-Resource can be accessed through the Web services interface.

The functionality of both an OGSI Grid service and a WS-Resource is essentially the same but the WSRF approach is more flexible in that it allows many-to-many mappings between Web services and any associated stateful resource.

14.3.3 OGSI Functionality in WSRF

For details of the conversion between OGSI and WSRF, see [183]. Briefly however, the WSRF is divided into five specifications along with the OGSI notification specification, resulting in six different areas:

- **WS-ResourceProperties:** covers the concept of WS-Resource and describes how one associates stateful resources using Web services. Further, it describes how a service's properties (i.e., stateful internal data) are retrieved, changed and deleted from a resource.
- **WS-ResourceLifetime:** allows a user to specify a lifetime for a WS-Resource.
- **WS-RenewableReferences:** describes how the WS-Addressing endpoint reference is annotated in order to provide the necessary information to retrieve a new reference when the current reference becomes invalid.
- **WS-ServiceGroup:** replaces the OGSI grouping mechanisms, described in Section 14.2.
- **WS-BaseFault:** replaces the OGSI representation for service faults or exceptions.
- **WS-Notification:** describes the publish/subscribe asynchronous notification models that can be used to listen for remote state changes or service data element updates. The WS-Notification has also been extended to include a variety of functions implemented in other event notification systems.

14.3.4 Globus Toolkit, Version 4

At the time of writing (February 2004), the GT4 toolkit is projected to be released officially (i.e., non-alpha or beta release) by mid-august 2004. This toolkit will consist of a transformation from GT3 OGSI-based services to WSRF-based services and associated documentation. Other near-term goals include providing *internationalization* support for languages other than English.

14.4 Conclusion

In this chapter, an overview of the Open Grid Services Architecture (OGSA) and corresponding specifications were given. OGSA is primarily concerned with extending Web services to include state information, necessary for distributed systems integration. There have been, to date, two specifications that have resulted from this architecture.

The first, the Open Grid Services Infrastructure (OGSI), extended Web services to create Grid services and used techniques which were outside the scope of current Web service standards and tooling but also duplicated other work within the Web services community. This resulted in the Web Services Resource Framework (WSRF) that addressed these shortfalls by subdividing the OGSI specification into six different areas and reporting to conform to current standards. We'll have to wait and see if this is accepted by the community at large.

A

Want to Find Out More?

This appendix contains a list of links to the core organizations and umbrella projects for many of the distributed systems discussed in this book. This list is by no means exhaustive but it does provide some pointers to on-line information for further reading.

A.1 Grid Computing

- **Global Grid Forum (GGF), http://www.ggf.org/** contains information about Grid-related events. There are three GGF meetings per year but the one held every October in Chicago is only for active working or research groups. The GGF is a forum of some 5000+ individual researchers and practitioners working on distributed computing or Grid technologies, and has a wide range of technical groups working on aspects of Grid technology and deployment.
- **GridForge, http://forge.gridforum.org/** is the working respository for GGF Working and Research Groups, housing the related documents through an open public comment process.
- **Globus: http://www.globus.org/** hosts the Globus middleware for Grid computing and all associated documentation.
- **GRIDSTART, http://www.gridstart.org/** contains information about the EU Framework 5 IST-funded Grid research projects. You can find links to CrossGrid, DAMIEN, DataGrid (EDG and EGEE), DataTAG, EGSO, EuroGrid, GRIA, GridLab and GRIP, along with a number of other projects that form the GRIDSTART cluster. The project's intention is to stimulate the widespread deployment of Grid technology by raising the awareness of potential users of the solutions already developed or being developed. They also organize IST Concertation Meetings on Grid Research, twice yearly, which hosts a number of plenary talks and European technical working groups.

- **UK e-Science, http://www.rcuk.ac.uk/escience/** is a cite where you can find more information about the UK e-Science program.
- **National e-Science Center: http://www.nesc.ac.uk/** is a site containing links to a number of projects within the UK e-Science program.
- **GridCafe, http://gridcafe.web.cern.ch/gridcafe/** is a place to learn various aspects of Grid computing, from the name and the dream to a list of concrete projects around the world.
- **Grid Technology Repository (GTR), http://gtr.globus.org/** was set up as a place for people to publish and discover work related to Grid technology.
- **The Grid Computing, http://www.gridcomputing.com/** information center is designed to promote the development of technologies which provide seamless and scalable access to wide-area distributed resources.
- **Grid Today, http://www.gridtoday.com/** provides daily news and information for the Grid community.
- **The Grid Report, http://www.thegridreport.com/** is a collection of news items about distributed and Grid computing. It contains the latest news and information about Grid computing; it's run by software engineers and its focus is for software engineers.
- **Grid Computing Planet, http://www.gridcomputingplanet.com/** is one of many sites run by JupiterWeb, the on-line division of Jupitermedia, which is a leading global provider of information, images, research and events for information technology, business and creative professionals. The Grid Computing Planet is in the EarthWeb information section and provides numerous articles, news events and so on, for Grid computing.
- **CCGrid, http://www.ccgrid.org/** is a yearly IEEE International Symposium on Cluster Computing and the Grid. It also hosts a number of workshops.

A.2 P2P Computing

- **Gnutelliums, http://www.gnutelliums.com/** provides a comprehensive directory of Gnutella clients for Windows, Linux/UNIX, and Macintosh, some of which are provided below:
  - **BearShare, http://www.bearshare.com** is a Windows file sharing program from *Free Peers, Inc.*
  - **Gnotella, http://www.gnotella.com** is clone of Gnutella for Windows.
  - **Gnucleus, http://gnucleus.sourceforge.net/** is an open Gnutella client for Windows.
  - **LimeWire, http://www.limewire.com** is a very popular Java-based Gnutella client.
  - **Phex, http://www.konrad-haenel.de/phex/** is also a Java client, based on William W. Wong's Furi.

- **Toadnode, http://www.toadnode.com** is an extensible platform for P2P networks. Its core functionality revolves around the ability to find, retrieve and distribute data between users across multiple networks.
- **Gnut, http://www.gnutelliums.com/linux_unix/gnut/** is a command-line client which implements the Gnutella protocol. It will run on a wide range of POSIX-compliant systems including: SunOS, Linux, FreeBSD, HP-UX and Win32.

- **P2P and XML in Business, http://www.xml.com/pub/a/2001/07/11/xmlp2p.html** provides an article discussing the integration of P2P and XML for businesses.
- **Peer-to-Peer Computing, http://p2p.ingce.unibo.it/** is a popular yearly conference on Agents and P2P Computing (AP2PC).
- **P2P4B2B, http://www.stratvantage.com/directories/p2pworkgroups.htm** is a site listing non-commercial peer-to-peer efforts. The sites listed are non-profit, open source or informational and have relevance to the business use of P2P technology. The sites also represent standards efforts.
- **O'Reilly OpenP2P.com, http://www.openp2p.com/** is a site dedicated to various articles on P2P-related technology. Always interesting!
- **Global and Peer-to-Peer Computing, http://gp2pc.lri.fr/** is an international yearly workshop held in conjunction with CCGrid.
- **Intel P2P Developer Center, http://www.intel.com/cd/ids/developer/asmo-na/eng/technologies/peertopeer/index.htm** is a site dedicated to technologies that can leverage the power of the existing end-user's resources on the Internet.

A.3 Distributed Object Computing

- **Jan Newmarch's Guide to JINI Technologies, http://pandonia.ca nberra.edu.au/java/jini/tutorial/Jini.xml** provides an on-line extensive guide to Jini Technologies.
- **The Distributed Component Object Model (DCOM), http://www.microsoft.com/com/tech/DCOM.asp** is a Web site for finding out about distributed DCM technology, which enables software distributed components to communicate in a reliable, secure, and efficient manner. It was previously called "Network OLE" and was based on the Open Software Foundation's DCE-RPC specification.
- **CORBA, http://www.corba.org/** is the home page for the Common Object Request Broker Architecture (CORBA) middleware. It contains a number of resources, CORBA success stories and pointers to the Object Management Group.

- **Object Management Group (OMG), www.omg.org** which is establishing a model-driven architecture through its worldwide standard specifications including CORBA, CORBA/IIOP, the UML, XMI, MOF, Object Services, Internet Facilities and Domain Interface specifications.
- **Jini, http://www.jini.org/** is a central place for finding out information about Jini. It contains new information, has discussion groups and allows users to exchange code and ideas.
- **Distributed Object Computing, http://www.yy.ics.keio.ac.jp/∼ suzuki/object/dist_comp.html** is a useful page containing a number of links and information about distributed object systems including CORBA, Jini, MOMs and distributed agents.

A.4 Web Services

- **The W3C, http://www.w3.org/** is the World Wide Web consortium, which is the foremost forum for information, commerce, communication and collective understanding for the Web-related technologies. The W3C develops interoperable technologies and releases specifications, guidelines, software and tools. For example, the W3C has developed the specifications for XML, SOAP and WSDL. It is the first stop on discovering standardized Internet technologies.
- **The W3C, http://www.w3.org/2002/ws/** is a starting point on the W3C Web site that lists Web service-related technologies on which W3C is currently working.
- **OASIS, http://www.oasis-open.org/** is a non-profit consortium, which attempts to drive the development and adoption of e-business standards. For example, it has developed specifications for ebXML and UDDI.
- **XML.com, http://www.xml.com/** provides various resources for XML including a section on Web services.
- **WebServices.org, http://www.webservices.org/** is a portal for finding out about Web services. It contains newsletters, introductions to Web services, news and numerous articles.
- **Web Services Architect, http://www.webservicesarchitect.com/** hosts a collection of articles and links for Web services from both a business and a technical perspective.
- **Microsoft's Web Services Developer Center, http://msdn.micro soft.com/webservices/** is a site dedicated to providing information to Web service developers. It hosts many useful articles of the use of various Web service technologies and lists the new Web service specifications.
- **IBM Developer Works for Web Services, http://www-136.ibm.co m/developerworks/webservices/** contains a number of technical articles and specifications about Web services and related technologies. It also has a download section and learning resources.

- **WS-I, http://www.ws-i.org/** is "an open, industry organization chartered to promote Web services interoperability across platforms, operating systems, and programming languages." It works with industry and standards organizations to respond to customer needs.
- **XMethods, http://www.xmethods.com/** lists the publicly available Web services. You can access the lists of Web services by using their UDDI server, for example, to dynamically discover and connect to available resources.
- **Web Services Journal, http://www.sys-con.com/webservices/** is an on-line resource that lists real-use cases of how various companies and organizations are deploying and using Web services. There is a news section that lists new incentives that are happening within the Web services world.
- **Java Technology and Web Services, http://java.sun.com/webser vices/index.jsp** covers the various Java tools and packages that can support the development and deployment of Web services.

B

RSA Algorithm

Figure B.1 shows an outline of the RSA algorithm for encryption, taken from Tanenbaum and van Steen [1]. For more information, please see the original text.

Find P and Q, two large (e.g., 1024-bit) prime numbers:

1. Choose E such that E is greater than 1, E is less than PQ, and E and $(P-1)(Q-1)$ are *relatively prime*, which means they have no prime factors in common. E does not have to be prime, but it must be odd. $(P-1)(Q-1)$ can't be prime because it's an even number.

2. Compute D such that $(DE - 1)$ is evenly divisible by $(P-1)(Q-1)$. Mathematicians write this as $DE = 1 \ (mod \ (P-1)(Q-1))$, and they call D the *multiplicative inverse* of E. This is easy to do -- simply find an integer X which causes $D = (X(P-1)(Q-1) + 1)/E$ to be an integer, then use that value of D.

3. The encryption function is $C = (T^\wedge E) \ mod \ PQ$, where C is the ciphertext (a positive integer), T is the plaintext (a positive integer), and $\wedge$ indicates exponentiation. The message being encrypted, T, must be less than the modulus, PQ.

4. The decryption function is $T = (C^\wedge D) \ mod \ PQ$, where C is the ciphertext (a positive integer), T is the plaintext (a positive integer), and $\wedge$ indicates exponentiation.

...and now:

- The *public key* is the pair (PQ, E).
- The *private key* is the number D.
- The product PQ is the *modulus* (often called N in the literature).
- E is the *public exponent*. D is the *secret exponent*.

Fig. B.1. An outline of the RSA public-key system, which is based on the difficulty of factoring large numbers that are the product of two prime numbers. This factoring problem has been studied for hundreds of years and still appears to be intractable.

References

1. Tanenbaum A and van Steen M (2002) *Distributed Systems, Principles and Paradigms*, Prentice-Hall.
2. Clip2, Gnutella Reflector Nodes, see *http://www.clip2.com*
3. SETI@Home, see *http://setiathome.ssl.berkeley.edu/*
4. Napster, see *http://www.napster.com/*
5. Jabber, see *http://www.jabber.org/*
6. Gnutella, see *http://gnutella.wego.com/*
7. Winamp, see *http://www.winamp.com/*
8. Nullsoft, see *http://www.nullsoft.com/*
9. Open Source Napster: Gnutella, see *http://slashdot.org/articles/00/03/14/094 9234.shtml*
10. AOL's Nullsoft creates software for swapping MP3s, see *http://news.com.com/ 2100-1023-237974.html?legacy=cnet*
11. Did AOL eat Gnutella for lunch?, see *http://dir.salon.com/tech/log/2000/03/15 /gnutella/index.html*
12. The Java Home Page, see *http://java.sun.com/*
13. J2EE, see emphhttp://java.sun.com/j2ee/
14. JMS, see emphhttp://java.sun.com/products/jms/
15. Jxta, see *http://www.Jxta.org/*
16. EJB, see emphhttp://java.sun.com/products/ejb/
17. Langley, A. The Trouble with JXTA, see *http://www.openp2p.com/pub/a/p2p/ 2001/05/02/jxta_trouble.html*
18. From P2P to Grids: Peers in a Client-Server World, Web site, see *http://www. cleverfish.co.uk/peerbook/*
19. Foster I, Kesselman C, Nick C, Tuecke S (2002) The Physiology of the Grid: An Open Grid Services Architecture for Distributed Systems Integration. Open Grid Service Infrastructure WG, Global Grid Forum, June 22, 2002. See website *http://www.gridforum.org/ogsi-wg/*. The OGSI working group. See https://forge.gridforum.org/projects/ogsi-wg
20. What is a Grid? a number of articles debating claims made by the original article [107], see *http://www.cs.cf.ac.uk/user/J.P.Giddy/debate.html*
21. Foster I, Kesselman C, Nick J and Tuecke S (2002) The Physiology of the Grid: An Open Grid Services Architecture for Distributed Systems Integration, see *http://www.globus.org/research/papers/ogsa.pdf*

22. Foster I, Kesselman C and Tuecke S (2001) The Anatomy of the Grid: Enabling Scalable Virtual Organization. *International Journal of High Performance Computing Applications*, 15 (3), 200-222.
23. Touch J (2001) Overlay Networks, *Computer Networks*, 3 (2-3), 115-116.
24. Foster I and Iamnitchi A (2003) On Death, Taxes, and the Convergence of Peer-to-Peer and Grid Computing. In *Proceedings of the 2nd International Workshop on Peer-to-Peer Systems*, (IPTPS '03), 2003.
25. The WS-Resource Framework home page, see *http://www.globus.org/wsrf/*
26. Grid and Web Services Standards to Converge, see *http://www.marketwire.com /mw/release_html_b1?release_id=61977*
27. IBM and Globus Announce Open Grid Services for Commercial Computing, see *http://www.ibm.com/news/be/en/2002/02/211.html*
28. The Globus Project, see *http://www.globus.org/*
29. The Triana Project, see *http://www.trianacode.org/*
30. Allen G, Davis K, Dolkas K, Doulamis N, Goodale T, Kielmann T, Merzky A, Nabrzyski J, Pukacki J, Radke T, Russell M, Seidel E, Shalf J and Taylor I (2003). Enabling Applications on theGrid: A GridLab Overview, *JHPCA Special issue on Grid Computing: Infrastructure and Applications*, August 2003.
31. Allen G, Angluo D, Goodale T, Kielmann T, Merzky A, Nabrzyski J, Pukacki J, Radke T, Russell M, Seidel E, Shalf J and Taylor I (2002). GridLab: Enabling Applications on the Grid: A Progress Report. *International Workshop on Grid Computing*, held in conjunction with Supercomputing 2002. Published as LNCS Vol. 2536, pp. 39-45.
32. Foster I and Kesselman C, eds. (1999) *The Grid: Blueprint for a New Computing Infrastructure*, Morgan-Kaufmann.
33. Foster I and Kesselman C, eds. (2004) *The Grid 2: Blueprint for a New Computing Infrastructure*, Second Edition. Morgan-Kaufmann.
34. The GridLab Project, see *http://www.gridlab.org*
35. Hughes, T.P. Edison and electric light, in Mackenzie D. and Wajcman J. eds. 1999. *The Social Shaping of Technology*. Open University Press: Philadephia.
36. XMethods.com. A "virtual laboratory" for Web services developers, see *http://www.xmethods.com*
37. Adar E and Huberman B (2000) Free Riding on Gnutella. First Monday 5 (10), *http://firstmonday.org/issues/issue5_10/adar/index.html*
38. BOINC, Berkeley Open Infrastructure for Network Computing (a generalized version of the SETI@Home project), see *http://BOINC.ssl.berkeley.edu/*
39. United Devices, see *http://www.ud.com/*
40. IBM, United Devices and Accelrys aid U.S. Department of defence in search for Smallpox Cure, United Devices press release, see *http://www.ud.com/company /news/press/02052003.htm*
41. Entropia, see *http://www.entropia.com/*
42. Windows P2P SDK release (2003), see *http://www.microsoft.com/presspass/ press/2003/Feb03/02-26SDKAnnouncesPR.asp*
43. Windows .NET. See website *http://www.microsoft.com/net/*
44. Pastry, see website *http://research.microsoft.com/~antr/pastry/*
45. Chord, see website *http://www.pdos.lcs.mit.edu/chord/*
46. Shirky C (2000), Modern P2P Definition, see *http://www.openp2p.com/pub/a/ p2p/2000/11/24/shirky1-whatisp2p.html*
47. Frankel J and Pepper T (2000) The Gnutella Protocol Specification v0.4, revision 1.2, see *http://www.clip2.com, protocols@clip2.com*

48. Oram A. *Peer-To-Peer: Harnessing the Power of Disruptive Technologies*, O'Reilly, March 2001. Notes from Chapters 8 and 14.

49. Gnutella Overview on Limewire, see *http://www.limewire.com/index.jsp/learn*

50. Gnutella articles and links, *http://www.oreillynet.com/topics/p2p/gnutella/*

51. LimeWire, see *http://www.limewire.com*

52. KaZaA, see *http://www.kazaa.com/*

53. Popular Power, see *http://www.popularpower.com/*

54. United Devices, see *http://www.ud.com/*

55. Entropia, see *http://www.entropia.com*

56. ICQ, see *http://www.icq.com/*

57. Netmeeting, see *http://www.microsoft.com/windows/netmeeting/default.asp*

58. Clarke I, Sandberg O, Wiley B, and Hong T. (2000) Freenet: A distributed anonymous information storage and retrieval system. In *Proceedings of the ICSI Workshop on Design Issues in Anonymity and Unobservability*, (Berkeley, California),

59. Clarke Ian, Miller Scott G, Hong Theodore W, Sandberg Oskar and Wiley Brandon. Protecting Free Expression Online with Freenet, *IEEE Internet Computing*, January, February 2002, 40-49.

60. Clarke Ian. Freenet's Next Generation Routing Protocol, 20/7/2003. See *http://freenet.sourceforge.net/index.php?page=ngrouting*

61. Freenet Web site, see *http://freenet.sourceforge.net*

62. Hong T (2001) Performance, Chapter 14 of *Peer to Peer: Harnessing the Power of disruptive technologies*, A. Oram, O'Reilly, March 2001.

63. Internet Firewalls Resources, see *http://www.cerias.purdue.edu/coast/firewalls/*

64. Distributed.net home page, see *http://www.Distributed.net*

65. OpenP2P.com, see *openp2p.com*

66. Minar N (2001) Distributed Systems Topologies, Parts 1 and 2, see *http://www.openp2p.com/pub/a/p2p/2001/12/14/topologies_one.html*

67. Gunther N. Hypernets, Good (G)news for Gnutella, see *http://www.perfdynamics.com/Papers/Gnews.html*

68. Rains M and Sloane N. On Cayley's Enumeration of Alkanes (or 4-Valent Trees), see *http://www.research.att.com/ njas/sequences/JIS/cayley.html*

69. Ripeanu M (2001) Peer-to-Peer Architecture Case Study: Gnutella Network, in *proceedings of IEEE 1st International Conference on Peer-to-peer Computing* (P2P2001), Linkoping Sweden, August 27 to 29, 2001 and on-line at *http://people.cs.uchicago.edu/ matei/PAPERS/P2P2001.pdf*

70. Transport Layer Security (TLS): IETF Draft, see *http://www.ietf.org/internet-drafts/draft-ietf-tls-rfc2246-bis-02.txt*

71. Data Encryption Standard, see *http://csrc.nist.gov/publications/fips/fips46-3/fips46-3.pdf*

72. Public-Key Infrastructure (X.509) (pkix), see *http://www.ietf.cnri.reston.va.us /html.charters/pkix-charter.html*

73. X.509 Certificates: IETF Draft, see *http://www.ietf.org/internet-drafts/draft-ietf-pkix-roadmap-09.txt*

74. RSA Cryptography Standard, see *http://www.rsasecurity.com/rsalabs/pkcs/pkcs-1/index.html*

75. MD5, see *ftp://ftp.umbc.edu/pub/unix/rfc/rfc1321.txt.gz*

76. OGSA Security: *http://www.globus.org/ogsa/Security/*

77. Overview of Certification Systems: X.509, CA, PGP and SKIP, see *http://mcg.org.br/cert.htm*

78. The Jini Web site, see *http://www.jini.org/*
79. Jini starter kit, see *http://www.jini.org/downloads/*
80. Understanding Reggie, see *http://www.kedwards.com/jini/reggie.html*
81. Sag, Dave. Crudlets: Making Peace Between Extreme Jini and XML View-points, see *http://www.onjava.com/pub/a/onjava/2001/02/08/jini_xml.html*
82. The Java Tutorial: A practical guide for programmers, *http://java.sun.com/do cs/books/tutorial/*
83. Wilson B, *JXTA* (2002), Que Press, also freely available on-line at *http://www. brendonwilson.com/projects/jxta/*
84. JXTA programmers guide: see Chapter 6 for system requirements, setting up and compiling JXTA programs and Appendix B for use of the JXTA Configuration Tool, *http://www.jxta.org/project/www/jxtaprogguide_final.pdf*
85. Configure your platform using the Jxta Configurator, see *http://platform.jxta. org/java/configuration.html*
86. Vogels W, Web Services are not Distributed Objects: Common Misconceptions about Service Oriented Architectures, *IEEE Internet Computing*, November/December 2003 (7, 6),59-66.
87. Newcomer E, *Understanding Web Services: XML, WSDL, SOAP, and UDDI*, Addison Wesley.
88. Fell S, PocketSoap, see *http://www.pocketsoap.com/*
89. Systinet, WASP, see *http://www.systinet.com/products/overview*
90. IBM, Emerging Technologies Toolkit, see *http://www.alphaworks.ibm.com/tech /ettk*
91. Microsoft, WSE: Web Service Enhancements, see *http://msdn.microsoft.com/ webservices/building/wse/default.aspx*
92. World Wide Web Consortium, SOAP Version 1.2 Part 0: Primer, June 2003 *http://www.w3.org/TR/soap12-part0/*
93. IBM, Web Services ToolKit for dynamic e-business (WSTK), see *http://www-4.ibm.com/software/solutions/webservices/overview.html*
94. Chappel D A and Jewell T, (2002), *Java Web Services: Using Java in Service-Oriented Architectures*, O'Reilly.
95. W3C Document, Extensible Markup Language 1.0. (1988), second edition (2000), *http://www.w3.org/TR/REC-xml/*, Third Edition, W3C Recommendation 04 February 2004, see *http://www.w3.org/TR/2004/REC-xml-20040204/*
96. W3C Document, XML Names, an XML v.1.0 Addendum, see *http://www.w3. org/TR/REC-xml-names/*
97. W3C Home page, see *http://www.w3.org/*
98. International Standard Organization, see *http://www.iso.ch/*
99. W3C Document, XML Schema: Parts 1 and 2, data types and structures using XML, *http://www.w3.org/TR/xmlschema-1/* and *http://www.w3.org/TR/xml schema-2/*
100. UDDI.org. UDDI Technical White Paper (2000), UDDI.org, September 6, 2000. See website *http://www.uddi.org*
101. Web Services Description Language (WSDL) 1.1 (2001). W3C Note, March 15, 2001, see *http://xml.coverpages.org/wsdl20000929.html*
102. The Web Services Description Language, version 2.0 draft, see *http://www.w3. org/TR/2003/WD-wsdl20-20031110/*
103. WS-Addressing, see *http://www.ibm.com/developerworks/webservices/library/ ws-add/*

104. Web Services Description Language (WSDL) Schema, see *http://schemas.xml soap.org/wsdl/*

105. Web Services Invocation Framework (WSIF), see *http://ws.apache.org/wsif/*

106. Web Services Architecture, a W3C Working Group Note, 11 Feb. 2004, see *http://www.w3.org/TR/ws-arch.*

107. What is the Grid? A Three Point Checklist. *Grid Today*, July 20, 2002.

108. Allcock W, Bester J, Bresnahan J, Chervenak A, Liming L, Meder S, Tuecke S, GridFTP Protocol Specification. The GGF GridFTP Working Group Document, September 2002. See *https://forge.gridforum.org/projects/gridftp-wg*

109. The Global Grid Forum (GGF). *http://www.ggf.org/*

110. Sun Microsystems, Sun Grid Engine, http://www.sun.com/software/gridware/

111. Platform Computing, Load Sharing Facility *http://www.platform.com/*

112. Catlett C and Smarr L, Metacomputing, *Communications of the ACM*, 35, 44-52, 1992.

113. Diachin D, Freitag L, Heath D, Herzog J, Michels W, and Plassmann P, Remote Engineering Tools for the Design of Pollution Control Systems for Commercial Boilers, *International Journal of Supercomputer Applications*, 10, 208-218, 1996.

114. Disz T L, Papka M E, Pellegrino M, and Stevens R, Sharing Visualization Experiences Among Remote Virtual Environments, in *International Workshop on High Performance Computing for Computer Graphics and Visualization*, Springer-Verlag, 217-237, 1995.

115. Nieplocha J and Harrison R, Shared Memory NUMA Programming on the I-WAY, in *Proceedings of the 5th IEEE Symposium on High Performance Distributed Computing*, IEEE Computer Society Press, 432-441, 1996.

116. Norman M et al., Galaxies Collide on the I-WAY: An Example of Heterogeneous Wide-Area Collaborative Supercomputing, *International Journal of Supercomputer Applications*, 10, 131-140, 1996.

117. Lee C, Kesselman C, and Schwab S, Near-Realtime Satellite Image Processing: Metacomputing in CC++, *Computer Graphics and Applications*, 16, 79-84, 1996.

118. The DataGrid Project (EDG/EGEE). See *http://www.eu-datagrid.org/*

119. de Roure D, Baker M A, Jennings N R and Shadbolt N R, The Evolution of the Grid, in Berman, F., Fox, G. and Hey, A. J. G., Eds. Grid Computing: Making the Global Infrastructure a Reality, Wiley, 65-100, 2003.

120. FAFNER, *http://www.npac.syr.edu/factoring.html*

121. Foster I, Geisler J, Nickless W, Smith W and Tuecke S, Software Structure for the I-WAY High Performance Distributed Computing Experiment, in *Proceedings of the 5th IEEE Symposium on High Performance Distributed Computing*, 562-571, 1997.

122. DeFanti T., Foster I., Papka M., Stevens R., and Kuhfuss T. Overview of the I-WAY: Wide Area Visual Supercomputing. *International Journal of Supercomputer Applications*, 10(2):123-130, 1996.

123. Grimshaw A, Wulf W et al, The Legion Vision of a Worldwide Virtual Computer. *Communications of the ACM*, 40 (1), January 1997.

124. The MENTAT project, see *http://www.cs.virginia.edu/ mentat/*

125. Condor, *http://www.cs.wisc.edu/condor/*

126. Common Object Request Broker Architecture, see *http://www.corba.org/*

127. The Distributed Component Object Model (DCOM), see *http://www.microsoft.com/com/tech/DCOM.asp*

128. The Object Management Group, see *http://www.omg.org/*
129. WC3 Semantic Web Activity Statement, *http://www.w3.org/2001/sw/Activity/*
130. The Access Grid. http://www.accessgrid.org/
131. Foster I, Kesselman C, Nick M N, Tuecke S, Grid Services for Distributed System Integration, *The New Net Cover Feature*, 37-46, June 2002.
132. Almond J and Snelling D, UNICORE: Uniform Access to Supercomputing as an Element of Electronic Commerce. *Future Generation Computer Science*, 15, 1999, 539-548, NH-Elsevier.
133. Allen G, Angulo D, Foster I, Lanfermann G, Liu C, Radke T, Seidel E, Shalf J, The Cactus Worm: Experiments with Dynamic Resource Discovery and Allocation in a Grid Environment, *Int. J. High Perform. Comput. Appl.* 15(4):345-358, 2001 Win.
134. Cactus home Page: *http://www.cactuscode.org/*
135. Sun Grid Engine, see *http://wwws.sun.com/software/gridware/sge.html*
136. White Paper 8: 1-Wire SHA-1 Overview, Dallas Semiconductor, Maxim, see *http://www.maxim-ic.com/appnotes.cfm/appnote_number/1201*
137. Broadband from Power Sockets, Scottish Hydro-Electric, see *http://www.hydro.co.uk/broadband/*
138. Withers, Stephen. An Overview of Distributed Grid Computing, Grid Today, November 4th, 2002, Vol. 1, No. 21, see *http://www.gridtoday.com/02/1104/10 0635.html*
139. Foster, Ian. Globus: What Will Come, Grid Today, February 2nd, 2004, Vol. 3 No. 5, see *http://www.gridtoday.com/04/0202/102590.html*
140. Moore, Gorden E. Cramming More Components onto Integrated Circuits. *Electronics*, 38, 8, April 19, 1965.
141. Intel comment on Moore's law, see *http://www.intel.com/research/silicon/moor eslaw.htm*
142. Gallopoulos, E, Houstis, E. H. and Rice, J. R. 'Computer as Thinker/Doer: Problem-Solving Environments for Computational Science, *IEEE Computational Science and Engineering*, 1(2), 1994. D. W. Shields, M and Huang, Y. Component-based Problem Solving Environments for Computational Science, Book chapter in *Component-based Software Development*, (Ed: Kung-Kiu Lau), World Scientific, 2003
143. G. Fox, D. Gannon, and M. Thomas, A Summary of Grid Computing Environments, *Concurrency and Computation: Practice and Experience* (Special Issue), 2003. Available at: *http://communitygrids.iu.edu/cglpubs.html*
144. The Globus Grid Security Infrastructure, see *http://www-unix.globus.org/secu rity/*
145. Resource Management in Globus, see *http://www-unix.globus.org/developer/resource-management.html*
146. MDS Features in the Globus Toolkit 2.4. Release, see *http://www.globus.org/mds/mds2/*
147. Data Management in Globus, see *http://www-unix.globus.org/developer/data-management.html*
148. Generic Security Service Application Program Interface, Version 2, see *http://www.ietf.org/rfc/rfc2078.txt*
149. e-Science Certificate Authority, see *http://ca.grid-support.ac.uk/*
150. The GridFTP Working Group within the GGF, see *https://forge.gridforum.org/projects/gridftp-wg*

151. Novotny, Jason. Developing grid portlets using the GridSphere portal framework, see *http://www-106.ibm.com/developerworks/grid/library/gr-portlets/? ca=dgr-lnxw11GSPortFrame*

152. GridSphere Design Document, see *http://www.gridlab.org/WorkPackages/wp-4/Documents/GridSphere.pdf*

153. Adamic L. A. et al. Search in Power-Law Networks, *Physics Rev. E*, 64, 4, article no. 046135, 2001.

154. Milgram S. The Small World Problem. *Psychology Today.* 1 (1), 60-67, 1967.

155. Berners-Lee, Tim. The World Wide Web, Past Present and Future: Exploring Universality, 2002, see *http://www.w3.org/2002/04/Japan/Lecture.html*

156. The Semantic Web Services Initiative (SWSI), see emphhttp://www.swsi.org/

157. Semantic Web Enabled Web Services (SWWS), see *http://swws.semanticweb.o rg/*

158. Bussler Christoph, Maedche Alexander and Fensel Dieter. A Conceptual Architecture for Semantic Web Enabled Web Services, see *http://www.acm.org/sig mod/record/issues/0212/SPECIAL/4.Bussler1.pdf*

159. Dumbill, E. Semantic Web and Web Services can live together, says Berners-Lee, see *http://www.xmlhack.com/read.php?item=1978*

160. Berners-Lee T, Hendler J and Lassila O. The Semantic Web: A new form of Web content that is meaningful to computers will unleash a revolution of new possibilities, see *http://www.scientificamerican.com/article.cfm?articleID=00 048144-10D2-1C70-84A9809EC588EF21&catID=2.*

161. The W3C Semantic Web home page, see *http://www.w3.org/2001/sw/*

162. Harold E.R, *XML Bible* 2nd Edition. Hungry Minds, 2001.

163. Ray Erik T. *Learning XML*. OReilly, 2001.

164. An Overview of SGML Resources, see *http://www.w3.org/MarkUp/SGML/*

165. The Stencil Group. Defining Web Services, see *http://www.stencilgroup.com/ ideas_scope_200106wsdefined.pdf*

166. W3C Working Group Note. Web Services Architecture, 11 February 2004, see *http://www.w3.org/TR/2004/NOTE-ws-arch-20040211/.*

167. Organization for the Advancement of Structured Information Standards (OASIS), see *http://www.oasis-open.org/home/index.php*

168. North American Industry Classification System, see *http://www.census.gov/ epcd/www/naics.html*

169. Using WSDL in a UDDI Registry, Version 1, UDDI Best Practice. May 2002, see *http://www.uddi.org/pubs/wsdlbestpractices-V1.07-Open-20020521.pdf*

170. The Castor project, see *http://www.castor.org/*

171. JSX, see *http://www.jsx.org/*

172. BEA/IBM/Microsoft/SAP/Siebel, Business Process Execution Language for Web Services, Version 1.1, 5 May 2003, see *http://www-106.ibm.com/developer works/webservices/library/ws-bpel/*

173. Feizabadi S. History of The Web, see *http://www.prenhall.com/abrams/demo/ chap1/*

174. Gamma E et al. *Design Patterns: Elements of Reusable Object-Oriented Software*, 1994, Addison-Wesley.

175. Computer Industry Almanac. On-line Article: Internet Users Will Top 1 Billion in 2005. Wireless Internet Users Will Reach 48% in 2005, see *http://www.c-i-a.com/pr032102.htm*

176. The Protean Research Group, SRSS project, see *http://cs.itd.nrl.navy.mil/55 22/*

177. Open Democracy: Free Thinking for the World, see *www.openDemocracy.net.*
178. Vaidhyanathan Siva. The New Information Ecosystem, parts 1-4, see *http:// www.opendemocracy.net/debates/article-8-101-1319.jsp*
179. Rainsford Miriam. P2P: Revolution or Evolution?, see *http://www.opendemo cracy.net/debates/article-8-101-1666.jsp*
180. Rimmer Matthew. The Genie's Revenge: A Response to Siva Vaidhyanathan, see *http://www.opendemocracy.net/debates/article-8-101-1639.jsp*
181. Drahos, Peter and Braithwaite, John. *Information Feudalism: Who Owns the Knowledge Economy?* W. W. Norton.
182. Baker Mark. Ian Foster on Recent Changes in the Grid Community, Distributed Systems Online exclusive, February 2004, Department Editor: Dejan Milojicic, see *http://dsonline.computer.org/0402/d/o2004a.htm*
183. Czajkowski Karl et al. From Open Grid Services Infrastructure to WSRe-source Framework: Refactoring and Evolution Version 1.0, Feb. 2004, see *http://www.globus.org/wsrf/#relevant*
184. Web Services Notification Framework for Publish-Subscribe Notification Events, see *http://xml.coverpages.org/ni2004-03-05-b.html*
185. XML Signature, see *http://www.w3.org/TR/xmldsig-core/*
186. XML Encryption, see *http://www.w3.org/TR/xmlenc-core/*
187. WS Security, see *http://www-106.ibm.com/developerworks/webservices/library /ws-secure/*
188. Nagappan R, Skoczylas R and Sriganesh R P. *Developing Java Web Services: Architecting and Developing Secure Web Services Using Java.* Wiley.
189. Apache Axis, see *http://ws.apache.org/axis/*
190. The Tomcat Servlet Engine, see *http://jakarta.apache.org/tomcat/*
191. XtremWeb Home page, see *http://www.lri.fr/ fedak/XtremWeb/introduction. php3*
192. Web Services Specifications Index Page, MSDN, see *http://msdn.microsoft.c om/library/default.asp?url=/library/en-us/dnglobspec/html/wsspecsover.asp*
193. The P2P Area within the GGF, see *https://forge.gridforum.org/projects/p2p*
194. Peer-to-Peer   Research   Group,   an   IRTF   research   group,   see *http://www.irtf.org/charters/p2prg.html*

Index